REIMAGINING BRITAIN

Foundations for Hope

Justin Welby

BLOOMSBURY CONTINUUM
LONDON • NEW YORK • OXFORD • NEW DELHI • SYDNEY

BLOOMSBURY CONTINUUM
Bloomsbury Publishing Plc
50 Bedford Square, London, WC1B 3DP, UK

BLOOMSBURY, BLOOMSBURY CONTINUUM and the Diana logo are
trademarks of Bloomsbury Publishing Plc

First published in Great Britain 2018

A catalogue record for this book is available from the British Library

Library of Congress Cataloguing-in-Publication data has been applied for

ISBN: HB: 978-1-4729-4607-2; EPDF: 978-1-4729-4605-8; EPUB: 978-1-4729-4606-5

2 4 6 8 10 9 7 5 3 1

Typeset by Newgen KnowledgeWorks Pvt. Ltd., Chennai, India
Printed and bound in Great Britain by CPI Group (UK) Ltd, Croydon CR0 4YY

To find out more about our authors and books visit www.bloomsbury.com.
and sign up for our newsletters

To our wonderful children, our children-in-law, and their children who have been such a support, such a reason for joy, and such a foundation of hope

Contents

Preface   ix

Introduction   1

PART ONE: WHY AND HOW TO REIMAGINE

1   Building on Our History   25

PART TWO: THE BASIC BUILDING BLOCKS

2   Family – Caring for the Core   63
3   Education – Life in All Its Fullness   85
4   Health – and Healing Our Brokenness   107
5   Housing – the Architecture of Community   127
6   Economics and Finance – Serving and
    Inspiring   149

PART THREE: VALUES AMID GLOBAL
CHANGE

7   The World Around Us   175
8   Immigration and Integration   195
9   For Those As Yet Unborn – Solidarity
    with the Future   215

10 The Key Actors   235
11 The Churches and Other Faith Groups –
    Healthy Disruptors   253

Conclusion   271

Acknowledgements   285
Index   289

Preface

When I finished my first book (*Dethroning Mammon*, Bloomsbury, 2016), I realized a couple of things. First, I write chiefly for myself. Second, actually letting go of a book so that others can read it is terrifying. In this, I suspect, I am like many others.

However, the enormous changes taking place around us, especially following the Brexit referendum of 2016, provoked me into thinking about the implications – especially in the context of a lot of talk about 'British values'. As I will discuss later, this phrase is used to apply to three values: democracy, the rule of law, and respect for others. Such values are obviously essential (who would want to argue for tyranny, anarchy and mutual contempt?), but the core of this book is to argue that, while they are necessary, they are not sufficient. They are not wide enough, not strong enough and not flexible enough to bear the weight of the necessity of reimagining Britain. 'British values' as often used is thus a phrase that always seems to strike the wrong note. I am not even convinced that there is such a thing as exclusively British values. I rather suspect, and argue here, that there are values that come out of our common European history and our Christian heritage, which have been tweaked and adapted in each country and culture. Wherever they exist, in every part of the UK – Scotland, Northern Ireland, Wales and England – they are seen in practices.

The number of books written on the subject of our future as a nation (or several nations), and the intensity of public discussion, seem to indicate that this really is one of those rare moments when we have both the risk and the opportunity of rethinking what we should do and be as a country. Of course, it is very far from being within our control, but collectively we have an influence on our future and, with sufficient courage, and determined leadership from among our politicians and others, it is something we can and must do.

Brexit is something that features frequently in these pages. The book assumes it will happen, and that 'making the best of it' is not good enough; there must be a process of reimagining that enables the UK to flourish in every possible way. However, as is said at least once, the need to reimagine how we live in hope may have been accelerated by the decision to leave the European Union, but it existed anyway, and would continue to do so even if, in some unforeseeable twist of politics, the UK remained part of the EU.

The views expressed here are my own, not an official position of the Church of England or the Anglican Communion. It is part of being Anglican that we accept a wide range of diverse opinions, and that no one person or group is entitled to decide definitively what the Church thinks. I would certainly not dare to imagine changing that happy accident of our history.

This book is therefore a personal contribution to the process that seems to be before us: of reimagining our future. It speaks above all of hope – that happy state where we can be realistic but positive about where we are going and how we get there. It is influenced by many things but especially by two recent books. One was a collection of essays edited by my remarkable colleague the Archbishop of York, *On Rock or Sand? Firm Foundations for Britain's Future*[1]; the subtitle of this book is a deliberate echo. The second is the magisterial work of Malcolm Brown and others on Anglican Social Theology.[2]

+Justin Cantuar:
Lambeth Palace
November 2017

[1]John Sentamu, *On Rock or Sand? Firm Foundations for Britain's Future* (London: SPCK, 2015).
[2]Malcolm Brown, *et al.* (eds), *Anglican Social Theology: Renewing the Vision Today* (London: Church House Publishing, 2014).

Introduction

For almost every nation on earth this is a time of extraordinary challenge amid rapid change. Our technology is driving us onwards in ways that would have seemed like science fiction within the last generation. Autonomous forms of transport are now practical, not only for vehicles but also for ships and aircraft. Artificial Intelligence is advancing very rapidly. Communications are unrecognizable: hugely powerful, and immensely subversive of existing orders and structures of many societies and institutions. Medicine is advancing ever more rapidly as the decoding of the human genome begins to bear fruit.

At the same time, the planet groans under the weight of the peoples and economies that it sustains. Social tensions grow as traditional societies and structures either resist or seek to adapt to change.

For most of us, the impact of these changes will be revolutionary – for jobs, development, life expectancy, as well as for the terrible possibilities of war or the wonderful gifts of peace. The United Kingdom, as well as Europe, has found its present form through wars and struggles of unimaginable cost in human suffering, and through brave dreams of reconciliation and reimagining of its future.

Now we must find fresh strength and passionate commitment to imagine ourselves afresh in the midst of such

change. To reimagine anything in such fast-shifting contexts and with so many impulses and pressures requires
us to be anchored in constant and flexible values. It has
happened before, and there is every reason to suppose
that we will manage with great benefit to our nation and
to the world. But it does not happen by accident.

Like other nations, the United Kingdom is understood, and understands itself, through stories about
itself, some of which are true. When great decisions are
taken, the stories become even more important. They
operate at a number of levels. There is popular history,
recounted again and again in films, and giving rise to
expressions like 'the Dunkirk spirit'. There are the more
nuanced and developed histories, asking awkward questions about the popular ideas. For example, in 2017 the
seventieth anniversary of independence for India and
Pakistan has led to much discussion of the merits and
vices of the British Raj. Deep down there are the formative stories, those that give a sense of what makes things
right or wrong. The impact of Christian faith on the
customs of the nation is foundational. These stories are
usually only accepted by a minority of the population,
but over time they set a pattern of self-understanding.

The history of Britain (I shall use Britain and the UK
more or less interchangeably), in common with much
of Western Europe, has been shaped to a very large
extent by the values, aspirations and virtues of what has
been called Western Christianity.[1] Of course, Western
Christianity itself was profoundly influenced not
only by the Gospels, but also, through its inheritance,

---

[1] By 'Western Christianity' I mean Christianity drawn originally from Rome,
much adapted, and distinguished from the forms and ideas of Christianity deriving especially either from the Celtic tradition or from the Orthodox traditions
centred originally on Constantinople.

via Rome, of Greek philosophy and culture. The Renaissance, the Enlightenment and the impact of the philosophical changes of the twentieth century have also been profoundly important in developing our current perception of our heritage. We see it through twenty-first-century eyes and are rarely, if ever, capable of stepping back in time to examine our values as if modernity had not happened. However, whether in terms of what we think is good, or in terms of art, or simply in daily expressions, in townscapes, in the presence of churches everywhere, and in a million other ways, Christian faith shapes us, whether or not we are believers. One of the biggest changes in recent British history and culture is that, whereas in 1945 there were fewer than a hundred thousand practising adherents of faiths other than Christianity, that figure today is well over three million. The influences of such a change are profound, as are the rapid increase in the number of those who hold no faith and the decrease in the number of practising Christians. Even so, Christianity is the foundation and inspiration of most of our ethics, values and actions. It is the formative story that gives us our knee-jerk reactions as to what is right and wrong.

In this book although I speak mainly about values and practices, they are inextricably bound up with virtues. Values guide practices, and practices build virtues; virtues also reinforce practices, and guide our understanding of values. The whole process is circular, self-reinforcing for good or ill. We cannot create virtue from nothing, but without it our practices will deteriorate. When I was a very small child, asking, after the first five minutes of a journey, 'are we nearly there?', my grandmother used to reply with a little nursery rhyme: 'Patience is a virtue/ virtue is a grace/ and Grace was a little girl/ who had a dirty face'. Patience came, however, through the practice of waiting, and the value of being quiet and doing what I was told. Our values and our virtues must interact with our practices.

This book is, unsurprisingly and unapologetically, written from a Christian perspective. Because of the Christian foundations of our society in Britain, it draws frequently on more or less well-known traditions and stories in the Bible. Underlying them all is the common theme of what it means to be a society whose members aspire to love one another, to love our neighbour, to find in today's complex world of multiple systems of belief and non-belief a story that is hospitable, challenging but welcoming. It seeks to speak of being a society of love, expressed in actions and practices that are tough and pragmatic, that is sufficiently confident of its own history, values and practices not just to accept but actually to welcome diversity.

Christians believe that the truth about Jesus Christ, unique in life, executed, resurrected and ascended, is intended to be the focus of their whole lives. Historically, the truth of Jesus Christ has been so dramatically lived out in individual human lives that it has become the narrative for movements, for groups, for societies and, in the end, for much of the world. At the heart of the story of Jesus Christ are restored relationships, first with God, but also with others. They are summed up in the phrase 'God is love'. The writer of that phrase, the Apostle John, does not use the word 'love' to mean romantic affection, but to denote active pursuit of the well-being of others, without seeking return. Good societies reflect this love-in-action. Values in a society that begin with moral exhortation or rules are doomed to failure, even to oppression and cruelty. Values spring from practices of love, and love reinforces values. That simple approach is at the heart of this book. In essence, it argues that a society that lives in love will flourish and develop, and will liberate the vast majority of its members, whether or not they themselves accept the premises of the Christian faith.

Despite our long cultural history, the way in which we live changes through the impact of war and peace, economics, climate change, demographics and many other factors. As a result, the truth of Jesus Christ has been re-expressed in different circumstances. It is a meta-narrative, an ever growing story of how the great virtues and benefits of gracious love are lived out in the hard pounding of a changing world. When changes are especially dramatic, they call for reimagining on a grand scale, for an interpretation of our ancient meta-narrative that is faithful to the past, that is adapted to the present and that guards the hopes of those to come in the future. Moments of great change require us both to keep in contact with the meta-narrative, and also to express what that means in new ways.

The opportunity, necessity and challenge to reimagine our society come rarely. Events, which so often drive us before their wind, very occasionally seem to throw up a choice of ways forward, in which our practices and values can direct where we go. The moment is not only rare but requires society-wide leadership and imagination to grasp it. It is not achieved by ample resources, but by a change of mood, a decision or a historic change. It cannot be forced but may be seized, or missed.

Within many religious traditions, including Christianity, it is believed that such moments are intended. They are offers from God – the God of all history, all nations and all people (whether they know it or not). In the ancient world, during the sixth century BC, the Persian Emperor Cyrus seized the chance to reshape the way his empire worked. Caught up by the decision, the Jewish people were given the chance to return from exile. The story is found in the

Old Testament in Nehemiah, Ezra, Haggai and other later prophets. It is a story of struggle and courage, of repeated failure, but above all of a faithful and loving God, seen and experienced through faith and events rather than through obvious and dramatic acts of miraculous power.

Moments of change are moments of great hope and opportunity, as was the Jewish return from exile. They are usually surrounded by threats, perceived or real, but the opportunity to spring-clean the detritus of culture and habit at a national level is a gift and not a danger. This is true provided that the hope for change may be built upon values of virtue and grace, of love and common humanity, and not on selfishness, inward-looking self-absorption, self-protection and fear. That is why we face choices.

In our history, there have been many such moments. Since the Reformation, examples include the time of the Elizabethan Settlement after 1558, which effectively established the Church of England in recognizable modern form, as part, despite its failings, of a balancing and moderating force in our culture and values. During the Civil Wars and Commonwealth of 1642 to 1660 there was an attempt to impose change. The result was one of the bloodiest wars, proportionate to population, ever experienced in our history. It was finally largely resolved by a shift of national mood and a national reimagining in 1688.

Between 1832 and the Great Reform Act through to 1870 and the Education Act (in which education passed from being mainly the responsibility of the Church of England as well as other churches into the hands of the state), Christian influence was among the formative influences in the reforms of society and, above all, the economy. Voting rights were extended, Factory Acts and health and safety legislation began, schooling widened, children and women were granted stronger protection, and slavery was abolished in the British Empire: the reimagining of society away from paternalism combined with *laissez-faire* liberalism started the long, slow progress that took over a century. Though long drawn out, it was a reimagining of who we are as a nation through a revolution in our values.

British liberal optimism grew in tandem with European modernism, although it had its own, typically more pragmatic aspects. As a result, the faults and strengths of modernity across Europe were seen in the UK. They gave rise to the vain hope of human-centred liberal progress: a sense that human beings and the world would get better and better, provided that Europe was in charge, which hypocritically concealed the cost of imperialism. Across Europe, and in the UK not least through the experience of the trenches, these hopes were dashed in 1914–18. What was left received its fatal blows when the idealism or nationalisms of the totalitarian regimes culminated in the Gulag and the Holocaust. As a result, by 1945 illusions were fading.

After 1945, both in Britain and across Europe, there were even more dramatic changes in social policy, in economics and in philosophy. The periods of the two world wars had seen Western European countries slaughter more than 10 million of each other's citizens. All infrastructure had been damaged; economies had disintegrated; vast numbers of people were displaced; hunger and disease were prevalent. Out of such ruins – the *reductio ad absurdum* of wars since the fall of the Western Roman Empire – came a desire to change. In Europe, Christian Democrats began the creation of what is now the European Union, which expanded into the largest democratic grouping of nations on earth, full of flaws but able to contribute significantly to fulfilling the dreams of peace that inspired its founders.

In the UK, the Labour government from 1945 to 1951 introduced massive reforms in social benefits, in the creation of the NHS and in the shaping of the economy towards low unemployment as a virtue in itself. They were guided to some extent not only by their own thinking but also by the views of Christian Socialists such as the philosopher R. H. Tawney, the Archbishop of York (and then Canterbury) William Temple, and the economist and social reformer Sir William Beveridge. Those three had been friends for years and cooperated deeply in the formation of their ideas.

Both in Europe and in the UK, the reimagining of society drew consciously and unconsciously on the ancient narratives of Christian faith, interpreted over the centuries. In Europe since 1893 the rapidly growing *corpus* of Catholic Social Teaching[2] had a powerful influence. In the UK the ideas of the nineteenth-century reformers and philanthropists (including Quakers like Cadbury) brought in a different stream of thought. Both were also influenced – reactively or in imitation – by Marx. There was, in the words of Edmund Burke, a reality to the idea that society is a contract taking the form of 'a partnership ... between those who are living, those who are dead, and those who are to be born'.[3] However, the great reimagining of Europe and the UK after 1945 was not a static contract, but a dynamic leap into new forms of relationship

[2]Well summarized in *The Social Agenda of the Catholic Church* (London: Bloomsbury Continuum, 2002). A version is available for download from http://www.thesocialagenda.org/. Catholic Social Teaching is the continually developing and very sophisticated body of thinking from the Popes that applies Christian belief to social, economic, cultural and environmental issues.
[3]Edmund Burke, *Reflections on the Revolution in France*, ed. Frank M. Turner (New Haven: Yale University Press, 2003 [1790]), p. 82, https://books.google.co.uk/books?id=OYkPY-EljDoC&num=13.

that nevertheless remained rooted in the underlying Christian faith and tradition of the countries involved.

The failure of the European agenda over the last few years is seen not only in the decision made in 2016 for Britain to become the first member state to leave the bloc (a process now known as 'Brexit'), but also in the lack of concern for the common good at so many levels, from the leadership of the European Union to populist movements. The expansion of the EU has led to a loss of its own, also very often Christian-driven, narrative. The stories of war and the compulsion to avoid the repetition of war have faded, as has the sense of escape from the totalitarian regimes of the pre-1989 Soviet bloc. The centrality of Franco-German reconciliation has been displaced by an often crude materialism. Different regions have different stories, separated by fault lines that resist action to improve the situation.

This book focuses on the UK, not the EU. However, the stories of both the UK and the EU are closely related. Brexit demands a reimagining of the EU as much as of Britain. Writing in the summer of 2017 it is possible that the reimagining is happening, following the election in France of President Macron. Yet the inertia in a system of 27 countries is enormous, and the profound inequalities make any change of heart far more difficult in Europe than in the UK.

The UK today is far distant from 1945. We are not in a world emerging from war, despite the many grave insecurities and fears that arise from terrorism, technological change, economic stagnation, cultural confusion and values in conflict with each other. We do not have an empire to lose or to which to give the opportunity for freedom. Our cities are not in ruins; we are not demobilizing millions of conscripts. Our economy is relatively healthy; we are not bankrupt. On the contrary, a long

period of stable government without great catastrophes
has given us a total national wealth (I will come back to
issues of inequality) for sharing that is greater than at
any point in our history.

Our society today is also far more complicated than
in 1945. To reimagine ourselves today requires a radical
effort that must take in a plurality of religions (William
Temple was dealing only with Christianity), that faces
a significantly more secular society and polity, that
engages with competing values and worldviews, and that
reflects the changes that will come with Brexit. But like
1945, this reimagining must recognize the needs and the
rightful demands of those left out of the rapid increase in
wealth over the last 25 years and the experience of social,
economic and political disconnection.

The impact of the Brexit decision is huge. Its economic
effect is open to debate and will almost certainly never be
agreed. By contrast, it is clear that there will be changes
required in how Britain works in terms of its relationships with the rest of the world. The British vision for
our diversity and for human flourishing needs establishing in the context of our past, the threats and difficulties of the present, and in faithfulness to our future. The
danger is of having a rootless and self-protective society
without generosity, arising from a lack of confidence
and an inward-looking and self-centred reimagining of
what it is to be British. One form of a Christian hope
faithful to our past is of a generous society rooted in history, committed to the common good in the present and
a steward of the hopes and joys of future generations
both in our own country and around the world.

The tasks of 1945 were much clearer, albeit profoundly
more difficult. There was a need to reimagine, to reform,
to redevelop a broken nation and broken Europe.

Everything had to start again. Houses needed building, healthcare and especially public health needed re-
establishing, education needed to restart. These three
tools – housing, health and education – have been the
principal agents in all times of national reinvention. They
address what Beveridge called the Giant Evils of squalor,
ignorance, want, idleness, and disease.[4]

By contrast, today, much looks good. Among the great
and beneficial changes have been radical improvements
in the status of groups that were previously oppressed:
women, ethnic minorities, those with disabilities, those
with varieties of sexual orientation and identity. The
development of a deep suspicion of power made government more difficult but served many groups well. The
changes were not only in culture. This was the period
of the rapid development of judicial review as a process
to hold the Executive to account. Human rights legislation came to centre stage. Status was no longer seen as
giving entitlement to power. The move began towards
devolution. A new move in philosophy either reflected
or triggered these changes (the argument is endless as
to which), in which hypermodernity or postmodernity gave more and more centrality to the individual, to
autonomous decision making and to suspicion of ancient
rules and institutions. The change has been uncomfortable for many of those institutions, but often powerfully
effective for those who in the past were marginalized,
and genuinely the victims of power groups.

There is legitimate debate about whether the problems
of our society require merely repairing and maintenance in
how we work, or whether there is a need for reimagining

[4]The Beveridge Report 1942, officially entitled 'Social Insurance and Allied
Services'. Available at https://www.sochealth.co.uk/national-health-service/public-
health-and-wellbeing/beveridge-report/.

and replacing. The Great Recession which followed the
financial crisis of 2008 has left profound damage, above all
to confidence. There is less acceptance of inequality, more
questioning of the failure of the economy to distribute
the rewards of growth more widely. The EU referendum
and the US presidential election of 2016 have raised huge
questions about those left behind, excluded and treated
as people to whom things are done and whose dignity
and humanity are thus diminished. Policies such as the
Northern Powerhouse were developed to try and even out
growth. Yet the UK general election of June 2017 seemed
to indicate an ever more divided and unequal society.

One of the most important and most rapidly emerging divisions is generational. In June 2017, those under
40 voted by a majority for the Labour Party (if under
30, by a huge margin of up to 50 per cent) and those
over 40 for the Conservatives. Among those over 65
years of age, the Conservative margin was similar to
the Labour one for the under-30s. In the 2016 referendum, the under-35s were mainly Remainers and the
over-60s largely in favour of Brexit. In 2016, however,
about 31 per cent of under-35s voted; in 2017, it was
more than 70 per cent. In Jeremy Corbyn they had
found motivation.

The emergence of this trend is not surprising, although
its timing was unforeseeable. The over-65s are the Baby
Boomers. They have good pensions, they have had relatively good jobs. Their debts and materialism were the
foundations of the 2008 crash, which led to vast unemployment for those then aged 18 to 25. They have not
constrained their consumption of the resources of the
earth. Voting as they did in 2016, they committed the
upcoming generation to a new adventure outside the EU,
which the majority of young voters had been against.

Many of the chapters of this book address this particular division. Investment in housing, education and mental health are especially relevant. Strengthening our endurance and resilience around climate change will protect our future long after the 'Boomers' are dead. Finding a way forward for our foreign policy and for immigration and integration will prepare a country to be proud of and seek to address issues that will not become critical for many years.

Globally, the number of people involved in forced or chosen migration has reached historic highs of well over 60 million, far greater than after the Second World War. There is a contrast between a deep sense of compassion for those fleeing hardship and a deep resistance to immigration. Hate crimes against perceived 'foreigners' (often those who had been in the UK for more than a generation) spiked after the referendum of June 2016.[5]

An influential group of economists is increasingly speaking of secular stagnation, of the rapid growth of much of the post-1945 period having been an aberration, and of a return to the previous centuries-long pattern of more or less non-growth economies with short bursts of change. Very low interest rates are pointed to as a sign of insufficient demand for investment matched by a surplus of savings. Historically, safer investments such as lending to governments of major economies have such low interest rates that many people have begun to look at new products, whose risks are uncertain, such as peer-to-peer lending, start-ups, venture capital and infrastructure projects.[6]

[5] See, for example, 'Hate crime "still far too high" post-Brexit – police', BBC, http://www.bbc.co.uk/news/uk-36869000 (22 June 2016).
[6] See, for example, Coen Teulings and Richard Baldwin (eds), *Secular Stagnation: Facts, Causes and Cures* (London: CEPR Press, 2014).

Since the 1980s, debt has become the default remedy for almost all economic stagnation. Yet as Adair Turner has demonstrated,[7] it was the inexorable growth in debt, at a rate faster than the growth of the real economy, that lay behind the 2008 crisis and that underpins much of the present lack of confidence. A large part of the crisis of the EU (and other developed economies) lies in the oppressive use of debt as a means of allowing the richer and more efficient to lend money to the poorer in order to enable them to buy the rich countries' goods. As a result, there is the gross immorality of having created out of some countries in Southern Europe the world's largest debtors' prisons. In nineteenth-century London, Charles Dickens challenged such vicious absurdities in *Little Dorrit*, in his depiction of the Marshalsea prison in Southwark. The imagination cannot grasp at what he would write today about Greece.

Inequality has re-emerged as the most destabilizing and unjust feature of our own society, particularly in terms of wealth inequality, and the most likely to result in damage to our future. Between July 2012 and June 2014 the wealthiest 10 per cent of households owned 45 per cent of total aggregate household wealth. The least wealthy 50 per cent of households owned 9 per cent of total aggregate household wealth.[8] Income inequality peaked in 2009 and has stabilized or slightly fallen since, an encouraging move, except that the fall is minute compared to the huge rise between the 1980s and 2009. Between 1990 and 2009, the income share of the top one

[7] Adair Turner, *Between Debt and the Devil: Money, Credit, and Fixing Global Finance* (Princeton: Princeton University Press, 2015).
[8] *Total Wealth, Wealth in Great Britain, 2012 to 2014* (Office for National Statistics, 2015), Chapter 2; http://webarchive.nationalarchives.gov.uk/20160105160709/http://www.ons.gov.uk/ons/dcp171776_428631.pdf.

per cent moved from less than 6 per cent to nearly 9 per cent, and there is some chance this is an underestimation. Since 2009, this share has fluctuated and was at 7.9 per cent in 2014–15. Income inequality overall remains much higher than before the rapid increase of the 1980s.[9]

Above all, there is today a lack of common values, due to the breakdown of what was once a shared narrative of virtue in the Christian tradition. The problem has been analysed to death, brilliantly in some cases.[10] The outcome of a plethora of incommensurable values has been seen in difficulties with decision making and the detachment of policies from virtues. This book is not a further analysis, but seeks to suggest ways in which policies could be more closely linked to historic virtues without crushing the diversity and freedom that are so attractive in modern life. In the end, the problem is as much one of inaction as of disagreement. Values are expressed in actions, in practices, not only in words. We know we are loved because someone acts lovingly towards us. Generosity is seen in the act of giving, not mere goodwill. Values do not make actions, nor do actions make values. They are in a dynamic and iterative relationship, mutually reinforcing or mutually destructive. A person or nation or group or society cannot stop the world while they sort out values, but they can express values through responding to the existential challenges they face.

Underlying the temporary values that spring from changing circumstances, there are the deep understandings of what makes for virtue, of what is good in absolute and permanent terms. It is what Aslan in C. S. Lewis's

[9]Chris Belfield, *et al.*, *Living Standards, Poverty and Inequality in the UK: 2016* (London: The Institute for Fiscal Studies, 2016).
[10]See, for example, Alasdair MacIntyre, *After Virtue: A Study in Moral Theory* (London: Gerald Duckworth & Co. Ltd, 1981).

The Lion, The Witch and the Wardrobe calls the 'deep magic'. In such deep values lies the force that drives us forward and corrects our errors. When the deep values are fractured then all hell breaks out. The deep values are those that set our boundaries and cause us instinctively to say 'that is not right', or 'things are falling apart', in more than the normal way of being uncomfortable with or failing to welcome change. The link between our policies and expressed values and the deep magic is what enables us to embrace change without losing all continuity with the past or the ability to make sense of the facts before us.

Reimagining will inevitably happen. It may occur thoughtlessly through the mere passage of time, in which case it is likely to be bad. Values in this case would be dictated by the powerful and rich, and imposed through self-interest. Economics would drive decision making. Vision would be tactical, not strategic. Hard choices would be avoided. Long-term investment in social, spiritual and moral capital would be feeble to non-existent. We saw this in the great adjustments of the 1970s and 1980s. There was huge change in many areas, from the rights of trades unions to the importance of the economy and the increasing size of the financial sector of the City of London. The long-term post-war trend towards greater equality began to reverse. Individualism became more important, not only in issues around personal morality but also in wealth accumulation. The result was a new definition of national purpose and values, arrived at by chance as much as intent. Some aspects were excellent. There was less moral hypocrisy, especially over sexual matters, and huge steps forward in individual liberty. Other aspects were terrible, especially for the poor. Values of growth became values of making money, mainly out of trading financial instruments. State support declined radically for areas where economic changes had destroyed traditional employment.

As structures changed, mainly for economic reasons, so did culture and also values, and the three forces interacted randomly, with very unpredictable results. The privatization of Christian faith and the consequent diminution of a national meta-narrative of virtue and vice, leading in some ways to the divorce of ends and means of policy, has led to an absolute lack of foundations to deal with numerous faiths, different cultures, globalized economies, and above all, to a world in which all values from around the planet confront us more rapidly and effectively than ever before. Public faith was and probably still is sometimes more surface than reality, at least in countries where its expression is a necessary part of holding power. Nevertheless, when faith is increasingly privatized, it leaves a vacuum which relativism in belief or a great plurality of incommensurable beliefs is unable to fill. That is not to say at this stage that the answer is to reverse the privatization of Christian faith (which is anyway not something within human gift) but rather that there is a need for a generous and hospitable meta-narrative within which competing truths can be held. It will be a suggestion of this book that Christian faith, centred on love-in-action, trusting in the sovereignty of God rather than political power, provides the potential for such hospitable and generous holding.

Being confronted by plural values is as old as human travel, thus as old as humanity. In the nineteenth century the British East India Company banned the practice of *sati* (the immolation of widows). It was a controversial move, both politically in its effects on the military alliances of the growing Raj, but also as a confrontation with another culture. The first major step was taken by William Bentinck, the Governor General, in 1829, much influenced by his own Christian faith and by evangelical pressure from missionaries and the UK. There was comment in UK newspapers, and in Parliament, but most people knew little of this huge decision.

The difference today is technology. In the days of the Raj, news and information was read by few, and seen by almost none except in the form of engravings in newspapers. Today, the whole world is found on a smart phone. The least important remarks of a celebrity or politician, a pope's apparently throwaway comments on a plane home after a tough journey, a tweet by a political candidate, all go round the world in seconds, and have deep effects for good or ill. We all know that the long-term impact of this wave of information is one that we cannot begin to imagine, any more than Caxton or the Emperor Charles V in the late fifteenth or early sixteenth centuries could have imagined the social, religious and economic impacts of printing.

Following Brexit (and for that matter, probably even if the vote had gone the other way), the need for a new economy is clear. That need by itself requires a change in education and in the infrastructure of the country. It also requires a renewal of values, a reinvention and reshaping of national purpose that is deliberate and integrated with actions at every level, which is reflective of the technological, social, moral and religious contexts. Reshaping and reimagining are often accidental but can be deliberate, as after 1945 or in the nineteenth century. When this has happened, it has been through a close relationship between values, virtues and practices, mutually reinforcing a new culture.

Almost half a century has passed since British entry into what was then the European Economic Community in 1973 (after a decade of efforts to this end). This means that there are few people in employment today who were employed before EEC membership, and almost none before it became an aim of UK policy. With no corporate memory of being outside the EU, it is no wonder that there is uncertainty about the future, as much within the groups that favoured Brexit as among those that opposed it. To some extent the fading of corporate memory makes space for corporate nostalgia and myth. Was there a simple world in which we were in control? Did things improve so much when we joined the EEC? Can loss of control or economic benefits be tied only or even largely to membership? The passage of time means that many ideas are put forward with too much simplicity by their respective adherents.

It is also no wonder that in such circumstances as I have briefly set out, the cracks in our society have begun to show, expressed in hate crime, in the growth of intolerance, and above all of an inward-turning. Brexit risks becoming not merely Britain's exit from the EU, but a catalyst of British introspection, xenophobia and self-pity if a self-regarding attitude leads to economic failure and international impotence, as well as being morally wrong in and of itself.

All the above is fairly general, and generalizing about the UK is invariably wrong. Certain cultural trends run throughout the different parts of the country, but the UK is above all a Union of differences. Whether one accepts that it has four countries as a minimum (England, Scotland, Northern Ireland and Wales) or in reality four countries and a number of ancient regions with distinct differences (for example Northumbria, Wessex, and Cornwall for England alone), the speed of cultural change and its direction are radically different across the country. In short, there are different narratives in each part of the UK, and generalizations will almost always have local exceptions.

Northern Ireland finds within it competing identities, shaped profoundly by centuries of twists and turns, traumas and triumphs. The Unionist and Protestant areas are more socially conservative than much of the rest of the Union and yet define themselves in part by attachment to certain aspects of that Union.

Wales is one part of the UK that has a significant linguistic tradition independent of England. Language matters. It shapes religion, politics and the arts, and changes everything from road signs to school curriculums. The experience of domination by England shapes identity, and gives a narrative of its own.

Scotland has been and remains distinct, with a clear national identity. It is different in religious tradition, in education and in culture. It has its own distinct sub-cultures within itself.

Some of this book applies across the whole UK, but even then it must be borne in mind that large-scale cultural, political and economic change interacts with national identity and culture in different ways. Most of the examples in the book are English, because at least where England is concerned my ignorance is conscious and not merely inadvertent. Hopefully, some ideas are transferable.

Much that is written above leaves out God and faith. Why does that matter, and indeed, regardless of which perspective for the future is right, what may the Church say or do that is useful?

It may be midnight, or morning and sunrise in the UK (to steal phrases much in vogue in the USA). Whichever it is, Christians believe in, and the Church globally witnesses to, the sovereignty of God over peoples and nations. The Church must never seek to compel but should always, in any political system, witness to the truth it believes that it knows and experiences. That draws it into the political (but not party political) sphere. Times of change require contributions from every part of society. There is no theocracy in orthodox Christian political thinking, but there is the obligation on the Church to live as the people of God in such a way that society is both preserved and illuminated.[11]

The Church should thus speak, but more importantly act, in a way that is coherent with seeking to bring light and healing.

More than that, the people of God are called to be a blessing to those places where they live.[12] Obedience to God is seen in imitation of God, and thus in love for those in the world around and in care for the concerns of God: the poor, the weak, and the creation.

Most of all, the people of God are to be a people of hope, of faith and of love, for one another, for neighbour and even for enemy.

Our values have been founded on virtues, developed and extended by the teachers of the Church, neglected and abused by church authorities, but always coming back at some point. They are the 'deep magic', often unmentioned, but requiring an engagement with society that is one of hope and confidence in the providence of God, that is unashamed of faith and that witnesses to the truth of Christ, in words but also in advocacy, in action and in sacrifice.

[11] Matthew 5:13–16.
[12] Jeremiah 29:8.

This book begins with a look at the reasons why reimagining is so important. It goes on to discuss the great and historic building blocks of reimagining the future of our country – housing, health, education, and the household/family – together with other factors that have always existed but which have new force and significance – immigration and integration, the environment, economics and finance, and foreign policy.

It is not a complete list, but neither does it attempt to set out a political programme. The aim is to contribute, from a distinctly Christian perspective, to the very widespread and exciting debates that are happening all around us in this most interesting of times.

PART ONE

Why and How to Reimagine

I

Building on Our History

Most people have some hope that their successor generations will have a better life. A desire for continual improvement, even Utopia[1], is hard-wired into our thinking. Politicians promise one. Economists plan for one. Religious people pray for a better future. Writers, artists and filmmakers describe it, or describe various forms of dystopias as a warning.

Utopia is seen to come in many ways, from some divinely ordained post-apocalyptic form to a steady state of economic and educational improvement that would leave most people working 15 hours a week and using their adequately funded leisure for self-improvement through the arts.[2] In different plans, Utopia is achieved through a range of options from a general coming together of people with a common and beneficial aim to its imposition by a wise but ruthless set of Guardians (Plato) who ensure that all is for the best in the best of all possible worlds.[3] The Christian understanding is that hope is an essential emotion and state of mind for all human beings, and to be

[1] Ironically, this literally means 'Nowhere'.
[2] See John Maynard Keynes, 'Economic Possibilities for our Grandchildren', in *Essays in Persuasion* (New York: Classic House Books, 2009), in which Keynes predicted a vastly increasing quality of life and a 15-hour work week.
[3] Voltaire, *Candide*.

deprived of hope is a tragedy, and a cruelty, of immense proportions. In the New Testament, hope means a convinced expectation, not merely a possibility.

It is something of a political truism to point to the absence of growth in prosperity for those on average incomes in the UK over the last 20 years. Depending on who does the measuring, real incomes in this group are seen to have stagnated since the late 1990s or perhaps since 2003,[4] a huge contrast with their parents' generation which saw continual growth in incomes, and now experiences growth in retirement benefits, so that in the UK the average income of a pensioner is now higher than the average working-age income.[5] Worse than that is the sense that for millennials and their parents, hope of change is diminishing. The absence of hope makes them more vulnerable to fear, and fear leads to being persuaded that the fault lies with the establishment, with political insiders, or worst of all, with the Other, the foreigner, or even in some cases the imaginary Jewish conspiracy (the oldest form of false fear and appalling racism).

Hope does not depend on experience. Our history demonstrates that it can be inspired by a vision – a new narrative of the future – that opens possibilities, rather than closes them down; that makes an individual or a group, or even a nation, producers in their own drama and not merely actors repeating the lines set by others or by some mysterious fate. Hope gives us purpose – it is life-giving.

[4]See, for example, 'Gaining from Growth: The Final Report of the Commission on Living Standards' (London: Resolution Foundation, 31 October 2012), http://www.resolutionfoundation.org/publications/gaining-growth-final-report-commission-living-standards/. Accessed 11 April 2017.
[5]Adam Corlett and Stephen Clark, 'Living Standards 2017: The Past, Present and Possible Future of UK Incomes' (London: Resolution Foundation, February 2017), http://www.resolutionfoundation.org/app/uploads/2017/01/Audit-2017.pdf. Accessed 11 April 2017.

A great British missionary in South India, Bishop Lesslie Newbigin, on his return to the UK from India in the 1970s, famously said: 'In the subsequent years of ministry in England I have often been asked "What is the greatest difficulty you face in moving from India to England?" I have always answered, "The disappearance of hope."'

François-Xavier, Cardinal Nguyễn văn Thuận, wrote an account[6] of more than a decade in prison in Vietnam after the Communist takeover of the south in 1974. His is a testimony of hope, despite torture, solitary confinement and a near certainty of death in prison, forgotten by the majority of the world. He was sustained by the presence of Christ, by Mass said each day with a grain of rice and enough rice wine to hold in the palm of his hand. He was sustained by the story, the narrative of hope that centres on the resurrection of Christ and his living presence with us now. He was not destroyed by circumstance, or a sense of fatalism, but neither did he have a false hope of survival, a vain optimism. The story of the resurrection of Jesus Christ is the most powerful narrative shift in world history, enabling a small and scattered group of disciples full of despair to set a pattern and style of life that conquered the Roman Empire without violence.

During the Northern Ireland Troubles, one minister of the British government in the Province was often asked during peace talks if he was optimistic. He used to reply that he was not optimistic, but he was hopeful. The difference is essential.

Narratives compete with each other. National elections are essentially competitive narratives, an effort to find the story that appeals most effectively to the electorate.

---

[6]François-Xavier Nguyễn văn Thuận, *Five Loaves and Two Fish* (Washington, DC: Morley Books, 2000).

Ronald Reagan was a master of finding a positive and hope-filled narrative that converted the national mood in the USA at the end of the 1970s from a deep sense of malaise to, in his phrase, 'It's morning in America'. Even grim experience may be overcome by a better narrative. In 1940, the speeches of Prime Minister Winston Churchill were crucial in resetting a national mood from near despair into determined hope, despite recognizing the enormous sacrifices to be made.

Narratives also fail and it is the failure of national narrative that is such an urgent problem at present. In the context of Britain, it has been failing for some time, struggling to come to terms with the post-imperial age. The US Secretary of State Dean Acheson once famously remarked that 'Great Britain has lost an Empire and has not yet found a role.'[7] For some time, within what became the EU, there did seem to be a new narrative emerging, of British leadership in Europe through the EU, and thus leadership in the world. While a leadership role is not essential to generating hope and determination, it must nevertheless be a role that gives a narrative of purpose and progress, of having significance.

Many narratives about our society have failed in the last ten years. The financial collapse of 2008 and the great and lasting recession that followed in most countries (and that remains a great and lasting depression in many such as Greece and Italy) exposed the vain optimism of 'the market state' – the idea that national success needs only to be measured in GDP, that financial engineering can be the basis for endless prosperity, or that materialism can repay

---

[7]Dean Acheson, 'Our Atlantic alliance: the political and economic strands', speech delivered at the United States Military Academy, West Point, New York, 5 December 1962. Reprinted in *Vital Speeches of the Day* xxiv, 6 (1 January 1963), pp. 162–6.

its followers and worshippers. In 2008, the idols of prosperity fell, exposed as the mere illusions that they are.[8]

Other narratives, while virtuous in themselves, have failed because they were overtaken by events. The liberal interventionism of the late 1990s, for example, set out with particular clarity and passion by Prime Minister Tony Blair in Chicago in 1998, failed because it could not be supported adequately by an overarching vision and story that would enable sacrifices sufficiently dramatic to pay the cost, and because it was overwhelmed by events such as the 9/11 terrorist attacks in the USA, and by the subsequent wars in Afghanistan and Iraq.

The narrative of Scottish independence took a knock in the 2017 election. The Grenfell Tower fire revealed the shallowness of our sense of being better run than other countries. The crisis in care provision has cast doubt on our self-image as a caring society, and on the possibilities of repairing the lack. Narrative moods rise and fall, usually for short-term reasons. Reimagining requires refinding the deep stories.

There are several threatening narratives. I wrote in the Introduction about the competing economic narratives of secular stagnation or renewed growth, to which one may add the historic competition between globalization and free trade on one side and protectionism on the other. Religious versus secular narratives struggle with each other in most parts of the world, with the former seeming more powerful (although by no means always more virtuous) in many regions other than Europe and some other of the world's economically most prosperous countries. However, frequently today the most dramatic

---

[8]A number of the chapters of my previous book, *Dethroning Mammon*, deal with the idolatry of finance in greater detail.

narrative is that of international terrorism, often apocalyptic,[9] and parasitical on aspects and dark elements of
all of the mainstream religious traditions of the world.

The narrative of apocalyptic terrorism begins with
contempt and disgust at the perceived valueless state
of those outside its supporters, and continues by establishing a sense of threat and persecution from outside.
It is the 'circle the wagons' approach of the old movie
Westerns, in which the wagon train forms a defensive
circle and keeps out the attackers. All within is good, all
outside is evil and dangerous. Groups such as so-called
Islamic State, or Boko Haram in Nigeria, have a very
clear apocalyptic narrative,[10] as do the equivalent forces,
albeit much less sizeable or powerful, inside Buddhism,
Hinduism and Christianity.

The response to religiously motivated and apocalyptic
terrorism has to be multi-disciplinary. It requires the use
of intelligence, security forces, anthropology, education,
psychology and economics. Theological literacy is essential and usually neglected. The mindset of the apocalyptic
terrorist cannot usually be understood without a sense of
the immanence of God, the call to establish a new world,
and the sense of the condemnation and imminent damna-
tion of all those who do not agree.

However, all of these skills are merely defensive. The
fundamental problem is that apocalyptic terrorism offers
hope, entirely coherently within its own terms (albeit

[9]That is to say, based on a narrative of the end of all things, often accompanied
by the imminent bringing in of a new world by God, and requiring active human
intervention in violent form to trigger the process. See Frances L. Flannery,
Understanding Apocalyptic Terrorism: Countering the Radical Mindset (Abingdon:
Routledge, 2016).
[10]See a booklet from The Centre on Religion and Geopolitics: Emman El-Badawy,
Milo Comerford and Peter Welby, 'Inside the Jihadi Mind' (October 2015), http://
www.religionandgeopolitics.org/crg-report/inside-jihadi-mind.

nonsense outside them), and is thus effective when faced with a mix of narratives that offer little or nothing, except perhaps more shopping.[11] For example, in north-eastern Nigeria there are very high levels (often over 70 per cent) of youth under- or unemployed. To be a young person in such a category prevents marriage, starting a family, or many other ways of building hope and finding happiness.

The traditional answer is wait, be faithful, and in time things may get a little better. Yet the young person sees deep corruption, great disparities of wealth, and hears through social media and through the web of Muslims being bombed and persecuted around the world by the richest nations. Into this sense of loss and frustrated anger the extremist says, 'take this AK-47 and we will turn the world upside down in a few years, and if you die you will be in Paradise'. It is deceit, of course, but a deeply attractive one, and one that many mainstream Muslim leaders struggle to combat (as do other religious leaders facing the equivalent in their own faith; there are also secular parallels, for example with the Khmer Rouge, the alt-right and so on).

For the UK, for Europe and for the USA, the narrative told against us that we are oppressors, morally bankrupt, exerting power with force and thus only answerable with greater force and fear, must be replaced by a narrative of greater moral virtue, of hope and inclusion. It must set out a pattern of life, in cooperation with others around the world, that gives the lie to the false narratives of apocalyptic theology. It must be resilient against extremism and other radical attacks on societies that accept diversity yet

[11]For a lengthy and brilliant analysis of what has brought many Western countries to the 'Market State', see Philip Bobbitt, *The Shield of Achilles: War, Peace and the Course of History* (London: Penguin Books, 2002).

hold to virtue and truth; that interact well with other traditions yet are faithful to their own. In short, it must be a narrative of hope (in the sense of a certain expectation) that is capable of overcoming all setbacks. All that we do has to build hope. Every government policy needs to reinforce the narrative of hope. Our housing, education, health, economy, foreign policy and approach to climate change must strengthen us as a hopeful society.

In post-Brexit Britain we need a more inspiring and better narrative that shapes in us a common purpose, not a sense of division and antagonism, let alone frightened isolation, both domestically and internationally. We need a narrative that speaks to the world of hope and not mere optimism, let alone simple self-interest, that enables us to play a powerful, hopeful and confident role, resisting the turn inwards that will leave us alone, despairing and vulnerable. A vision of this kind will promote community, be courageous and be lived out consistently, notwithstanding the events that come. It is to these three values and their significance within our 'deep magic' that I now turn.

COMMUNITY

Community is one of the great antidotes to insecurity because it speaks to us of the assurance that 'we are all in it together'. It is achieved with a sense of commonality, of common goals. It is open to and welcomes arguments and diversity, but sets parameters, a boundary line, within which actions are taken. There are many great episodes of community in the Bible, and numerous stories of seeking to establish it. Two leading examples are the exodus of the people of Israel from Egypt (found in the books of Exodus, Leviticus, Numbers and Deuteronomy) and the early years of the New Testament community of the Church, in the Acts of the Apostles chapters 2–6.

The impact of both these stories has been monumental, and they are deeply embedded in those countries where Christian faith has taken root. In the UK, the exodus story is reduced in impact for most of us because – at least at the national level – we have not known slavery, occupation or oppression for a very long time. By contrast, the story held huge power and promise for African Americans in the states south of the Mason–Dixon line during the time of slavery and subsequently in the Civil Rights movement of the twentieth century, and to this day in the *favelas* and slums of Latin America, where the gap between rich and poor is among the largest in the world. It resonates in Northern Ireland, Scotland and Wales, and with many minority communities across the UK, whether around ethnicity, disability, gender or sexuality.

In such circumstances, where inequality and the abuse of power are great, the exodus speaks of the care of God for the poor and oppressed, and the power of God to deliver through those who will serve him faithfully and courageously. The Israelites in the wilderness after the exodus had many problems, from enemies without to their own divisions and sin within the community. Yet there was a commonality which the rest of the Old Testament looks back to with celebration and almost nostalgia. Food was held in common, given by God as manna and quail each day. God's love is expressed in community and provision.

The author of the Acts of the Apostles, Luke, deliberately sets out a similar pattern of life. The earliest Christians had all things in common, and no one was in need. There are two summaries, at the end of Acts 2 and

Acts 4, in which the love, generosity, inclusion and common vision of the new community is seen. Even deep-set ethnic differences are overcome, and where people seek to take unfair and deceitful advantage, God steps in powerfully (Acts 6).

At other points in the Bible there are conscious efforts to recreate such communities of equality; and at the very end, in Revelation chapters 18–21, there is the vision of a new heaven and a new earth in which the common good is achieved, and a society perfectly filled with love is created. Nehemiah, the leader of the Jews following their exile in the two decades after 600 BC, tackles the issue of rebuilding not only the physical walls of Jerusalem but also its moral and spiritual walls, which are founded on the exodus and the Law of Moses. He knows that physical walls will not by themselves protect the people unless their lives are lived communally in obedience to God and love for one another.

The inspiration of these passages, and their echoes above all in the psalms and in the lives and aspirations of Christians, has set patterns for revolutionary and peaceful living throughout Christian history. St Benedict founded his monastic rule on this ideal, a rule which not only gave the context for Christian living in an age of barbarism, but incidentally helped save European civilization in the early medieval period we call the Dark Ages. In the 1930s, Pastor Dietrich Bonhoeffer formed a community not only to train pastors but to do so by living a life in common, in resistance to the oppressive and demonic power of the Nazi state.

In all these examples, there was freedom to be different, but not freedom to damage the common good, or to imperil the common vision. As a result, they set a pattern of community swelling up from below rather than imposed from above. Whether autocratic, totalitarian, theocratic or democratic, narratives that are imposed do not bring community but, at best, mere compliance, which lasts only a little while. In the City of London during the crisis of 2008–09 the length of a company's ethics code was often in direct and inverse proportion to the likelihood of it failing ethically.

In 1891, Pope Leo XIII published an encyclical – a letter to all the faithful – entitled *Rerum Novarum* (or known by its English title 'On Capital and Labour'). It was the beginning of a series of encyclicals, continued to this day, in which are set out the main aspects of what is often referred to as Catholic Social Teaching: the applied outworking of the good news of Jesus Christ in terms of social structures and social justice.

The teaching originally arose from the impact of the European Industrial Revolution, and in response to the threat of Bolshevism and socialism, as it was perceived in Rome. Its aim was community in society, but it did not seek that end by obligations imposed on the weak and the poor but by a series of brilliant reflections on the nature of a functional and just society.

It is a complex body of thought, but among the key and most influential aspects are five principles which need a renewed focus in a reimagined set of shared national values, applicable to all parts of life, including the economy. They are: the universal destination of goods, gratuity, the common good, solidarity and subsidiarity.

The universal destination of goods says that all that exists is given by God for all. It is not against private property, far from it, but sees all ownership, whether individual or collective, as containing an element of stewardship or trusteeship. What we own, whether as a person, a company or other body corporate, or even as a nation, is there

not only for ourselves, but also for the rest of those living and for the generations to come.

The knee-jerk reaction of many, especially on the
political right, on hearing such ideas, is to say 'told you
so, leftie, trendy vicar stuff, a recipe for Marxism with a
pointy roof'. The universal destination of goods imposes
moral more than legal responsibilities, and calls on individuals and governments to ensure that they do not act
selfishly to the detriment of the rest of the world, now or
to come. The 'how' of its implementation is not set out,
but the value and aim of it is. Christian social teaching is
never of the 'left' or 'right' in political terms (and never
was; it predates such labels by the larger part of two
millennia), but has as its aim the revealing of the values
and nature of the kingdom of God, of a society where
what is good and wonderful and fruitful for all people is
lived out. The German philosopher Friedrich Nietzsche
would have hated such a body of work, because it is a
doctrine of love and self-giving, not a desire for power.
As Benedict XVI said, 'A humanism which excludes
God is an inhuman humanism. Only a humanism open
to the Absolute can guide us in the promotion and building of forms of social and civic life – structures, institutions, culture and ethos – without exposing us to the risk
of becoming ensnared by the fashions of the moment.'[12]

Gratuity is at the heart of being human. 'Gratuitousness
is present in our lives in many different forms, which
often go unrecognized because of a purely consumerist
and utilitarian view of life. The human being is made for
gift, which expresses and makes present his transcendent
dimension.'[13] In its ancient use, it means love given freely,

---

[12]*Caritas in Veritate* (Vatican, 2009), paragraph 78.
[13]*Idem*, paragraph 35.

an abundance of generosity without hope of return, not a tip or something got for nothing. It is based in understanding the nature of life as more than exchange and equivalence, a giant zero-sum game in which what you gain I lose: rather, it is based on the idea of abundance and gift, of life as having more than enough for all and thus gift being a way of increasing what we all have.

We see gratuity in the carer looking after a child with disabilities, or an incapacitated parent. Too often, as Benedict XVI says, we do not recognize the care as gift, a virtue and good in itself, but talk in terms of economic effect alone. In 2016, a government-generated questionnaire (*The Times*, 17 August 2016) designed to measure deprivation asked whether the respondent had been a carer while still a child. Those who have lived with such things know that it is severe hardship, and deeply unfair, but not *solely* by itself a test of economic deprivation as a human being (although normally associated with it). Love given and received is not deprivation. To call it such is to reduce relationships to the crudest of economic calculations.

Gratuity looks for ways of sharing excess, that which is more than we need. It recognizes that companies may have a return on capital employed that is adequate, although they could have more, and that they thus have a social duty to restrain their monopolistic search for market control, and instead to pay a living wage, to improve services to customers, to ensure that they operate cleanly and safely, to remunerate shareholders for the risk they have taken by investing, and thus to restrain senior executive pay.

Gratuity is not merely about philanthropy (although it is a part of it), but about finding ways of life that satisfy what is required – for example, that the return on capital is at least equal to its cost – and are also sustainable. Corporate social responsibility budgets are not the same thing, nor even is the individual who tithes all that they have. Gratuity springs from a sense of 'love-in-action', a reaching out simply because there are other human beings around us with needs.

The common good is the sharpest and most uncomfortable challenge to our financially centred society. We are accustomed to speaking of the general interest, a sort of average of the needs and claims of a given group of people. We hear about the general interest when the latest economic report tells us that our Gross Domestic Product (GDP) has risen and that it is good news for everyone. Averages, like all statistics, have to be treated with great care. In a group where one person earns one million pounds a year, and nine earn ten thousand each, the average income is £109,000, a very generous income indeed. Yet no one is earning it. The common good looks not to averages (or even the mean, or median income) but to the totality of flourishing in the group. In our example, the millionaire would be asked to take a very large pay cut, not necessarily to the same level as all the others, but so that everyone, albeit with differences, had enough, and, incidentally, there was a significant surplus for the purposes of gratuity.

A living example of the problem is in the Eurozone, to which I alluded in the Introduction. Average incomes across Europe are high compared to the rest of the world, yet Greece in particular (along with other countries, especially in Southern Europe) is imprisoned by debt. The reason for this is not important in this context, even though there is a strong argument that previous Greek governments, with the collusion of the European institutions and international banks, created the disaster that has happened. Yet no one can look at Greece and find that they are able to see the common good as a priority in the formation of policy, or fail to see how a failure to actively pursue it led to the current situation.

In the United Kingdom, one of the questions that must be asked as we leave the European Union is whether we will have a culture that tolerates huge disparities of wealth, a growing inequality, regions left behind so that in times of growth they grow less quickly than the prosperous areas and in times of recession they shrink more quickly and more definitively.

The common good is not seen in a 'bread and circuses' set of values, which seeks to keep the poor quiet with charity or handouts, so that the rich may get on with becoming richer. The common good is a foundation of stability in society, and a source of hope. It liberates skills in every corner of society, and refuses ever to treat people as a means to an end, or an inconvenience to be looked after.

In wartime it is easy to see how it must be achieved. In 1940, the idea that victory in the war would be for the benefit of only some Britons was clearly absurd. Defeat meant defeat for all. So strong was that sense of the common good that it spilled over into the reimagining of society after the war. What was seen as essential at a time of battle could not be forgotten when the struggle was against Beveridge's five evils.

Solidarity is a cousin of the common good. The word sprang into popular consciousness when it became the title of the Polish trades union, *Solidarność*, set up in the 1980s to resist tyrannical communism in Poland. Led by Lech Walesa, it became, closely allied with the Catholic Church, a centre of the resistance to the government; and, after the fall of the Berlin Wall in 1989, it achieved its aim of a democratic and free Poland for the first time since 1939. In English, the concept is summed up beautifully and succinctly by John Donne:

No man is an island,
Entire of itself,
Every man is a piece of the continent,
A part of the main.
If a clod be washed away by the sea,
Europe is the less.
As well as if a promontory were.
As well as if a manor of thy friend's
Or of thine own were:
Any man's death diminishes me,
Because I am involved in mankind,
And therefore never send to know for whom the bell tolls;
It tolls for thee.[14]

The challenge of solidarity is the challenge to care for those with whom we have connections. In the age of social media that essentially covers the whole world, the capacity to apprehend loss and need must be developed not so as to paralyse us before the endless suffering of human beings, but to call us to belong to one another.

A friend of mine, a bishop in the Democratic Republic of the Congo (DRC), when asked some years ago about the number of refugees in the area where he lives, said, 'Oh, around two million.' When I asked him how he coped, and what he did in the face of such unmeetable needs, he said, 'We do what we can, what God enables us to do.' That is true solidarity.

The greatest danger of the changes affecting our country at present is that we turn inwards and lose a 'global economy' perspective. Economically and politically, there would be collateral damage to such an approach,

[14]John Donne, 'Devotions Upon Emergent Occasions: Meditation XVII' (1624).

as it would lead to our increased vulnerability, to impoverishment, to domestic instability and failure. Far more than that, it would mean that we did not recognize our solidarity with one another or with the world around us, thus never acknowledge that we lose greatly when others suffer: we would not hear that the bell tolls for us. Solidarity breaks down barriers, drawing us to love and care actively for those with whom we disagree, separated by nationality, history, gender, race and sexuality.

Solidarity is a value which resists gross inequality but seeks for the gain of others so that all may gain. Despite Donne's words, he is not being called in aid of resistance to Brexit, but rather in aid of commitment to finding a new way in which as a country we are bound to the rest of the world.

Finally, another European word, far more spoken of than acted on, is *subsidiarity*. The principle is simple. All actions and decisions in any group or organization should be handled by the smallest, lowest, most local or least centralized level that is practical and efficient. It sounds obvious, but everything militates against it, especially our growing capacity in information technology and in systems.

A few years ago, I was visiting the Chief Executive of the local County Council. He had just returned from London, over 200 miles away, after a visit to the Department of Education. There he had been shown a system which was able to tell him how many children in a certain primary school Year 3 group in his area had learning difficulties, and what progress they were making. Rather than being impressed, he was concerned, and asked why the Department kept information on such a granular basis. The reply was that they needed to monitor his efficiency, and to know what could be done. Just because we can do something never means we automatically should. By all means let the head teacher hold the Special Educational Needs coordinator to account, with the class teacher, for the progress of those children. Let the governors of the school oversee what is happening. But once you get much further away than that, you are asking for bureaucracy, lack of local knowledge, and things being done *to* people rather than *with* them.

Subsidiarity is difficult because it accepts that there will be failures because of local difference and incapacity, while claiming that local responsibilities, and local knowledge, will be more important in resisting oppression, misjudgement and cruelty than central systems. Subsidiarity puts suffering in three dimensions – tangible, audible and visible – right in front of us. We cannot switch it off, because it is close. We cannot find another page with less concerning questions, because it is present. Of course, the reverse danger is local collusion, the tyranny of the neighbourhood. The complexity of modern large-scale institutions makes a partnership of central and professional expertise with local and informed voices an essential aspect of ensuring values are turned into practices, and practices inform values. A striking example is found in the Francis Report, 'It is a significant part of the Stafford story that patients and relatives felt excluded from effective participation in the patients' care. The concept of patient and public involvement in health service provision starts and should be at its most effective at the front line.'[15] In other words, local input mattered and matters.

[15]The Mid Staffordshire NHS Foundation Trust Public Inquiry, chaired by Robert Francis QC, Executive Summary February 2013, paras 1.9 (p. 44) and 1.17 (p. 46).

The Church of England operates on a strong system of subsidiarity. The authority of the archbishops is profoundly limited: they can guide, make suggestions, encourage, but very seldom give instructions. Happily, they neither hire nor fire the bishops. The bishops are in a similar position with the majority of their parish clergy and chaplains. The results are usually messy, often inefficient, but they give a deep resilience and sense of local responsibility to those who have to make things happen. They do not always prevent trouble, and in some areas they have failed, most seriously in the prevention of the abuse of children and vulnerable adults. At the same time, the resilience of the Church is not based in a few people at the 'top', whatever that means (it is a concept disliked by Jesus), but on the 15,000 and more local parishes and groups, who will continue doing what they do pretty well regardless of what happens at some self-imagined grand central level of decision making.

Community is what makes us stick together. The five principles of community are the core values for enabling a society to know that it is not an atomized collection of individuals, but that its deep magic comprises unbreakable bonds of mutuality, of permitting diversity, of rescuing the weak, of letting local communities flourish, and of generating a non-economically based sense of human value and dignity.

COURAGE

A vibrant, flexible and dynamic culture needs more than community. The values of community do not start with where and what we are; that is to say, they do not start with our nature, which tends to be selfish, but assume an acceptance of self-discipline that imposes selflessness on ourselves.

The values of Catholic Social Teaching have become implicit in our culture when at its best; they have emerged from the Christian tradition that has shaped Europe and thus become part of our nation's heritage. Yet they risk being static in a world that is intensely fluid and changing as a result of technology, communications, travel, migration and other forms of globalization. The love of God is dynamic, flowing powerfully through different places and times.

The dynamic group of values which relate most closely to the needs of our future, to the calls of love-in-action and to the nature of human beings, are those I call courage. Three values merit special consideration; aspiration, creativity and competition.

Aspiration is seen in the desire to make a mark, to change things, to achieve at some level or another. It is reflected in the Bible, in stories with which we are deeply familiar. Abraham sets out from his own home and family with the God-given aspiration to find the land promised by God, and to see the fulfilment of God's promise to him. His heroic status is found in his faith, trusting God's promise for something he would not see completed.[16] The impulse for the aspiration is God's, but its expression is seen in the life of Abraham.

King David celebrates not only the throne of Israel, but more than that the knowledge that he is founding a dynasty (2 Samuel 23:5). The Apostle Paul aspires and strives to reach the finishing line set for him by God, using images of an athlete in a race straining for the tape.

---

[16]For a brilliant and brief comment see Rabbi Lord Jonathan Sacks, *Lessons in Leadership: A Weekly Reading of the Jewish Bible* (New Milford: Maggid Books, 2015), pp. 23–6.

Beyond the Bible, much of our most celebrated litera-
ture that is profoundly influential in shaping our values
is grounded in aspiration. The Homeric heroes, especially Achilles, engage in war to create a name that will
outlast them. Shakespeare reflects on the contradictions
of pride and aspiration in *Coriolanus*, and on its power
and capacity for evil when unbridled in *Richard III* and
Henry VI.

A society without aspiration that is embedded in
the virtues of community will become inward looking
and complacent. It will become disposed to protect the
status quo at the expense of desirable change for the
common good.

Creativity is the necessary companion of aspiration
in a world that does not work on a 'zero-sum' model. If
all I need to fulfil my aspirations is to seize what belongs
to others, I need not create, but if I want to add to the
world then something new must appear. The first chapters of the Bible speak of a God whose very nature is
creative, and who imprints that nature in human beings.
In our creativity of all kinds, from engineering to art, we
show ourselves to be made in the image of God. As a
carpenter, Jesus himself made a living in a creative industry for the majority of his life.

Creativity is the greatest gift to the common good.
Its side effects may be damaging (as in the Industrial
Revolutions and much modern industry and economic
activity), but its capacity to improve health and life,
to give generously to human flourishing, is colossal.
Values that do not include creativity or fail to liberate the creative spirit will inevitably constrain human
flourishing.

Creativity implies taking risks, and thus accepting
failures as a normal part of human experience and of the

experience of society. A set of values that rejects failure, or refuses to recognize it, will condemn itself to deceit and ultimate and decisive failure.[17]

Competition is natural to human beings and must be recognized in our values as something that may lead either to human flourishing or to selfish mutual destruction. It has always existed in terms of access to resources, in sport and entertainment, in business and trade. Its benefits in a healthy economy with reasonable regulation are understood by economists as driving up services and improving the efficiency of what happens in economic transactions. St Paul tells the Roman Christians to 'outdo one another in showing honour'.[18] It is a dangerous value, for unless combined with the others it leads to oppression. Yet when suppressed it breaks out in forceful and often destructive paths. In the Soviet Union of the 1930s, the pretended absence of economic competition was matched in its failures and falsity by the ruthless competition for power which gave access to the resources and pleasures denied by a supposedly 'competition free' economy.

Competition recognises, and seeks to dispel, the natural complacency of human beings. Throughout history, monopoly has led to abuse of power and laziness, whether organisational or individual. Organizations that are subject to competition will normally seek either to replace or to acquire the competitor, or – if prevented by regulation from doing so – to outperform it. They may act through raising productivity and thus reducing costs, improving quality, or cutting prices. The element

[17]*We Never Make Mistakes: Two Short Novels*, by Aleksandr Solzhenitsyn (Columbia, SC: University of South Carolina Press, 1963), is a powerful reflection on exactly the problem of lack of creativity and acceptance of failure.
[18]Romans 12:10.

of competition compels the organization to address the interests of its consumers, sometimes at the expense of its producers.

The impact of competition is also significant at an individual level. The desire to rise to the top, to be the most recognised, to excel is one that drives athletes to better performance, and is used to challenge teams at work. Competition is part of being human, and when disciplined is a catalyst of achievement.

All systems of values must link not only to the tradition of the virtues, as expressed implicitly in a particular culture, but also to the nature of the human being. The social (and I would argue theological) anthropology is as important as the ethics. Without understanding a little of what makes a human being, values are no more than ethical castles in the air. However, there are natural and almost insuperable contradictions between values of community and the values of courage, and they must be linked and harmonized by the third group, the values of stability.

STABILITY

Aspiration, creativity and competition all generate conflict and uncertainty. Within limits, this is not serious, but the inevitable corruption that attends all human activity leads necessarily to enmity, to seeking monopoly and market fixing, to falsification and to abuses of the weak.

Values of stability are those that give an overall system of values the capacity to be generative of healing when things go wrong. Reconciliation, resilience and sustainability enable the mechanisms and impulses that bring together community and courage for the common good rather than conflict.

Reconciliation is the transformation of destructive conflict into creative and dynamic diversity which encourages growth and development. It rejects coercion and embraces difference within the broadest possible limits that still maintain community. It encourages competition, aspiration and creativity, but enables them to be constructive values, dealing with failure and diversity by enabling a mutual acceptance, rather than being a means of gaining power at the expense of others.

The costs of failing to have systems and mechanisms for reconciliation are huge, and a society in which the concept does not exist is doomed to anarchy. Every household develops some sort of technique of reconciliation, although they are not always healthy ones. In nation states, the development of democracy is a means of reconciling competing stories of how flourishing should happen between competing groups who seek power. General elections are, in effect, reconciled civil war, the seizing of power without the gun.

The example of elections reveals the difference between reconciliation and mere peace-making. A healthy democracy recognizes that the common good is served by diversity, and that elections enable the diversity to be experimented with over time. As we know in the UK, in moments of tragedy or crisis political differences can be put aside. A notable example was the coalition government of 1940–45. By contrast, in one country with which I am familiar, the period since the last civil war has not resulted in reconciliation. Neither side fully accepts the legitimacy of the other, and as a result there is a grave danger of renewed hostility.

Reconciliation is often seen as an 'event', whereas it should be part of the ongoing process of self-healing of any group, a living and dynamic process which is always operating at some level. Those groups and nations that have arrived at means of settling disputes creatively and not destructively are distinctive in their ability to cope with new circumstances, movements and groups.

There is no single, effective model for reconciliation, but there are some basic principles. Reconciliation is the process by which diversity is accepted and even welcomed, without sliding towards oppression by the dominant power. It starts with a rejection of unanimity or absolute conformity, let alone the use of coercion.[19] In their constant struggle against the human desire for dominance, the reconciled as well as the reconcilers must sacrifice their own rights and advantages. It is a costly business with an outcome *that will not normally fully satisfy anyone*, but which enables all to flourish to a degree compatible with the flourishing of those with whom they disagree, and as a whole, to the benefit of the wider society.

In Christian understanding, the paradigmatic act of reconciliation is found in the life, death, resurrection and ascension of Jesus, with the empowering sending of the Holy Spirit. The cost is huge: the life of the Son of God. There is no coercion: the party with all the power, the one offering the means of reconciliation – God the Father, through Jesus Christ – is bound by promise to the offer of reconciliation. The ones to whom it is offered (every single one of us) are free to choose whether to pursue its aims. Its outcomes are new relationships with God, with the community of believers, with the world, even with enemies, all of whom are loved with the overflowing love given by the Father through Jesus in the Holy Spirit.

[19]For a fascinating case study and discussion of this point, see Chapter 9, 'Tolerant Cranmer?', in Diarmaid MacCulloch, *All Things Made New: Writings on the Reformation* (London: Allen Lane, 2016), pp. 118–35.

Reconciliation is the core of Christianity. Its cost and challenge are seen in the interminable failures to live it out within the Church, and even in societies with very high proportions of professing Christians. The shame of the actions of the Church through its history of persecuting other Christians and those outside Christian faith is an appalling burden which weighs on any credible witness to the good news of Jesus Christ. Reconciliation demands honesty about our own failures and our pasts – individually and collectively.

The cost of reconciliation is mirrored by the enormity of its possibilities. The greatest example to date in human history is the reconciliation of the countries of Western Europe since 1945. When the two halves of the twentieth century are compared in that region, one of them demonstrates almost nothing but tyranny, bloodshed and cruelty beyond words. The other shows mainly (not entirely) steady growth, concern for the weak, the reduction of barriers of all sorts, and the development of generosity of spirit which has created what may well be argued to have been a golden age for Europe, at least in comparison to the centuries preceding it.

To achieve such a change will always require huge sacrifice: in Christian understanding, the very example of Jesus is that the cost of bringing about such a change is enormous. That sense of cost has become part of our culture. Peace-making is seen as a virtue; the achievement of reconciliation, a triumph. Reconciliation is sometimes impossible, the nature of human evil means that there are those who seek only to be able to rule or act without accountability and without concern for others. Yet without reconciliation as an assumed value, the only other road leads to the Hobbesian description of human life without order, or to avoid such a disaster, to coercion and the use of power as the only final resort:

> In such condition there is no place for industry, because the fruit thereof is uncertain, and consequently, not culture of the earth, no navigation, nor the use of commodities that may be imported by sea, no commodious building, no instruments of moving and removing such things as require much force, no knowledge of the face of the earth, no account of time, no arts, no letters, no society, and which is worst of all, continual fear and danger of violent death, and the life of man, solitary, poor, nasty, brutish, and short.[20]

Resilience is more often spoken of as a need for individuals, especially those in political leadership. The resilience of societies and of nations is measured in their capacity not only to deal with shocks and traumas, but also to maintain their values in times of prosperity and flourishing. This virtue is captured by Rudyard Kipling in his poem 'If': 'If you can meet with Triumph and Disaster / And treat those two impostors just the same ...'

There is a strong argument that the financial catastrophe of 2008, not only in the UK, Europe and the USA but all round the world, resulted from a lack of resilience to the lures and dreams of prosperity. The increase of debt in the economy, and the ever growing financialization of the largest economies (their dominance by finance as a sector all on its own, not merely in service to the

---

[20]Thomas Hobbes, *Leviathan: Or the Matter, Forme, & Power of a Commonwealth Ecclesiasticall and Civill* (1651), http://www.bartleby.com/34/5/13.html. Chapter XIII, paragraph 9.

real economy), undermined resilience. They became less able to cope with shocks, and margins of safety in case of human error were reduced until banks could be toppled by historically small and prospectively likely losses.

Approaches to the threat of terrorism often show a need for resilience, for a capacity to respond vigorously and actively but without allowing those things we value to be destroyed. Resilience is shown by a system not needing serious change even when threatened. The argument for the use of torture in the UK or USA, forbidden in the far more threatening times of 1939–45, demonstrates a lack of resilience.

Resilience and hope are closely linked. Without hope, resilience is mere obstinacy and will be ground down by stronger forces. When hope is part of the equation, even great suffering may be endured in the consciousness that it is for a purpose, even when that purpose is itself questionable. The 'Blitz Spirit' of 1940–42 in many UK cities was matched by equivalents in the German cities in 1942–45. Resilience is a very natural human condition, and thus when it breaks down the results are especially horrific.

Resilience as a value springs from an inner sense. It finds the right way to act even when circumstances change, but is adequately flexible when faced with the unexpected. In 2 Samuel 15, King David deals with a rebellion by his son Absalom (a rebellion which, as it happens, is the fruit of inadequate reconciliation). Absalom's revolt takes David by surprise and he has to flee from Jerusalem. The narrative describes encounters with supporters and enemies as he flees down towards the Jordan valley. Yet, after an initial sense of panic, David's moral actions are resilient, caring for his followers, not – despite the urging of his companions – seeking revenge against a man insulting him, and acting justly.

At the heart of resilience is the determination to do what is right, however much it costs the individual, or even the nation. Winston Churchill's greatest gift to the UK in 1940 was a capacity to inspire resilience, even when the majority of his cabinet and his advisers were advocating negotiation.

Sustainability underpins everything else. There are limits to human endurance and to the endurance of societies. There comes a time when, even in the greatest causes, human beings feel that they can do no more. Values must be sustainable under pressure, whether pressure of fear, of exhaustion or of the natural human desire to protect oneself and those closest around.

Sustainability comes not only from the narrative that a group or country projects, but above all from company and fellowship. A society or a country with sustainable values must know how to support those who struggle and to forgive those who fail. Above all, as discussed later, the world is increasingly aware of the need for the global ecosystems to be sustainable.

In the days before his crucifixion Jesus warns his disciples that they will not be resilient in sustaining their loyalty to him. They protest and St Peter says that he will die rather than betray Jesus. When the time comes and Jesus is arrested, Peter follows at a distance by himself. As he stands by a fire warming himself outside the house where Jesus is being held, he is challenged by various people. He denies that he knew Jesus, three times.[21]

Peter could not sustain loyalty for a number of reasons. He was unprepared and had not mentally faced the reality of what would happen. He was alone. In the weeks after the resurrection of Jesus, however, he was

[21]See Mark 14:66–72.

restored. He received forgiveness; he joined in with the company of disciples; he recognized his own weaknesses.

To be sustainable, values must be mutually encouraged, they must provide for failure and not condemn people who fall short, and they must make honesty about ourselves easier. They must also be seen in our actions, in order that they be embedded in our thinking. The greatest test of modern governments and modern society is not policy (which we have coming out of our ears), but implementation – the things we do because they reflect what we are.

The three groups of values work together. Community, made up of the universal destination of goods, gratuity, solidarity, the common good and subsidiarity, enables us to stick together. Courage, with aspiration, creativity and competition, gives us strength to move forward. Stability, built on reconciliation, resilience and sustainability, enables us to cope with the chances and changes of a rapidly moving world.

THE BUILDING BLOCKS OF A HOPEFUL SOCIETY

The building blocks for implementation of values include ones that have existed for all of the twentieth century and much of the nineteenth. At a governmental level, whether local or national, they are educational policy, housing and health, especially public health and now mental health. Three of the chapters further on in this book look in more detail at how these areas can help to reimagine Britain today, and what needs they must meet to do so.

However, since 1945 the enormous changes in our own country, across Europe and in the structures and nature of society in richer countries have combined to make a number of other building blocks as important as the trinity of housing, health and education.

The nature of families has changed enormously. The introduction of equal marriage in many countries including (since 2014) the UK, the transformation in habits of cohabitation before marriage from something regarded as daring or scandalous to something accepted as normal, and other trends and changes, have all combined to challenge the image of the classical family. In many ways, because the image was probably a myth, and where it existed was often patriarchal, hypocritical and deceptive, these changes have often been more honest. My grandmother used to remark that my generation thought we were the first to discover sex. When she was growing up, the risk of pregnancy was very inhibiting for sex before marriage, but where she lived, when there was a party the unmarried young women always had a married chaperone. With her friends, they cruelly nicknamed their chaperone 'the promiscuous carrot' because of her striking red hair and willingness, her husband being away, to sleep with a number of different people.

The nature of what we recognize as family has changed remarkably, and there is a great need for households to be safe places for children and the vulnerable, to be places of healing and of stability. The family is the base community of society, and its values are crucial to the values of a society or nation. Too often the family is neglected or treated as merely an economic unit, or a group to be appealed to by politicians.

In 1945, the stability of the climate and the environment was taken for granted. Today it is overwhelmingly accepted that climate change is human-generated, and represents a massive threat to our future.

The economy and the role of finance are areas of such power that the values which they adopt tend to be the values all of us follow. They may build a sense of materialistic selfishness, unaccountable profit seeking, or they may develop the common good and the universal destination of goods. They are truly international. One of the last major economies that sought to strike out on its own in economic policy was France in the early 1980s. It rapidly became evident that the pressure of international and globalized markets was stronger than any one sovereign state, and that the choice was either impoverishment in a siege economy or partnership internationally. The nature and development of economic and financial policy defaults to being market driven and not values driven: any country that wants a just and good society will require immense courage to challenge the power of Mammon.[22]

In 1945, the issues of foreign policy were relatively clear. Europe needed reconstruction. Demobilization was urgent. Peaceful relations had to be started almost from scratch between many countries. The Stalinist occupation of Eastern Europe had to be faced. Much of the Empire needed independence. In the light of the EU referendum result, but far more as a result of the development of international law and relations in the years since the Second World War, most of all since the fall of the Berlin Wall in 1989, foreign policy is now a key building block for national values. The history of the UK makes this especially true. Throughout our history since the late seventeenth century, we have had an expansive and courageous (but often not virtuous) foreign policy. For centuries it was

[22]For more background on the biblical character of Mammon, see the Introduction to *Dethroning Mammon*.

built around the taking and holding of imperial power as well as the preservation of security at home. In the last half-century, it has progressively become more linked to seeking to find our role, to encourage values abroad, and more recently in developing soft power through the use of international aid, in which we are one of the leaders in the world. What we do and how we act beyond our borders reflects who we are within them, and so a 'proactive' foreign policy is a key part of a reimagined Britain.

Finally, the issues of immigration and integration have emerged as of crucial importance both in terms of policy and to the electorate. This will be dealt with more fully later in the book. Immigration is consistently raised in polls as a primary concern of the people of this country, and the challenge of dealing with more people on the move around the world as refugees of one kind or another than at any time in history is one that is a primary policy issue everywhere. Almost no country has yet shown that it is capable of addressing this in a way that satisfies both its own population and a general sense of obligation.

All these different areas of life help to define values as well as other issues too numerous to deal with in this book, but they include such subjects as defence and policing, the prisons and penal system, and transport. They are all of immense importance, but this book is not a political manifesto, nor a grand blueprint for society, and the number of areas of application is necessarily thus limited.

THE ACTORS AND THE PLAY

Values do not, however, exist in isolation, but by interaction with practices. Good values feed good practices, and the evidence of good practice builds good values.

Certainly within the UK the strength of values has been recognized pragmatically. Simply to state them, however often and however clearly – as being, for example, democracy, the rule of law, individual liberty and mutual respect and tolerance of different faiths and beliefs – does not make them.[23] They need actors, who play them with such conviction and effect that they become what they claim. It is said that to become an expert in something requires 10,000 hours of practice. How do we practise our shared values, and do we consider ourselves to be experts?

That 'becoming' will not happen with the values listed above (good as they are), because they are not part of our history, and there is a barely acknowledged hypocrisy in them. Where was democracy in the Empire? Do we respect Dr Martin Luther King, Archbishop Tutu, Nelson Mandela or Gandhi because they observed the rule of law or because they broke the law in the service of deeper values? How do we find the limits of tolerance? These are values near the surface, useful but not strong enough to bear the weight of a complex and shifting society. The values of the 'deep magic' are so important because they are weight-bearing.

The actors in the drama of our country have also grown in number and diversity. In addition to government at all levels, the churches and the private sector, there is now a large civil society, great institutions like the NHS and a diverse multiplicity of faith groups. No longer held together by a single story (however true or false) of what it means to be British or by a widely held set of values,

---

[23]List of 'Fundamental British Values', as set out in HMG's *Prevent* Strategy, published in 2011, https://www.gov.uk/government/uploads/system/uploads/attachment_data/file/97976/prevent-strategy-review.pdf, p. 107.

these varied actors have to seek ways of interacting powerfully and effectively. In looking at the building blocks of our values, I will also be arguing for the intermediate institutions that collectively bring these actors on to the stage and enable the drama of the practice of values to be reimagined. Values are developed and refined above all in intermediate institutions, which is where democracy is founded, and our diversity preserved and nurtured for the common good. Intermediate groups are where we build social capital, integrate, learn loyalties, practices and values, learn to disagree well – to build hope and resilience. Intermediate institutions are repositories of practices and loyalties fundamental to who we are, even with their idiosyncrasies and untidiness.

SUMMARY

- We are in a time of great economic, political and technological change in which our values, virtues and practices will be reshaped. We must draw on our history and culture to ensure the inevitable reimagining builds hope.

- Whether Brexit happens or not, there is the same need for reimagining.

- This book proposes that we find in our history three groups of values, common to much of Europe, but adapted by the practices of the UK. The three groups are community, courage and stability.

- Each constituent part of the UK has its own particular narratives of value, which interact with each other.

- Our values are expressed in our practices, which today must include the environment and immigration.

- The key players in reimagining are our intermediate institutions.

PART TWO

The Basic Building Blocks

2

Family – Caring for the Core

In almost all circumstances of human life the greatest source of hope, and the main location of despair, is found in the family. By family I also mean something close to household and use both or either terms to mean much the same, and include where appropriate extended families, because the shape and nature of family life has varied enormously through history and continues to vary in different social contexts today. The structures of families range from the oppressive and abusive to the utterly liberating and healing.

Families are (and always have been) flexible groups, with somewhat elastic boundaries. People can find themselves part of a family or household by reception or adoption, as well as by birth. Especially in an era where a high proportion of family units break up, many children grow up with a step-something, and a complex pattern of what they understand as family.

We should not have illusions about families, nor should we collude in idolizing them. These errors have led to such sins as ignoring issues of abuse and domestic violence. Yet the answer to bad families is not no families but good families. Too often the response of the state in different parts of the world to family life, good or bad, has been to see families as a threatening counter-centre of power, or a source of harm, and to seek to control, direct or interfere with them.

Everyone knows the bad statistics. In the UK something close to 80 per cent of all abuse happens in families. In some parts of the world they are the main source of patriarchal and demeaning treatment of women. The complexities of family life are found in the biblical stories, from Cain and Abel, through the patriarchs to David; in the very family-ambivalent teaching of Jesus, and in the letters of Paul and other writers of the epistles. Yet while the Bible is realistic about families, it is also profoundly positive. The idea of family begins with the Creation story. The stories of the patriarchs are based in family. God's promises to Abraham revolve around family, as do David's. Jesus upholds the value of family and the obligations of fidelity between husband and wife. In the Acts of the Apostles, households are places of worship, of conversion and of mission (some of the New Testament epistles set out the nature of relationships in the family of the time).[1] The family or household (because the family in biblical times normally looked nothing like the family in the UK of the twenty-first century) is never an idol to be worshipped, but it is at the centre of what is needed for a good life.

We also know, as Catholic Social Teaching puts it,[2] that the family is the 'fundamental nucleus' of society, the Church in micro form, the training ground for generosity, for courage, for community life, for stability and

[1] For example, Ephesians 5:21–33, Colossians 3:18–25, I Peter 3:1–7.
[2] See *The Social Agenda of the Catholic Church* (London: Bloomsbury Continuum, 2002). A version is available for download from http://www.thesocialagenda.org/.

above all, for hope. A happy family life, lived out amid difficulty and challenge, is among the deepest satisfactions of human existence, and when it is prevalent in a society it lays the foundations for hope and national character in a way that is impossible to replicate in any other form of human institution. Some of life's greatest gifts – stability and fidelity, the knowledge of love and community – are often 'givens' within the family or household, so that the values lived in the micro are practised for the macro.

The good family is the foundational intermediate institution in society, and one to which every human being necessarily belongs in one way or another. It addresses issues of care, isolation and rootlessness. It is a gift of God in any society, bearing burdens, supporting the vulnerable and stabilizing both those who believe themselves autonomous and those who feel themselves to be failures.

Within the UK and much of Europe, the changes in the understanding of the household have been especially rapid since 1945, and even more so since the millennium. In 1947 there were about 62,700 divorces in the UK, and this was experienced as a serious problem[3] although it was clear that the war had some very significant impact. In 2013 there were 126,717[4] for a population of around 64 million, as opposed to 50 million. At the same time, the number of people cohabiting (living together as partners but not married or in a civil partnership) reached 5.8 million in England and

[3]Found in Andrew Chandler and David Hein, *Archbishop Fisher, 1945–1961: Church, State and World* (Farnham: Ashgate Publishing, 2012), p. 119.
[4]Data retrieved from 'Dataset(s): Vital Statistics: Population and Health Reference Tables' (Office for National Statistics, 2016), https://www.ons.gov.uk/people-populationandcommunity/populationandmigration/populationestimates/datasets/vitalstatisticspopulationandhealthreferencetables/current.

Wales alone in 2015.[5] The figures for 1951, in contrast, were too small to be statistically significant.

The number of single-parent households with children has also risen sharply, partly through the break-up of relationships, or sometimes through choice. As many parish priests know and all schools are aware, family life is full of step-parents, or some kind of significant other, and working out who has the responsibility at home (whatever that may mean) can be complicated. It is a generalization, and there are important exceptions, but far more often than not the burden of the care of children in single-parent or reconstituted households still falls on the mother. As generations pass, in many areas this becomes the grandmother, and in my pastoral experience, I have found that there are often networks of essentially matriarchal groups raising children.

I have commented on the rapid growth of the fluidity of traditional family structures, sometimes with a strong core surrounded by various people who appear and disappear like random comets. In addition, there has been a radical reimagining of the social and legal nature of marriage through the Marriage (Same Sex Couples) Act of 2013 (which came into force in 2014), and similar measures in many other countries. Here the change has been even faster than the shifts in the experience of traditional households. Same-sex, or as it is often called equal, marriage is now understood to be normal, acceptable and unchallengeable in many countries, whereas as late as the 1990s the very idea would have been heard

[5]'Statistical Bulletin: Population Estimates by Marital Status and Living Arrangements, England and Wales: 2002 to 2015' (Office for National Statistics, 2016), https://www.ons.gov.uk/peoplepopulationandcommunity/population-andmigration/populationestimates/bulletins/populationestimatesbymaritalstatus-andlivingarrangements/2002to2015#toc.

as incomprehensible, revolutionary and perhaps absurd. The speed of change has led many constituencies such as churches and other faith groups to find themselves living in a culture with which they have not even begun to come to terms. Every Christian denomination and church struggles with the results.

Faith groups are a minority (albeit a significant one of several million people) in the UK, and in many parts of Europe. In other parts of the world they are the over-whelming majority, and they still consider some of the changes we are experiencing to be not only unwelcome but abhorrent. In more traditional countries, many peo-ple still feel that same-sex marriage is a denial of nature and a revolt against God's laws. In a world that is still estimated to be 80 per cent religious in one form or another, ideas of being unnatural and sinful carry weight. It is important to realize, of course, that like many judgements in the UK around sex and sexual activity, in a vast number of countries and cultures there are double standards, concealed sexual orientation, fear and shame which lead to much suffering.

As I suggested in the Introduction, all these changes would not have so much cultural impact if it were not for the fact that the distance of geography that once insulated cultures from radically different views has now been eliminated through information technology and especially social media. When a gay activist is mur-dered brutally somewhere in the world, it is all round the news here, and the Church of England (which com-monly but wrongly in the media tends to mean the Archbishop of Canterbury) is expected at the very least to express a view, and often to do something about it (usually the content of the action is not defined). Policy on international aid may be influenced by the use of social media to change laws overseas where, for example, former parts of the British Empire have inherited from the British occupation criminal sanctions against same-sex practice. In the UK, and in many of the more prosperous parts of the world, such measures are seen as morally required uses of soft power, as LGBTI people here feel a profound sense of solidarity with LGBTI people overseas. In the countries concerned, however, such threats of withdrawing or limiting aid are seen as the twenty-first century equivalent to sending a gunboat: the threat is considered immoral in its exercise of power and imperialistic in its means.

In addition, the impact of immigration is such that, within two generations, large communities have come to the UK from abroad and feel a deep sense of conflict or even threat between the values of their homeland and their adopted countries. Joined as they are by links of blood and communicating endlessly through social media with relatives still in their countries of origin, there is sometimes a conflict between embrace of the stability of traditional values there and the seemingly endless recalibration of households here.

The issue is one of values. It is impossible and absurd to pretend that the changes here have not taken place or that they can be ignored. A simple restatement of 'British values' will not work. Neither can there be a 'value-free' approach, as that in itself is a value: 'do what you will' is a choice of values as much as 'do what society has always said'.

If fluidity of relationships is the reality of our society, then this should be our starting point for building values, because all values must connect with where people are and not where other people might like them to be. (Though equally, value development must emphatically not end there.) Our understandings of what makes for good values around households, marriage and the family must allow for flexibility and even contradictions in order for us to make sense of the world around us and relate to that world. A liberalism of approach that rejects all other approaches that are not equally liberal is stifling, unenforceable and self-contradictory. A 'one size fits all' approach, whether originating from the state, secular views or faith groups – even those whose tradition is deeply embedded in the culture – will be overthrown by numerous contradictions.

The answer must be found in values that emphasize and incite community, courage and stability. To maintain a tradition, changes must have an organic link to the past as well as to the present and the future. The outcome must link the expression of values to the historic moral instincts of society in a way that enables those understandings to be sufficiently flexible to change and develop. In Christian understanding, the core concepts of households and family include holiness, fidelity, hospitality and love above all, because God is holy, faithful, welcoming and overflowing in love, and any human institution that reflects these virtues also in some way reflects God.

In the Gospel of Luke chapter 15,[6] Jesus tells the profound, beautiful and open-ended story of the prodigal son, a description of love-in-action given as gift. This is one of the best known and most approachable of Jesus' parables. It is a story of a normal family with normal problems. The younger son wants now what is coming to him later. In effect he says to his father, 'I wish you were dead, so that I could have my share of the will.'

[6]Luke 15:11–32.

Dad, abandoning the rights and privileges of fathers of the time,[7] gives his son the money. The son wastes it on parties and wild living, runs out of cash, out of food, out of dignity; and resolves to come back and get a job with his father, a rich man. Note that he does not want to come back as a son, but with a little independent income, albeit with some humility. So he comes back, and before he can even ask for forgiveness and make his pitch, his father abandons his own dignity and runs to meet him, overwhelms him with love, reinstates him publicly, but as a son (with both privilege and duties; is this what he wanted?), and throws a party. The elder brother, always dutiful, always resentful, comes back from work. Losing his temper, he refuses to come in (humiliating his father), and his father, abandoning dignity for a third time, goes out and pleads with him.

There, like all the best stories, it ends, hanging in the air, leaving us to make up our minds about how to react. What we see is a family whose head (in the terms of the time) is principled yet flexible. No one says that the younger brother is right, or that what he did does not matter. The elder brother is not told that his work and dutiful service were wrong or wasted, or that his insult to his father is in its turn justified. Yet, from the father there is a conspicuous absence of the exercise of power and privilege or even of following the conventional processes of family life. Love conquers sin, yet only for the moment: here there is no neat answer, no 'happily ever after', any more than in normal life.

The father in the parable is seen as an image of God. Jesus is challenging the idea that God only deals with

---

[7]For a wonderful extended commentary on this passage, see Kenneth E. Bailey, *Poet and Peasant: A Literary-Cultural Approach to the Parables in Luke* (Grand Rapids, MI: William B. Eerdmans Publishing Co., 1976).

good people and is revealing a God who gives anything in order to find those who are lost. In this parable, the values of reconciliation – which include forgiveness and restoration – are deeply embedded. They are there first to call us to God himself, to turn to God and find God's love reaching out to us. They are there also to enable us to see ourselves as the younger brother, who needs to repent, to turn around and return, and as the elder brother who needs to accept the return and reinstatement of the younger and realize that no amount of good and hard work can make our Father love us any more than our siblings.

Best of all, the parable does not claim to be the end of the story, but is only the end of the beginning. Does the younger brother settle back at home, not as a hired labourer with some independence, but as a son, sneered at by the neighbours, resented by his brother, and with responsibilities? Or does the elder brother come into the feast, rejoice at restoration and play his proper role in reconciling disputes in the family? In this parable, there is all the complexity and contingency of normal family life: therein is its genius.

Of course the history of interpretation of the parable has been to highlight the strengths and weaknesses of Christians in relation to each other and to God. The nature of the family as a divine creation, however, enables us to let the parable shine a light on what is needed in families.

First, they require unity in order to support each other. The elder brother is not merely selfish, but far worse, is causing division. Tackling isolation and loneliness, facing the issues of immigration and integration, and developing courage, all require strong and hospitable social networks which are most effectively found in families. The elder brother isolates himself more than his father or his sibling. He condemns himself to being outside. It is in the family that we best learn of the common good, of solidarity, of goods being for all. Second, families need to be equipped to inspire courage as well as aspiration and creativity. It is in familial love that the father sets a counter-cultural pattern of re-establishment. Family ties inspire a courage to break down social conventions of honour and shame. Third, families need to generate resilience. Life is sustained and love is renewed both by such simple means as sharing a meal with laughter, or the complex sacrifice of being a carer. A family that loves unconditionally and expresses that love-in-action, reveals and interprets what is meant by the dignity of the human being to a culture living by the idea of radical autonomy.

The 'family' is, as we have seen, in the midst of great turmoil and change – a crisis in the best sense of the word – that can lead to something better emerging. Of course, families and family life are always under pressure, not only in our time. War and economic crisis, or the need to work for long periods far from home (as in many economically poorer countries), produce enormous strains on household life. Change is also normal. The move in Victorian times towards a nuclear family was a vast change from the more rural eighteenth-century models of household. So we must not imagine that the crisis today is especially severe. Yet there are fundamental changes, of which the increase in cohabitation on a serial basis, and changes in approach to sexual orientation, are among the most significant.

Underlying the crisis are demographic factors as well as economic ones. The Baby Boomers are rapidly approaching the age where they become dependants, relying on others for care. The NHS is struggling under the impact of the rapid increase in the number of elderly people in absolute terms, and as a proportion of the population as a whole (see Figure 2.1). As always, the household will have to bear the brunt of the change. Already there are estimated to be 6.8 million full- or part-time carers in households, saving the national exchequer up to £132 billion each year.[8] If all carers one day decided to abandon the historic duty of compassionate love to the members of their family and

FIGURE 2.1 *Population growth and age distribution projections, based on ONS 2014 projections*[9]

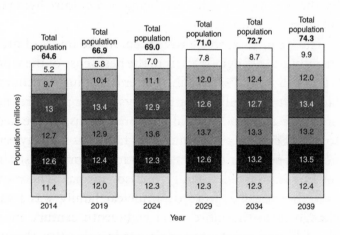

[8]Lisa Buckner and Sue Yeandle, 'Valuing Carers 2015: The Rising Value of Carers' Support' (Carers UK, 2015), pp. 8–10. Available at http://www.carersuk.org/for-professionals/policy/policy-library/valuing-carers-2015.
[9]Chart taken from the Government Office for Science publication 'The Future of an Ageing Population' (Crown Copyright, 2016). Available at https://www.gov.uk/government/collections/future-of-ageing. Contains public sector information licensed under the Open Government Licence v3.0.

household and leave it all to the state, the NHS could not absorb the extra burden.[10] The family is essential to preserving other institutions, for its failure brings down all else in the ruins.

The changes in the make-up of households and the variety of cultural backgrounds, as well as the redefinition of marriage, call for a flexibility of approach which deepens commitment and yet allows for diversity. Three particular areas need attention. First, the issue of supporting extended families as well as nuclear families. Second, the challenge of how we support the care of children and vulnerable adults. And third, the issue of living with integrated and at the same time distinct values across different cultural groups.

THE SUPPORT AND AFFIRMATION OF FAMILIES AND HOUSEHOLDS

The scope of the household and family in the modern eye have diminished to include only those with one degree of separation from us. We care for and link ourselves closely with parents, siblings and children. The next steps along the family tree are often less emphasized in a society of greater mobility. Though in some areas family networks remain strong, especially with grandparents and sometimes with cousins, this is no longer the norm.

In recent years, it has become increasingly clear that isolation is one of the great evils of our land, akin to the

---

[10]The burden falls disproportionately on women and, sadly, child carers. Those who can afford care, pay for it, and those who are more vulnerable and cannot afford it, have to put themselves in an even more vulnerable position and give care freely. This is a profound and yet hidden injustice.

five giants attacked by Beveridge.[11] Family breakdown, serial monogamy and unstable relationships all lead to isolation, and the resulting loneliness is often behind depression and other forms of mental health problems in older people, and insecurity of relationships may contribute to mental ill health in younger ones. The nuclear family is unable to bear the burden, but the extended family can.

Extended families can be strengthened further by legislation, by incentive and by affirming and encouraging choice within family networks. Legislation that supports grandparental access in cases of divorce – for example, through the use of mediation with grandparent contact orders as a fall-back – maintains the affections that bind people together across generations. Incentives can relate to tax allowances for carers, with a significant degree of flexibility and ease of administration. Carers' allowances should be portable and attached to the person being cared for so that they take the financial support with them.

In terms of choice, there is a great need for recognizing both the economic value and the social contribution of carers. The prodigal son's elder brother in the parable had been caring for the family business, the wider household, and it was perhaps the lack of his recognition of his role that led to growing bitterness. Governments both national and local, the National Health Service and Social Services all benefit in terms of cost and effort through the work of carers, and yet carers are so often treated with indifference, pity or even contempt rather than being celebrated for their contribution.

[11] See Malcolm Brown's paper for the Church of England House of Bishops, 'Thinking Afresh about Welfare: The Enemy Isolation', 2016. Available at https:// www.churchofengland.org/media/2524695/welfare.pdf.

Our Christian tradition reinforces the family as a place of selfless giving and of love shown as grace (gratuity), not for hope of reward. Yet even within the Church, the prevailing culture has often tended to protect the nuclear family at the expense of the extended family. Extended families should be inclusive groups, valuing all equally, without treating individuals either as a useful asset (the English Victorian view of the youngest unmarried daughter) or as objects of pity. Households come in all forms, from single people to large and numerous groups. All need to be valued and esteemed. Love, hospitality and compassion, as well as the biblical emphasis on respect for the elderly, should lead to a much stronger emphasis on extended families liturgically and socially within the Church as an example to society. The celebration of the extended family reflects the grace that it brings.

The care of children and vulnerable adults is a sector of life in which there has been great improvement in some respects, especially for women, although much remains to be done. The proportion of women in remunerated employment has increased from 55 per cent in 1976 to 70 per cent in 2016.[12] This correlates strongly with the increasing availability of childcare, with the number of providers in England of all-day care having increased from 2,100 in 1988[13] to 17,900 in 2013.[14] For many women this has been experienced as a great liberation, although it is essential to remember that the gender pay gap remains

[12]'Time Series: Female Employment Rate' (Office for National Statistics, 2017), https://www.ons.gov.uk/employmentandlabourmarket/peopleinwork/employ-mentandemployeetypes/timeseries/lf25/lms.
[13]'Statistics for Education: Children's Day Care Facilities at 31 March 1998 England' (Department for Education, 1999), p. 5. Available from http://webarchive.nationalarchives.gov.uk/20130401151655/ http://media.education.gov.uk/assets/files/pdf/daycarepdf.pdf.
[14]'Childcare and Early Years Providers Survey 2013' (Department for Education, 2014), p. 2. Available from https://www.gov.uk/government/uploads/system/uploads/attachment_data/file/355079/SFR33_2014_Summary.pdf.

considerable and that even though more women are in employment, their employment is usually more precarious, poorly paid, and is less likely to reflect their qualifications. The 'double-day' argument (women who go out to work and then return home to carry the major part of the domestic burden) is an additional social conundrum.

This chapter is mainly about family and household structures, not the prevention of abuse and violence. However, healthy families and households are profoundly intolerant of such evils, and the strengthening of the household and family implies improved behaviour within them.

It is clear that the majority of caring is done by women, increasingly so as care hours increase: 71 per cent of those claiming carers' allowance are women.[15] Households and families will be strengthened the more we value care that springs from family ties regardless of the circumstances. It is right and proper that years in receipt of Child Benefit or Carers' Allowance count towards the state pension. Focusing resources in these ways, and adding to them, is cheaper, usually better, and more expressive of our values than simple state-paid provision alone.

THE SUPPORT AND PROTECTION OF CHILDREN
AND VULNERABLE ADULTS

Although it is not the primary aim of this chapter, and indeed would require a whole book in and of itself, it has to be recognized that the protection of children and vulnerable adults is both one of the greatest strengths and most profound vulnerabilities of families. The twin dangers of this reality are complacency and control.

[15]Calculated from Department for Work and Pensions time series data, available at http://tabulation-tool.dwp.gov.uk/100pc/ca/ccdate/ccsex/a_carate_r_ccdate_c_ccsex.html.

It is widely believed that up to 80 per cent of child abuse occurs in the family rather than through the major institutions which are so often in the limelight. To be complacent about the family as a place of safety would be the height of folly. The response to the realities of family life are already in place potentially, and often practically. There needs to be training in recognizing the signs of abuse, and support in developing healthy and open family lives. The best guardians of good family practice are other members of the family, provided they have the courage to speak up (which is too often not the case).

Second, however, there is the risk of diminishing the healing power of good families by treating the very institution as suspicious, and of giving too much power to outsiders to break in and direct events. Every family has its own sorrows and every family develops means of dealing with them. Incentivizing good practice as suggested above, especially the practice of caring, affirms the role of the household, while resisting the urge to channel all action through outside agencies, necessary as they are for more extreme cases.[16]

DEALING WITH THE DIVERSITY OF TRADITIONS: HOW DO WE UNDERSTAND FAMILIES?

The challenges to our historic understanding of household and family come from many different sources. Some are cultural, the result in part of living in a far

---

[16]As seen in the chapter on Housing (Chapter 5), the example of neighbourhood coaches developed by Bromford Housing Association is a good example of how to help.

more diverse society. Some are philosophical, the results of a radical turning towards the self, and the sense that the way one lives is how identity is created. More than that, the identity we create by our actions is often seen as changeable by other actions; there is no such thing as a fixed identity in this way of looking at life. Two examples illustrate this point.

First, the tax advantages of being a household (for example, the exemption between married people for inheritance tax purposes) have led to suggestions that the same help should be given to all types of households. Each person's choice of identity and household formation, it is argued, is particular to themselves, and neither the state nor any other institution should prefer one choice to another through giving particular advantages. It is the exact opposite of the case being argued for in this chapter.

Second, the levels of immigration of those with an Islamic understanding of family have an impact on the accepted pattern for choosing a partner, on assumed ages of maturity and sexual activity, and especially on issues of polygamy. There has been and remains a demand for the introduction of those aspects of *Sharia* law that affect family and inheritance.

On the face of it, the move from the very static patterns of family and household in the past to the fluid and dynamic views of sexual orientation, family and even gender all argue for an open approach, almost without boundaries. Household arrangements have moved from being a social construct to an individual one. The younger brother in the parable was doing the same thing. He sought to remake his life in his way, breaking rules of inheritance, and disregarding conventions of loyalty, subservience and duty. It is easy to take the high moral ground, assuming that tradition is right, but we are confronted in the parable by the father who does not do this, but takes the course of sacrificial love.

The nature of shifts in the content of tradition, of their development and alteration, is of change working when it retains a recognizable sense of where it has come from. Tradition that is static dies. Tradition that abandons the past in a paradigm shift loses stability.[17] The same applies to traditions of values, and thus to the importance of embedding our reimagining in what we have been, as well as what we will be. Thus, for example, same-sex marriage builds on the presumption that marriage is stable and lifelong (the rootedness in the tradition), while also responding to the massive shift in cultural acceptance with regard to the understanding of human nature and sexual orientation. By contrast, some of the shifts now being proposed either abandon all tradition or introduce a different story of the family and household, based in a different history. The idea of new formations of identity, without boundaries, creates insecurity. In terms of the deep values and virtues, it also lacks resilience and stability. Some of the proposed changes may well be courageous but their inward focus neglects the common good and the wider community.

A personal example may help in this case. In 2016, through a series of accidents and some clever work by a journalist, I discovered that my father was someone other than the person whom I had, up until that point, believed to be my father. There was a good deal of press

---

[17]For more on the need for faith traditions to reconceptualize their heritage, see Vincent Brümmer, 'Escaping from the Ghetto', *Verbum et Ecclesia* 33 (2) (December 2012), http://verbumetecclesia.org.za/index.php/VE/article/view/729/1032.

attention. The comment I made at the time was that I found my identity not in DNA but in Jesus Christ. Whether one is a person of Christian faith or not, the underlying principle is that of identity being neither a fixed given, as with genetics, nor self-created, but securely held in the narrative of being known perfectly and loved unconditionally. With that security, one can develop and discover identity, neither constrained nor lost in a desert of infinite choice.

An important example of proposed changes is that of the Islamic system of law and practice of faith known as *Sharia*. *Sharia* is more than a system of law. For some Islamic scholars it is a mark of an Islamic society that it lives within the *Sharia*, although exactly what that means is not universally agreed within Islam. Other Islamic scholars have argued variously that Western legal systems already reflect many aspects of *Sharia* law and that *Sharia* cannot be enforced by the state because it must be voluntarily adhered to in order to retain its religious character.[18] Under such views, Muslim minorities in non-Islamic states are permitted to live without *Sharia* being legally institutionalized. The system of *Sharia* is both complex and sophisticated, with clear demarcations between civil law and criminal law (demarcations that include but are much more wide-ranging than the *hadad* punishments of amputation and stoning, and usually reject these).

On the face of it, the request is reasonable in a country that is tolerant of different cultures and traditions, and which is developing very rapidly shifting patterns of household. The problem is that reimagining Britain

[18] For examples, see the work of Tariq Ramadan, Abdullahi Ahmed An-Na'im and Khaled Abou El Fadl.

through values applied in action can only work where the narrative of the country is coherent and embracing. To put it another way, it is possible to welcome and accept diversity from within the security of a story about ourselves, an identity that is intuitively recognized, and is traceable through our history. To go back to the prodigal son, the father restores the prodigal to the place of a younger son, and offers restoration to the elder brother as an elder son, saying, 'all that I have is yours'. He is generous in love but from within a pattern of life that is established. Stability in household and family requires the confidence that comes from understanding who we are or should be.

Sharia, which has a powerful and ancient cultural narrative of its own, deeply embedded in a system of faith and understanding of God, and thus especially powerful in forming identity, cannot become part of another narrative. It is either formative or different. Accepting it in part implies accepting its values around the nature of the human person, attitudes to outsiders, the revelation of God, and a basis for life in law, rather than grace, the formative word of Christian culture. Household and family, and the expressions of love within them, are the basic foundational communities of society. They face enormous pressures and need one legal basis of oversight and one philosophical foundation of understanding. For these reasons, I am especially sympathetic towards those Islamic groups that do not seek the application of *Sharia* law into the family and inheritance law of this country.

There are many failures within families and households, above all those relating to abuse and violence. In the parable of the prodigal son, failure and dysfunction are apparent, but within the context of the aspirations of the family and household as a safe place of return and healing. Households and families are changing rapidly, and will continue to do so. Whether or not one agrees with the changes, it is when they are tested against a benchmark of values of community, courage and stability that it becomes clear whether these new forms relate back to existing structures.

SUMMARY

- The family or household is the base unit of society.

- It is immensely powerful, both for good and for evil.

- It is changing shape very rapidly, and without any overall sense of direction.

- Any reimagining of the country must have a clear sense of the values of family and household and put them at the centre of policy.

3

Education – Life in All Its Fullness

Along with households and families, education, housing and health are the cornerstones of reimagining Britain. They ensure the possibility of human flourishing for all and offer the possibility of aspirations for a better future being turned into reality. They convert values of solidarity and the common good into practices of forming households, and of establishing care and development.

No society or country can flourish without an education system that is world class, and that offers every person who chooses to take it the possibility of living 'life in all its fullness', a phrase used by Jesus.[1]

It seems characteristic of many prosperous nations to believe that their education system had a glorious past that no longer works, and the UK is no exception. The myths around the quality of education after the Butler Education Act of 1944, or the equally strong myths about its total failure (linked either to the supposed success of grammar schools or the failure of governments after 1944 to put enough resources into technical education), demonstrate that education in the UK, like health, is a highly political issue. In the 1960s, the Wilson

[1] John 10:10, Good News Translation.

government sought to deal with the inadequacies and inequities of the divide between grammar schools and the rest through the comprehensive system. That again was not seen as having succeeded. Indeed, it is hard to think of any government since 1945 that has not sought to face the challenge of education. Every government enters office with a promise to resolve the issues, and none leave office feeling that it is 'job done'. Tony Blair, Labour Prime Minister from 1997 to 2007, announced at the start of his first term that his three priorities were 'education, education and education'. John Major, his predecessor as Prime Minister, quipped that his priorities had been the same, but not necessarily in the same order. The 1988 Education Reform Act has to some extent stood the test of time, but demonstrates that the question of education was a challenge for the Thatcher government.

The reality is a much more mixed picture, as one might expect. Looking at final outcomes in terms of the ranking of universities on some measures today, it is noticeable that in the top 100 globally the UK share is disproportionate (although it is worth noting that measures vary and that UK universities do less well on student satisfaction or teaching quality than research). According to the *Times Higher Education* rankings, the UK has three universities in the top ten, seven in the top 50 and twelve in the top 100, despite only offering 9.3 per cent of the universities assessed.[2]

---

[2]Figures from 'World University Rankings 2016–2017' (*Times Higher Education*, 2017), https://www.timeshighereducation.com/world-university-rankings/2017/world-ranking#!/page/0/length/25/sort_by/rank/sort_order/asc. Accessed 16 March 2017.

Within the QS World University Rankings, the over-representation is greater, with four in the top ten, nine in the top 50 and eighteen in the top 100, despite only 7.8 per cent of universities assessed being UK institutions.[3]

The proportion of people achieving university degrees has risen sharply, especially since the 1990s.

The number of undergraduate qualifications awarded in the UK in a given year has increased from approximately 357,000 in 2000/01 to 480,500 in 2015/16, with an average year-on-year increase of just over 3 per cent – though numbers have actually been declining slightly since 2012/13.[4]

The major development of the last 20 years in the state sector of education has been the growth in the number of academies. Having started as part of the Major reforms, they were taken up under Mr Blair, and their number accelerated rapidly in the latter years of the Labour governments of 1997–2010. Lord Adonis was centrally involved in the process, writing persuasively and power-fully about his experience of introducing academies in the face of pessimism and obstruction from many in the education establishment.[5]

As a result of all the changes, the structure of education in the UK has changed considerably in some respects, but not all. The following figure shows the diversity of schooling in the UK.

---

[3]Figures from 'QS World University Rankings 2016–2017' (QS Quacquarelli Symonds Limited, 2017), https://www.topuniversities.com/university-rankings/world-university-rankings/2016. Accessed 16 March 2017.

[4]Data from 'Qualifications Obtained' (Higher Education Statistics Agency, n.d.), https://www.hesa.ac.uk/data-and-analysis/students/qualifications. Accessed 16 March 2017.

[5]Andrew Adonis, *Education, Education, Education: Reforming England's Schools* (London: Biteback Publishing, 2012).

FIGURE 3.1 *UK schools fact sheet*[6]

Primary schools	Secondary schools	Independent schools
There are 16,778 primary schools in England. <18% of these are academies.	There are 3,401 secondary schools in England. <65% of these are academies.	There are 2,311 independent schools in England, which is <10% of total schools.
36.8% are religious: 26.1% C of E; 9.8% RC; 0.6% other Christian; >0.3% Jewish, Muslim, Sikh, non-/interdenominational	18.7% are religious: 6.1% C of E; 9.4% RC; 2.3% other Christian; <1% Jewish, Muslim, Sikh, non-/interdenominational	Independent schools educate >5% of primary aged children and <8% of secondary aged children in England.

Other schools

Special schools offer tailored education for children with SEN for <1% of primary age and <2% if secondary age. There are 1,039 special schools in England and <18% of these are academies.

Alternative provision schools/pupil referral units exist for children who cannot be educated in mainstream schools. They educate 0.1% of primary age and <1% of secondary age. There are 353 such schools in England and <22% of these are academies.

Other UK nations

Wales has 1,561 publicly funded schools. 17% of Welsh schools are religious.

Scotland has 2,163 publicly funded schools. 17% are religious – mostly Roman Catholic with 3 Episcopalian and 1 Jewish.

In Northern Ireland, 43% of 1,076 schools are Roman Catholic (maintained or voluntary grammar schools). State-controlled schools are traditionally Protestant. There is a small but increasing number of integrated schools educating from both Protestant and Catholic traditions.

The complexity of the data is itself revealing. British education is a collective noun, not an expression of a single system.

When we look at the statistics for Further and Higher Education (FE and HE; for these purposes, post-16 for Further) we see that life does not get simpler. I have deliberately left FE aside until now, partly to make the point that it has a Cinderella aspect (meaning that it is neglected despite its virtues) to its existence. Although hugely important for a very large number of people, it is not often mentioned.

The struggle to include other forms of education and qualification than the purely academic has been one that

---

[6]Data from https://gov.uk, https://statswales.gov.wales, http://www.gov.scot and https://www.education-ni.gov.uk, all published by Crown Copyright, 2017, under Open Government Licence v3.0. Accessed 28 March 2017.

has existed at least since the 1944 Education Act. Success in this endeavour requires cultural change as well as widespread partnerships between businesses, government at all levels and the education services. A good result would involve establishing a number of principles: not only fullness of life, but also values of courage and stability. It is an especially important struggle with respect to the low UK levels of productivity, which has stagnated since 2007, and in output per hour, where the UK ranks in Europe ahead only of Greece, Italy and Portugal.[7] To offer an opportunity for fullness of life to all those in education requires flexible and imaginative training based on aptitude. The culture of the UK has looked down on technical skills, to our great cost and shame.

Education is necessarily based on the history and culture of a society. Within British society, there is a combination of cultures, Scotland, Wales and Northern Ireland being very distinct, and Scotland's education system being one of the defining characteristics of its nationality. Within England, the legacy of the class system has been and remains a huge challenge and often a major handicap to education, which seeks to be cohesive, aspirational and sustainable. It is all very well to look at the increasing number of students in university, but the breakdown of those attending Russell Group institutions[8] shows that those educated privately have a very disproportionate share of places. Oxford and Cambridge are split out to show an even stronger effect.

[7] Martin Wolf, 'Britain is no world-beating economy' (*Financial Times*, 29 September 2016), https://www.ft.com/content/cd1c369c-84c7-11e6-8897-2359a58ac7a5.
[8] A rough-and-ready proxy for those universities widely seen as among the top in most subjects, though it must be borne in mind that other universities will also excel in particular fields and that this definition is increasingly problematic.

FIGURE 3.2 *University destination by KS5 institution type*[9]

	Total percentage attending university/HE institution	Of which attending Russell Group university	Of which attending Oxford/ Cambridge
Educated through state-funded schooling at Key Stage 5	48%	11%	1%
Educated through independent schooling at Key Stage 5	60%	38%	5%

It is easy to be overly depressed by these numbers, and a more worrying statistic is discussed below. There is a globally established and ancient reality that the children of privilege tend to inherit privilege, especially in terms of access to health, housing and education. For example, at Harvard, around 12 per cent of children have parents who are alumni.[10] There is anecdotally a similar pattern in China. Life chances always have been and always are improved by ancestry, except in times of global war, pandemic, economic collapse or revolution. The

[9]Data from Department for Education, 'Destinations of KS4 and KS5 Pupils: 2015 (revised)' (Crown Copyright, 19 January 2017), https://www.gov.uk/government/statistics/destinations-of-ks4-and-ks5-pupils-2015-revised. Accessed 30 March 2017.
[10]Justin C. Worland, 'Legacy Admit Rate at 30 Percent', *The Harvard Crimson*, 11 May 2011, http://www.thecrimson.com/article/2011/5/11/admissions-fitzsimmons-legacy-legacies/. Accessed 30 March 2017.

Four Horsemen of the Apocalypse are the only inevitable equalizers.

There is a degree to which poverty and deprivation also pass through the generations. The Casey Review of late 2016, although mainly about cultural integration, described other challenges facing an integrated society. One of the most striking tables, set out below, is of the ethnic breakdown of children on free school meals (which can be used as a proxy for poverty levels) who achieved five A*–C grade GCSEs at 16. The levels vary enormously, but the white British category comes third

FIGURE 3.3 *Proportion of Free School Meals-eligible pupils achieving 5+ A*–C grades (including Mathematics and English GCSEs) by ethnic group, 2014–15* [11]

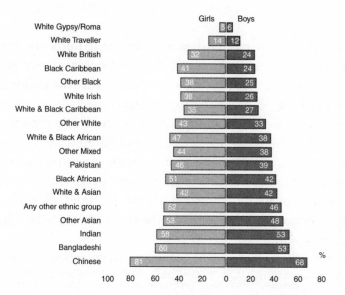

[11]Dame Louise Casey, DBE CE, 'The Casey Review: A Review into Opportunity and Integration' (Department for Communities and Local Government under Crown Copyright, December 2016).

last out of 18 categories, with only 32 per cent of girls and 28 per cent of boys achieving this standard.

One rather provocative way of looking at this number is to see white British from poor backgrounds as among the least well equipped for integration into a rapidly changing world where skills in science, technology, numeracy, literacy and IT will be essential. White British in England are also by far and away the largest group. For this and other groups at the bottom of the table to be born of poor parents in an area of poverty is unjustly to have one's life chances significantly reduced unless you somehow acquire exceptional ambition, courage and discipline. The geographical areas where concentrations of poverty are found are increasingly well defined. All large urban areas have areas of very severe deprivation, often right next to areas of extreme wealth, as in London. Many areas near the coast or on the edge of the UK have significant deprivation, very often accompanied by poor infrastructure, including that of IT. To be born into many of these areas and into households caught up in poverty reduces one's opportunities yet further. The injustices of these obstacles to educational performance (which are not based in any sort of inherent lack of ability) are an affront to any sense of being one nation at birth, to the value of solidarity, or to the universal destination of goods. It is, in a word, wrong.

The answer is often seen as meritocracy. Surely a fair system would be one in which all are born with equal chances and may rise if they have the talent? Obviously there is something important in this approach. It is certainly better than birth being a key determinant of the outcome of education. Yet it is far from sufficient and is potentially utterly demeaning of many individuals.

People are not born equal. Some children suffer the consequences of divorce or family dysfunction, or are simply born with learning difficulties or varying levels of physical, emotional or intellectual disability. They may have suffered from the alcohol or drug abuse of parents, or simply have less ability in some areas than others.

Historically, our education system has been careful to nurture to some degree those with disabilities, and that has been a sign of the strong values of our society. In fact there is anecdotal evidence that we have looked after those with disabilities rather better than those of exceptionally high ability. In the last 20 years the separate special schools have been reduced in number and many children with less severe special educational needs have been educated in mainstream schools. It is widely and reasonably believed that this has been beneficial for all and leads to a far greater acceptance of children with learning difficulties as well as to a better sense of the benefits of diversity. In a well-organized school with proper funding for special educational needs and streaming by ability, this has no negative academic impact on those of high ability. We have experience of the benefits of this in our own family.

Such changes in approach reflect a significant improvement in the nature of comprehensive education, and a practice that seeks the fullest and most abundant possible life for each human being regardless of their ability. Far more than that, the practice supports the idea that, all other things such as resource allocation being equal, good communities are not made up exclusively of those who are alike, but include diversity. Of all the communities in our country, schools are the best to teach that lesson.

Selective schools or other forms of separation of education do not achieve the same aim. They make a statement about our understanding of the purpose of education which is dangerous and that has proved very often to be deeply damaging. That statement is not principally about privilege or ability, or even about opportunity, let alone about success and failure: all these realities are part of every child's growing up. They will run faster or slower than others, play more or less easily, accomplish more or less at science or maths or English. Even if there is no ranking, they will know that others do better than them – perhaps all do, or others do worse. Even if there is no competitive sport, they will recognize that, when they kick a ball around, some people do it better and have more fun and pleasure in doing so.

Especially in an age of instant information, they will hear about the brilliant, and about the disastrous. They will see reality TV shows and watch people being expelled for one reason or another. Above all, in our age, many will be conscious of the (falsely) perceived failure of their self-image, or the shape of their body, and many will be harmed by that feeling.[12] All those things are part of the bittersweet experience of being human in the UK today. The intensity of experience will vary, as will the balance between bitterness and sweetness, but there is no vaccine against the experience.

The wrong and harmful statement is not about any of these things; it is far more fundamental. It is about the purpose of being human, and about the nature of living in community. Education is a process of shaping human beings to be able to reach out for and enjoy abundant

[12]The Children's Society *Good Childhood Report* here (http://www.childrens-society.org.uk/sites/default/files/pcr090_summary_web.pdf), which looks at this in some detail.

life and to do so in such strong communities that ide-
ally they and all around them flourish. Education fails
equally when it neglects those of lesser ability, or does
not give the fullest opportunity to those of higher ability, or does not enable all to develop a sense of community and mutuality, of love-in-action, fullness and
abundance of life.

The etymology of education is the Latin 'edu-
care': meaning to bring out or lead out – not to cram
in! Education should be about drawing the best out of
people, about leading them out into life.

A focus on grades alone contributes to an inadequate
sense of self-worth and does not diminish issues of mental ill health. A system that was focused on human flourishing would reduce many causes of mental health in the
education system.

Abundance of life is not measured simply in any way
at all. Money, productivity, success, beauty, wit, intelligence are not merely bad proxies for abundance. When
put to the wrong purpose, they are false gods that lead
to despair. When put to the right purpose, they are gifts
that overflow to all around.

The early chapters of the Acts of the Apostles describe
a flourishing community.

> Now the whole group of those who believed were
> of one heart and soul, and no one claimed private
> ownership of any possessions, but everything they
> owned was held in common. With great power the
> apostles gave their testimony to the resurrection
> of the Lord Jesus, and great grace was upon them
> all. There was not a needy person among them, for
> as many as owned lands or houses sold them and
> brought the proceeds of what was sold. They laid it

at the apostles' feet, and it was distributed to each as
any had need.[13]

The argument as to the historicity of this description is
irrelevant. It is clear that there was at least some extraordinary group, since the infant Church grew so rapidly.
It is also clear that there was a sense of *voluntary* commonality of goods and gifts. Community is formed in
sharing and flourishing communities that gather up the
weak and strong, enabling all to benefit from all.

It happens seldom, but it happens. When it does, there
is the experience of abundant life.

So what is needed? To be clear, education that prior-
itizes culture, values and inclusion but only demands
second-rate training is not the aim of schools (though
if it does not prioritize those things, it is not good education). Nor should we subscribe to an airy-fairy optimism that good education will make good people. The
process of enabling abundant life is infinitely complex
and requires a combination of flexibility and skills, but
also requires a clear objective: that every child should
reach their highest potential, with a decent and reasonable respect for all other communities in our nation.

To demonstrate the practice of values which are
implicit in our society and explicit in our history, an
education system requires a clear internal sense of values. That is the greatest obstacle we face. The community of the Acts of the Apostles shared everything
because of the narrative that drove them: that in Christ,
the whole world had changed and that they were above
all called to love one another. That led to a generosity of spirit in their holding of property. We live in a

[13] Acts of the Apostles 4:32–35.

country where the idea of an overarching story, which is the framework for explaining life, is rejected by many people. There are many good reasons for the suspicions which over the last 70 years have progressively eroded that idea of a single story. It seems too simple in a complicated world. Meta-narratives have so often meant tools of repression and control rather than means of liberation and flourishing.

Historically, in England, national education of all classes in society moved forward decisively with the vision of the National Society, formed within the Church of England, in 1811. By 1870 there were too many children and schools for the churches (education had been sponsored by many denominations beyond the Church of England), and the first of the great Education Acts brought the schools under state control, although still with a very strong religious participation from churches and Jewish groups. The Education Act of 1944 set out the requirement for Christian worship to be a normal part of the day in almost all schools (with some protection for children whose parents objected), and this form of religious settlement did not come under severe challenge until the 1970s and 1980s. Scotland, Northern Ireland and Wales developed differently, but again largely church-based, with Scotland especially having a world-famous standard of universal education.

By the 1990s the changes in society had led to the loss of a sense of an essentially Christian country, and in many non-church schools the idea of daily acts of worship was giving way to a time of corporate reflection. Religious Education (RE) as a subject remained popular, although the number of teachers specializing in the subject dropped considerably. An All Party Parliamentary

Group report in 2013[14] found that in primary schools, RE was often taught by a teaching assistant while the class teacher took Planning, Preparation and Assessment time (PPA) time, and that 67 per cent of RE coordinators had no RE qualification or only to GCSE/O-level. In secondary schools, where a higher level of specialism is generally expected, 27 per cent of RE teachers were found to have no relevant post-A-level qualification.

Many problems arose from this shift in attitudes among the majority group in our country, and I shall discuss four that seem especially important.

First, no alternative narrative has replaced the Christianity-based story. G. K. Chesterton is reputed to have remarked that when people stop believing in God, they don't believe in nothing; they believe in anything. A world of competing and incommensurable narratives of life offers no means of choosing what is best except individual choice and freedom – unguided, untutored, and without intrinsic values. There is no argument that can be made, as a Christian, for compulsion in religious belief, but within schools it has become very clear that confidence in any personal sense of ultimate values is diminishing and the damage that this causes to a national sense of value and to the ability to form communities is very great.

Second, and partly as a result of the absence of a meta-narrative, in a value-neutral or multi-value system without commensurability, the rest of education ceases to be moored to a final purpose in terms of human flourishing and development and becomes merely functional.

[14]'RE: The Truth Unmasked – The Supply of and Support for Religious Education Teachers' (Religious Education Council, March 2013), http://religiouseducation-council.org.uk/media/file/APPG_RE_-_The_Truth_Unmasked.pdf. Accessed 30 March 2017.

Utilitarianism rules. Skills move from being talents held for the common good, which we are entrusted with as a benefit to all (the pattern of the community in the Acts of the Apostles), to being personal possessions for our own advantage. The disastrous move of privatizing university education through increasingly high tuition fees, so that I buy my skills on the never-never, paying back loans as and when I can, compounds the damage. By the time someone graduates, they 'own' their degree. After all, they paid for it, not only with work but also with money. It must serve therefore as an income enhancer, and poor marks have recently become the cause of litigation for lost earnings.[15] What I own is mine, for me. The natural selfishness of human beings is compounded and the sense of moral and social responsibility diminished. The 2017 Labour Election Manifesto motivated students in its recognition of the need for a return to non-fee-based funding of universities, although the cost implications of such a step are clearly considerable.

Third, the vacuum in values is filled by government-imposed ideas (as discussed in Chapter 1) which exist not merely for convenience but to ensure social cohesion in a way that is based on function over substance. As has already been said, but is especially true in education, without a religious meta-narrative the debate is potentially between an extremist religious narrative on the one hand and a patently secular, functional narrative on the other. A weak, secular challenge will sadly only serve to fuel the perceived need for the imposition of an extreme religious meta-narrative. Moreover, such imposed values will not flourish if they are imposed or

[15]https://www.theguardian.com/education/2016/dec/04/graduate-sues-oxford-university-1m-failure-first-faiz-siddiqui.

remain abstract. As with all things in life – from learning that the stove is hot, to learning how to ride a bike – learning and living values requires their practice, in communities such as the classroom, where the value of every human is taught by example and experience.

Fourth, our society continues to change, and religious influence has not declined as much as expected, not least as a result of immigration. The vast majority of those who have been immigrants in the last 60 years have come from countries with a strong religious tradition (it is estimated by the Pew Research Center that about 80 per cent of humanity is linked to a religious tradition[16]). The second generation of incoming migrants, although British-born, are on the whole also deeply committed to faith traditions other than those which have historically existed here in the UK. Inserting children with strong faith backgrounds into an education system which has lost the capacity to handle faith issues – not least because many teachers themselves are not religiously practising – is bound to throw up challenges. At worst, as with the 'Trojan Horse' cases of 2015 and 2016, the vacuum has been filled with extremism. At best, in many Church of England schools in areas of high immigration, although in some cases almost all the children belong to a non-Christian faith community, the ethos of the school has remained Christian while respecting religious diversity. In the vast majority of cases, the incidental outcomes have included very good education and a growing capacity to relate to difference, while building genuine community.

[16]'The Global Religious Landscape' (Pew Research Center, 18 December 2012), http://www.pewforum.org/2012/12/18/global-religious-landscape-exec/. Accessed 30 March 2017.

Education is an area of immense complexity. The range of abilities, characters, ethnicities and backgrounds of children and students is as great as the number of individuals: the demands of society, of employers, of the future of the nation, are insatiable. So, to conclude this chapter, here are five principles for the development of values.

First, all education must be seen as a principal place confidently to develop values that are widely held. We must not be fearful of developing the narrative of who we are and why it matters. Our culture is always dynamic and changing. As I argued earlier, that is why we begin with practices, and not with grand statements. Yet we can only change what we have if we recognize explicitly what it is.

Second, schools, FE and HE institutions are intermediate communities which exist to bring fullness of life and are nurseries of community living. They need to develop stories of the common good, of community, not merely tolerance. They need to generate inspiration and aspiration. They need to enable the creation of resilience and sustainability. It is achievable but it depends crucially on the education system remaining diverse in provision, enabling different streams and approaches. The non-judgemental, inclusive values of schools, including Church of England schools, create in our education system a community of communities. This can only work if it is well funded and diversity is nurtured, with a structure of accountability. In a very diverse society, centralized and dictatorial decision making on curriculums, teaching methods and values are more likely to do harm than good, while an encouragement of local imagination and inspired practice, provided that there are clear boundaries and principles at the centre, leads to the emergence of shared values. The Academy and Free School movements, properly managed to ensure that they do not marginalize other schools, have the potential for the requisite subsidiarity. One contentious example of the dangers of centralization is around sex education, especially in cross-cultural contexts. What in some schools may be too late in Year 4, in others will be considered inappropriately early in Year 6.

The essential issue is confidence in the values we hold. The identification of values by an OFSTED statement cannot lead to ownership and is likely to receive no more than lip service, especially when the 'values' lack historical and cultural depth. At best they become a veneer beneath which the real work is done. At worst they provide an excuse for lazy thinking and inadequate definition amid the immense complexity of a school.

Third, there cannot be Cinderellas. The history of the education system at least since 1944 has always been of some part being neglected. For many years it was the Secondary Moderns. At other times it has been those above or below average. Today it is often FE and technical education, and also adult learning. The counter-cultural struggle to enable lifelong learning and training, and to develop the prestige of technical education, has to be won if we are to reimagine our country with less division and with the flexibility and capacity necessary for 'the fourth industrial revolution'.[17] Our education system is indispensable to a successful future, as much as are roads, armies, housing and health. To invest in education not merely for economic advantage but as

[17]See, for example, Klaus Schwab, 'The Fourth Industrial Revolution' (Geneva: World Economic Forum, 2016), which describes this revolution as marked by the 'fusion' of technologies and 'their interaction across the physical, digital and biological domains' (p. 8).

part of an expression of values is both economically reasonable and socially essential.

Our education system has been diminished by the undervaluing of FE, the neglect (since the 1944 Act) of technical education, and the relative lack of prestige around apprenticeships compared to 'academic' routes of education. The good news is that these problems are recognized. The bad news is that no solution has yet been found. They are, of course, issues of values as well as of practices. Aspiration and creativity are nurtured as well and often better technically than in purely academic qualifications. The resilience and sustainability of the UK's economy and of the life chances of those educated will require flexibility and aptitude to learn new skills. The most recent innovation to be announced is T-levels for technical subjects.

To face these challenges requires the collaboration of several forms of intermediate institution, especially companies and FE colleges. This collaboration is already happening well in many areas. However, the biggest change is a cultural one, and that will only happen as practices change, which will in turn redefine the importance of the values just mentioned.

Fourth, education must develop ever stronger partnerships, as is already happening in FE and HE and some secondary schools. Partnerships with potential employers are well established, but there also need to be developments with cultural, charitable and social institutions. Intermediate groups need to work together so that cultural practices and values are constantly challenged and developed. The advent of Free Schools and Academies is controversial, but among their great advantages has been the partnerships formed with local companies and other intermediate institutions.

Finally, and most foundationally, there is a profound need for training and development to improve, especially in the areas of anthropological and religious literacy, in history and in ethics, so that the indispensability of confident values is recognized and the tools for their development are offered. To that end, the Church of England has set up The Church of England Foundation for Educational Leadership in order to begin to tackle the need for deeper and more effective training in issues of values and practices, as well as in the hard skills of leading schools and developing the pipeline of new leadership for the future.

Education has to combine the provision of skills with the creation of values and of practices that enable those values to be developed. Where that happens 'life in all its fullness' becomes accessible for those affected, and there can be a profound change in national mood and confidence. It is not a magic wand, but it is an essential building block.

Our vision for education needs to be at the centre of a policy to reimagine Britain. Failures within education (as, for example, outlined in the Casey Review in Figure 3.3 above) are national crises. A fresh vision for a decentralized, accountable and diverse education system must aim to resolve this crisis in a way that builds not just skills but community. Values within schools and colleges and universities, whether relating to behaviour, inclusion or outcomes, need to be grounded in a vision of what the country should be.

SUMMARY

- Education is far more than an instrument for creating an effective and productive workforce: it exists to open the way to abundance of life.

- The education systems of the UK are a common good, but must also serve the interests of the country, especially in equipping people to cope with change and providing a clear sense of identity.

- Whilst they are varied and flexible, they increasingly lack an overall narrative. Some areas (such as FE) are 'Cinderellas', neglected and overlooked.

- Inequalities in education threaten community, demotivate courage and prevent stability. Without a value-confident and adequately funded education system, the long-term outlook for this country is poor.

4

Health – and Healing Our Brokenness

Caring equally for the health of all, regardless of perceived economic or societal value, is a clear sign of our values. The first people to suffer when a sense of community is lost are those who we may value less – the poor, especially the young and old, and the mentally ill or those in prison. Healthcare is a key marker of our values.

Since the establishment of the National Health Service (NHS) in the UK at the end of the 1940s, emergency and critical care has sought equality of outcome regardless of where people live. It is taken as a basic value that all those in this country should receive medical care free at the point of delivery. Such an aspiration, hard though it has been to put it into practice and maintain, reflects a deep concern for the common good, and for the solidarity of society. As with the provision of lifeboats on a sinking ship, when people are ill, care should be available equally for all. Nonetheless, the aspiration has often been unachievable through lack of resources as well as problems of local delivery. Moreover, the commitment to equal care for all has always been under threat, both by pressures within the NHS and also through advances in medical sciences which enable a vastly greater range of treatments, both medical and surgical, at significantly higher cost.

The NHS has lived in an almost permanent state of fear of not being able to cope,[1] as well as being under political attack that its costs are untenable in our economy. In the decade up to 2010, the very large increases in government spending on healthcare[2] led to sharp reductions in waiting times for treatment.[3] Yet the GP service was not widely perceived (rightly or wrongly) as greatly improved (although GP pay went up significantly), and the increase in money spent was not accompanied by concomitant increases in productivity.[4] At the same time, three areas of healthcare slipped into the shadows of the public gaze, two of which are now producing major crises, reflected in the general election of June 2017.

The first was social care, especially for the elderly. Largely the responsibility of local government, funds available to support those who needed residential or sheltered care have diminished on a per capita basis. Political pressure grew against the idea that the savings of elderly people should be deployed in their care over the last few years of life, leaving very little to bequeath. However, the result has been that those who cannot

---

[1] Nicholas Timmins, 'Back in the Emergency Room', *Prospect*, April 2017, p. 36, is a good historical perspective on, and analysis of, the history and current problems of the NHS.

[2] UK public spending on healthcare moved from 1,360 USD per capita, 4.96 per cent of GDP in 2000, to 2,624 USD per capita, 7.22 per cent GDP at its peak in 2009. Source: Health Spending (indicator) (OECD, 2017), https://data.oecd.org/healthres/health-spending.htm. Accessed 5 April 2017.

[3] Seán Boyle, 'United Kingdom (England): Health System Review', Health Systems in Transition 13 (1), pp. 1–486 (European Observatory on Health Systems and Policies through World Health Organization, 2011), http://www.euro.who.int/__data/assets/pdf_file/0004/135148/e94836.pdf?ua=1. Accessed 5 April 2017.

[4] Ibid.

afford the high costs of private residential care have been left behind. Accounts of 'elder abuse' have grown rapidly; we have seen increases in the number of nursing or residential home providers closing as a result of government-funded revenues being lower than the cost of providing the service. Domiciliary care finds it very hard to recruit good workers given that they are normally on low wages, often with zero-hour contracts, and with lack of support and training. The statutory coverage is patchy, with an obligation to look after vulnerable children but not the same obligation for vulnerable elderly. The unpredictability of payments for supported living leads to housing associations being cautious in their provision, and the growing number of isolated and vulnerable elderly people inevitably adds to the pressure on the NHS, both in A&E and for GPs.

The lifeboat of social care appears to be adopting a class- and wealth-based preference system. It no longer reflects a commitment to the common good, or solidarity between generations and between the rich and the poor. It is not consistent or resilient, or – on its present basis – sustainable.

The second neglected area has been public health, although this has often also been the way in which huge advances in the health of the nation have occurred. In 1854 a severe outbreak of cholera in London around the area of Soho led to Dr John Snow and a local curate, the Reverend Henry Whitehead, realizing that contaminated water from a particular pump was the cause of the cholera. This was a crucial turning-point in both epidemiology and public health, as the discovery contributed to the decision to build a sewage system, under the guidance of the engineer Joseph Bazalgette. The system, begun in 1859, was completed by 1875, and the impact on the health of Londoners was immense. In the twentieth century, the 1956 Clean Air Acts in the UK contributed to a huge change in air quality, especially in London. It is estimated that as many as 12,000 premature deaths resulted from the London Great Smog of 1952:[5] that disaster led to the concentration on improving air quality through the use of smokeless fuel.

Most changes in attitudes to public health have been as a result of great disasters, such as the cholera epidemics or the Great Smog. Inequalities of diet, health education, lifestyle and general quality of life have a long-term and chronic impact on life expectancy, but it has required a crisis to change the way we work. The indifference to massive life-quality differentials today needs to change as dramatically as the indifference to smog or cholera. We must learn, in public health, to prevent disaster, not only to react well to it. Historic attitudes may have needed a crisis to change them, but the response drew on a sense of the common good and solidarity. Health has become rightly seen as something that should not be strongly affected by relative wealth. The next table shows the variations in life expectancy at birth between different parts of the UK. Within the relatively small but still significant regional variations are intra-regional differences which can be much more extreme. Almost all the gaps are explainable through poverty, but poverty was also behind many of the concentrations of poor health in previous times. One part of the answer was public health.

[5]Michelle L. Bell and Devra Lee Davis, 'Reassessment of the Lethal London Fog of 1952: Novel Indicators of Acute and Chronic Consequences of Acute Exposure to Air Pollution', *Environmental Health Perspectives* 109 (June 2001), pp. 389–94.

FIGURE 4.1 *Life expectancy at birth of females and males born 2012–14 by UK region*[6]

Region of birth	Life expectancy, females	Life expectancy, males
London	84.2	80.3
South East	84.0	80.5
South West	83.9	80.2
East	83.8	80.4
East Midlands	83.0	79.4
West Midlands	82.9	78.9
Yorkshire and the Humber	82.4	78.7
Wales	82.4	78.5
Northern Ireland	82.3	78.3
North West	81.9	78.1
North East	81.7	78.0
Scotland	81.1	77.2

In the nineteenth century, solutions to public health issues could have been different. The rich could have moved to safer areas, leaving the poor to suffer in slums. The refusal to tolerate this approach alone sprang from governments

[6]Data on England and Wales available from 'All Data related to Life Expectancy at Birth and at Age 65 by Local Areas in England and Wales: 2012 to 2014' (Office for National Statistics, 2015), https://www.ons.gov.uk/peoplepopulationandcommunity/birthsdeathsandmarriages/lifeexpectancies/bulletins/lifeexpectancyatbirthandatage65bylocalareasinenglandandwales/2015-11-04/relateddata. Data from Scotland available from 'Life Expectancy for Administrative Areas within Scotland' (National Records of Scotland, 2015), https://www.nrscotland.gov.uk/statistics-and-data/statistics/statistics-by-theme/life-expectancy/life-expectancy-in-scottish-areas/time-series-data. Data on Northern Ireland from 'Health Inequalities Regional Report 2016' (Department of Health, 2016), https://www.health-ni.gov.uk/publications/health-inequalities-regional-report-2016. All contain data published under Open Government Licence v3.0. Note that this regional data masks more localized disparities; for example, life expectancy in Kensington and Chelsea is F:86.4, M:83.3, whereas in Tower Hamlets it is F:82.5, M:78.1. These two London boroughs should therefore appear at opposite ends of the table.

seeing such inequality as solvable, and the obligation to confront it as ethically essential, a question of values. Much of the impetus came from the churches and then from Christian Socialism.

The tensions between economic pragmatism and the need for good care systems and good public health continue today. There is also an added complexity, which is that social care, public and mental health are increasingly obviously linked. Mental health is the third Cinderella of healthcare. Its issues afflict those throughout society, of all classes and incomes, especially the growing number of the elderly afflicted with side effects of isolation, such as depression, but the resources to deal with it are less available for those on low incomes. In addition, prisons are notoriously places where a large proportion of those held would benefit from good mental health provision. Mental health issues can affect everything from a pupil or student's capacity to study to the possibility of obtaining and holding a job, the ability to form and maintain stable long-term relationships, and the quality of life towards its end.

One of the most severe and stark passages of the Gospels is at the end of St Matthew chapter 25. Jesus describes the Last Judgement, not as a parable but as the way it will happen and the criteria by which the world is judged. It is a passage that has had a deep effect on the struggle for social justice, and for the common good. At its heart is the call for love to be seen in actions that reflect the values of community above all, but also courage and stability.

Jesus describes humanity divided into two groups, the sheep and the goats. The King, sitting in judgement, tells the first group that they will enter eternal joy because they fed him when he was hungry, gave him drink when thirsty, welcomed him when a stranger, clothed him when naked, cared for him when sick and visited him when a prisoner. They are puzzled, asking when they did these things for him; his response is that when they did it to the least of his family they did it to him. The same dialogue happens with the others but in reverse: they are condemned, because by not doing any of those things for the needy whom they encountered, they had also neglected him.[7]

As in the parable of the talents a chapter earlier in Matthew's Gospel, there is a moment of judgement. However, the criterion set out by God is not whether we have been 'naughty or nice', like some Father Christmas figure deciding whether to hand out Christmas presents or not, but whether we have seen the reality of the divine image in the poor and marginalized, and have had compassion leading to action for the common good. In other, non-religious, words: have we recognized the call on our compassion and action in the humanity of those we encounter?

All three of the groups of values that historically have underpinned, and have grown and developed in, British society are expressed in this account of judgement. Compassion requires a sense of solidarity and the common good, a 'being with' and 'belonging to'. Compassion also requires a willingness to set aside the surplus, over and above what we need, in an act of gratuity. Courage is required to act, to be creative and adventurous – like Bazalgette; or the creators of the NHS, imagining whole new ways of care, and refusing to be intimidated by the unlimited scale of potential demands, or indeed by initial resistance to the very idea of a national health service.

[7]Matthew 25:31–46.

Stability is essential for any society to continue to be compassionate through structures of resilience and sustainability as well as reconciliation between those with needs and those without. There must be structures that share burdens, a universality that avoids only the fashionable, or the immediately urgent, cases of need being addressed.

A reimagination of Britain as a country in which human beings flourish has to put high-quality social care, public and mental health at the heart of its objectives. If we look afresh at the description of judgement in Matthew 25 (which has been so formative in the development of modern social policy), the two groups to be judged look alike.

They are capable of action. In today's terms, they are powerful and wealthy. They are from all the nations on the earth. The Christian narrative of a just society is neither utopian nor particular. It is achievable and universal; every nation and every sort of person is implicated. The poor are not judged. This is an issue of justice towards the oppressed. The test is both of awareness and of love-in-action in response.

The separation is very clear indeed. One group is condemned and the other is rewarded. No one can accuse this judge of lacking jurisdiction, or say that since they did not believe, they are exempt from a court appearance. The standards set are those that should apply in all circumstances everywhere.

Neither those who are rewarded nor those who are condemned demonstrate that they knew that what they were doing was to do with God. They simply acted or failed to act humanely, in solidarity with the most deprived of the earth. The values that shape us have a historic meta-narrative. Like Jesus' words, they do not contain get-out clauses, and they are not optional. They hold to absolute right and wrong, and we are condemned out of our own values when we ignore them.

Yet our culture in the twenty-first century resists such absolutism. Inescapable standards of the common good are sidelined by our own interests. Public health is a Cinderella service exactly because it is for the common good. Since all benefit, no special group recognizes the value. Sewage-free streets are seen as normal. Clean drinking water is considered a right, not an exception.

Significantly shorter life expectancy among the poor (simply because they are poor) than among the rich is the sort of hidden evil and injustice that it is too easy to be blind to unless it causes a great crisis that impacts more widely, such as the Great Smog, or a cholera epidemic. Critical care in hospitals naturally gets high attention. The ability to see a GP quickly is assumed. Standards of public health are simply expected. The mentally ill are, and always have been, easily stigmatized. Failures of social care are too easily hidden in homes and residential centres.

Today's culture does not honour old age, but sees it at best as an inconvenience. Anyone who doubts that needs to consider the regular calls to legalise euthanasia, without adequate consideration of the risk that – in a society where age is not respected – the possibility of assisted suicide will too easily become the duty to ask for death. Leading figures in the various groups campaigning for assisted suicide have pointed to the increasing number of elderly and the economic burden that represents as a reason to support their cause.[8]

[8]E.g. Matthew Parris, *Spectator*, 19 September 2015.

Mental health suffers from similar invisibility. Unless you know someone well, they can hide mild mental ill health quite easily. Their depression may be seen as being the neighbourhood Eeyore, or just being pessimistic. In Victorian times, people who would now be seen as bipolar were understood to be highly strung. A breakdown was called 'brain fever'. If people were obviously 'lunatics' they were sent away to an asylum and hidden. In our own society today, there is a high proportion of victims of mental ill health among the prison population. They are literally hidden away.

Those rewarded in the Gospel story also have no idea that they are doing anything exceptional. For them it is obvious that you visit the sick, clothe the naked, care for the prisoner, or in general terms support those who cannot support themselves. Those needing support are not described as deserving or otherwise, but simply as the poor or vulnerable. They may or may not merit help, but in their circumstances it is required that they be helped. For Christ, there is no deserving or undeserving, but people with needs to meet.

The shocking thing to both groups is that they have done, or failed to do, something intrinsically good. The declaration of Jesus about the Last Judgement became the central motivation for social reformers and those who sought to challenge the inequalities of society.

Health and healing are deeply related to our values, especially when founded on the solid rock of social care, public health and mental health provision as a priority.

Public health is the greatest catalyst for solidarity. Its absence on a sustained and fair basis across all sectors of society is likely to increase inequality dramatically, and to diminish solidarity. Its absence is a powerful symbol of a society that relies on personal strength and good fortune, not common values. The struggle to survive tells those struggling that they matter little, and the costs in terms of early mortality, sustained illness and burdens and griefs for those in such a situation diminish any feeling of common good. Those in the Gospel's description of judgement do not respond to a *conscious* sense of the presence of Christ. Intuition or indifference drive the choice to see or ignore that the reality of human dignity is disguised in the weak and struggling people they see. That sense of solidarity, of belonging to the same category and class of person, or its absence, sets a pattern for society that is infectiously effective or contagiously corrosive in creating good and evil among us.

The struggle to survive not only diminishes solidarity, but also reduces the capacity for innovation, for courage, aspiration and creativity. Human dignity is constrained by the lack of liberty to use talent, and the lack of opportunity for any except the strongest characters. It reduces us to Hobbes's description of uncivilized life: 'nasty, brutish, and short'.

Finally, the absence of good public health is not sustainable. Just as its presence is a strength and blessing to all, so its absence ends by threatening all. Some of the responses to the cholera epidemics may have been out of love and kindness for the poor. Some may have been out of the obvious calculation that what was in Soho yesterday may be in Mayfair tomorrow. The Clean Air Acts benefited every inhabitant of London, not only the poorest. Public health is a universal good, and its absence a danger to all.

It is possible to reduce significantly the overwhelming proportion of the gaps in life expectancy. A number of steps need to be taken.

First, public health must be made a cross-discipli-
nary priority involving education (from behaviour to
good school meals to regular PE to specialist provision,
especially in prisons), leisure activities (sports, arts, and
whatever promotes physical and psychological well-
being), medical culture (check-ups, and proactive rather
than reactive care), quality housing, the economy (taxes
and benefits), and employment.

The greatest difficulty in government (or indeed any
large organization or institution including the churches)
is not creating good policy but implementing it, and the
challenges are increased many times when the actions
require crossing departmental and budgetary boundaries. It is noticeable that a silo mentality has for decades
been identified as one of the greatest problems in government. Solidarity and the common good demand the
breaking down of silos and in many of the most pressing
issues facing us, from health and housing to education
and climate change, cross-departmental collaboration is
the greatest challenge.

Research on premature mortality has demonstrated
clearly that the reasons are complex, sometimes inescapable, but normally attributable to a relatively small
number of causes, all of which inter-relate. The main
ones among them are diet, exercise, housing, mental health, employment conditions and security, and
relationships.

To put it fairly graphically, those who have had a poor
educational record, limited job opportunities, suffer
from mental illness as a result in part of lack of hope and
healthy relationships, are themselves damaged by lack
of money, rarely take any exercise, and have a poor diet,
are likely to die much sooner than those without such
problems. It only has to be written for people to say,

'obviously; tell us something we don't know'. Yet if it is so obvious, why has nothing been done for so long, so that the reality is that the issue of inequality is not improving and in some areas is getting worse?

In Sweden, nutrition is part of the curriculum, and school meals are compulsory.[9] Eating together improves health and relationships, and the cost of providing reasonable school meals for all children, based on a good diet about which education is provided, should be a cost that offsets future needs for medical care.

Sport is always deeply unpopular when compulsory. The poet Sir John Betjeman, speaking of school days' dreads, wrote of the 'dread of games'. Yet they are also a source of health, especially if they don't only consist of kicking people – and occasionally a ball – on a freezing cold pitch while being yelled at by bad-tempered teachers. I too remember the dread! Levels of Type 2 diabetes are now at epidemic levels,[10] and the costs to the NHS will be vast unless the issue is tackled with exercise and diet.

The arts and music have been well funded in the past but recent cutbacks have hit hard at this area. This is during a time when music therapy for those with disabilities and for those with mental health challenges is turning out to be highly effective. Similarly, the use of art to express feelings is both very low cost and very beneficial. It is routine in refugee camps, and a powerful source of therapeutic support.[11]

[9]'School Food Policy Country Factsheets: Sweden' (European Commission, 2013), https://ec.europa.eu/jrc/sites/jrcsh/files/jrc-school-food-policy-factsheet-sweden_en.pdf. Accessed 5 April 2017.
[10]There are an estimated 4.5 million people living with diabetes in the UK, an estimated 90 per cent of which are cases of Type 2 diabetes. Obesity accounts for 80–85 per cent of the risk for developing Type 2 diabetes. Source: 'Diabetes UK: Facts and Stats' (Diabetes UK, October 2016), https://www.diabetes.org.uk/Documents/Position%20statements/DiabetesUK_Facts_Stats_Oct16.pdf.
[11]I saw this for myself in Jordan in June 2017.

These are only examples to demonstrate that the issues run through most areas of government. Only a public health service that is freestanding and powerful will be able to compel the spending of the requisite funding in a way that enables future economies while also forcing all areas of government to look beyond their immediate interest. One irony of the NHS is that the vast majority of those working within it strain every sinew to make it work, and yet the frictions in the system and the lack of well-directed resources present a continual extra challenge. It is especially noticeable that the gaps between departments in government render the hard work of all less effective, especially at the interface of the NHS and care systems.

The Churches through education, chaplaincy and the parish system are in a good place both to draw attention to issues of public health and also to be effective in supporting imaginative and community-based approaches to resolving them. It is often forgotten that many housing associations were started by churches; sports teams (including many football clubs now in the Premier League) started with churches; and the presence of more than one million children in church schools today gives a vast opportunity for tackling early-years onset of diabetes, ill health from obesity, issues of diet and education in self-care.

The areas that require a significant level of attention and action are those of social care and mental health; the latter is rapidly becoming *the* public health crisis of the twenty-first century. It could be as serious in its effect as physical health crises in the nineteenth century, and its causes may well be linked to social issues and especially the use of social media and modern technology for communications. Within mental health, I include not only the issue of mental illnesses that are diagnosed but also personality disorders and similar issues that may well contribute to mental health problems.

MENTAL HEALTH

This is a time of revolution both in the acceptance and in the treatment of mental health problems. Although this is still, along with public health and social care, a neglected service, the general culture is changing, led by a wave of celebrities, politicians and other well-known figures being transparent about their own issues. The intervention of Prince Harry and his joint work with the Duke and Duchess of Cambridge in early 2017 felt like a watershed moment for open conversations about mental health, certainly in the UK. The Scottish Mental Health Strategy introduced in 2017 has the ambition for mental health to be treated with the same 'commitment, passion and drive' as physical health, and sets out plans to increase the availability and quality of mental health services across GP surgeries and hospitals, police stations and prisons, and schools. Its capacity to cross departmental boundaries speaks to the benefits of subsidiarity. Should it be effective, it is to be hoped that other parts of the UK will follow the example.

The effects of mental illness are enormous, especially in terms of life chances. A period of depression in adolescence, especially prevalent among young women,[12]

---

[12] A longitudinal study found that in 2014, 14-year-old girls were more than twice as likely to be psychologically distressed than their male counterparts, and that this disparity had increased compared to the previous cohort of 2005. Source: Carli Lessof, *et al.*, 'Longitudinal Study of Young People in England Cohort 2: Health and Wellbeing at Wave 2' (TNS BMRB, July 2016), https://www.gov.uk/government/uploads/system/uploads/attachment_data/file/599871/LSYPE2_w2-research_report.pdf. Accessed 5 April 2017.

may well affect exam results, and if not well treated lead to a lifetime of periodic sickness, immeasurably reducing earning capacity, and leading to an ever lower sense of self-worth and even social isolation.

Untreated depression and other forms of mental illness in the workplace are also not only costly to the economy but more importantly reduce the capacity of individuals to perform well, and lead to isolation and, in some cases, family breakdown.

Family life itself is nearly always affected by chronic or severe illness at some stage, but the absence of physical symptoms, and the fear that still accompanies mental illness, again affects not only the sufferers themselves but their carers and wider family networks.

One of the most neglected areas of understanding and action on mental health is its relationship with those in the criminal justice system. The Department of Health estimates that 90 per cent of offenders are affected by mental illness and personality disorders or substance dependency and that 80 per cent are affected by more than one of these.[13]

Addressing mental and public health attracts few votes, but prison reforms even fewer. NOMS (the National Offender Management Service) has suffered enormous cuts since 2009,[14] and that has affected every area. It is both a morally flawed and unsustainable approach. Offender management that takes mental health seriously is likely to reduce reoffending, cutting the long-term cost of the service. There is a moral assumption that those in

[13]Nicola Singleton, *et al.*, 'Psychiatric Morbidity Among Prisoners' (Office for National Statistics, 1998).
[14]'Prison: The Facts – Bromley Briefings Summer 2016' (London: Prison Reform Trust, 2016), http://www.prisonreformtrust.org.uk/Portals/0/Documents/Bromley%20Briefings/summer%202016%20briefing.pdf.

prison or other parts of NOMS are punished by being detained or serving their sentence in some other way. To be deprived of proper healthcare would properly be considered unacceptable for physical health issues, and the same should apply to mental health.

Jesus' words in Matthew 25 have shaped the approach of society, led by the Church, over the centuries and have entered deeply into our shared values. The NHS sprang out of a concern that the poor should be able to be treated as well as the rich. It is the most powerful and visible expression of our Christian heritage.

What then has gone wrong with care in mental health, and where can we start enabling the system to heal itself?

First, the cultural change that has begun must be encouraged. In the same way as the L'Arche[15] communities for those with learning difficulties have had a major positive impact on the public attitude to their human dignity, there is a need for good examples and practice in dealing with mental illness. Historically, one of the problems has been the sense – too often colluded with by the Church – that mental illness was in fact diabolical in origin, or some sort of divine curse.

Cultural change is encouraged by good public examples, by laws about the treatment of employees with mental illnesses, by education, and by proper equipping of centres of care. There must be the same intentionality about the treatment of mental illness and attitudes towards it as there is for other serious diseases and physical illnesses.

[15]A global network of mainly Christian communities in which those with learning difficulties live in community with those without, learning how to express a common good.

Second, the effects of mental illness need tackling. Using the imagery of the judgement of Jesus on the nations, those who are mentally ill often find themselves imprisoned in dungeons which grow ever darker with isolation and lack of human contact. The walls of such a prison are scaled by having someone to talk to, and knowing oneself to be part of a community. Much the same applies to social care.

Solidarity in our society, a sense of being one people, should impel the tackling of mental health issues to be one of the great tasks of our time. Any society that wants sustainable households and innovative industries will seek to enable those struggling with mental illness to find a place that reflects their humanity and dignity, demonstrated by the gift of work and creativity in their own lives.

SOCIAL CARE

The issues of social care are of immense complexity and the growing demand is only now being experienced. The values of solidarity and the common good are expressed not simply by funding (the provision of which is a very large-scale problem without, as yet, an obvious solution) but also by practices that reduce isolation. Many of these will be expressed privately at the family level through the normal expressions of affection. It is essential that the dignity of all is taught clearly through education and example; nothing less is required than a significant culture change, especially towards the elderly. One of the benefits of changing our approach to social care is that it is a major opportunity for job creation, for the development of apprenticeships and for creative and aspirational approaches. Social care has often been seen as a dead-end and last-resort occupation, which is demonstrably false in terms of its importance for human dignity. The development of proper structures of training and pay, with opportunities to progress through both academic and experiential routes would increase its prestige. It is one of the most significant expressions of our historic values in an ageing society, where fragility of health – mental or physical – is seen less and less as something to be tolerated, and more and more as a diminution of the value of the person concerned.

SUMMARY

- Health inequalities are a significant sign of injustice in UK society. They are evident in, for example, life expectancy, mental health, and elderly care: key indicators of problems with values.

- The neglect of public health, mental health and social care arise from the lack of a coherent and values-based approach to health issues.

- The impact is seen most clearly in the penal system.

5

Housing – the Architecture of Community

The Grenfell Tower disaster of June 2017 in North Kensington, London, became almost at once a symbol of many of the greatest problems in housing. First, it was clear that the building was unsafe, and similar dangers were promptly discovered all over the country. Second, it was apparent that the voices of tenants had not been heard either by the tower-block managers or by the local council. Third, it was obvious that the number of people living in such a dangerous block was unknown, with numerous examples of sub-letting, of unregistered tenants, of refugees and people on low wages. There was an enormous voluntary effort to help those made homeless, without possessions and often bereaved, all in a few hours; yet while the emergency services acted with speed and immense courage there was a perception that the government response, at all levels, had been neither fast enough nor adequate.

The fact that the tower was a few minutes' walk from some of the richest neighbourhoods in the world, and the suspicion that the voices of tenants were not heard because they were poor and often from minorities, only added to the anger. Whatever the findings of the enquiry may be, there is a sense that values of solidarity and the common good – the basic values of community – had been lost somewhere along the way, especially in relation to social and rental housing.

An article in the *Financial Times*[1] set out the change in patterns of housing provision since 1945. House building peaked in 1968 at more than 400,000 homes. Around a quarter of homes were lived in by council tenants. By 2009, the system was far more fragmented, with large numbers of private landlords, many housing associations, and about two-thirds of properties owner-occupied. One consequence of this was that councils to some degree lost direct oversight of standards in public housing – standards which themselves had become vaguer and outdated. It is clear, tragically, that a fresh revolution in housing is needed and it must be values-led.

If the purpose of housing was understood as creating communities and not merely building accommodation, the whole nature of the industry would be changed. The revolution would be even more profound if the incentive for housing was to have a good and safe shelter in a safe and convenient location, not principally an investment (or two). It is in the area of housing that the most far-reaching reimagining is needed. In this chapter, having looked at the general situation, I will discuss some aspects of social housing and then turn to the private sector.

Housing has always been a major part of national reimagining. In 1945, after six years of an economy devoted to wartime production and of widespread aerial bombardment, British housing stock was very poor.

[1] 30 June 2017, p. 9.

The creation of the post-war estates in the 1940s was one of the main signs of a return to normality. The aims of the housing activity in the years after 1945 went far beyond the replacement of destroyed buildings, or even of slum clearance. They created a vision of a new Britain – more equal, more healthy and with greater opportunity.[2]

FIGURE 5.1 *Percentage of UK dwellings owner-occupied over time*[3]

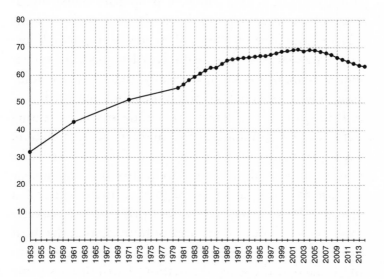

[2]The 1945 Labour Manifesto stated: 'Housing will be one of the greatest and one of the earliest tests of a Government's real determination to put the nation first.'
[3]Data on 1980–2014 from 'Table 101: By Tenure, United Kingdom (Historical Series)' (Department for Communities and Local Government, 12 January 2017). Available at https://www.gov.uk/government/statistical-data-sets/live-tables-on-dwelling-stock-including-vacants. Accessed 2 March 2017. Data on 1953, 1961 and 1971 available at 'Home Ownership Down and Renting Up for First Time in a Century' (Office for National Statistics, 19 June 2015), http://visual.ons.gov.uk/housing-census/. Accessed 2 March 2017.

For the first 35 years of the post-war period, home ownership was growing steadily, albeit from a low base. The
major change was in the years after 1979, in which there
was a very rapid increase in the proportion of people
owning their homes, following the government's drive
for full home ownership and linked in part to the sale
of council houses to their tenants. In the context of an
economy where home ownership is promoted as the best
tenure and where land is limited, planning consent slow
and local authorities not able to build, a one-way market
became inevitable, in which continual demand pushed
up housing prices in the absence of adequate supply. The
pattern seemed to be part of the way of the world. A
house would be a safe investment. It thus became obvious and reasonable that most people would prefer to
pay the costs of a mortgage, through which to buy their
home, rather than pay rent. Yet, as in most economics,
there are multiple consequences of the growth of home
ownership. The benefits have been strongly argued,
ranging from a greater stake in the condition of a house,
more stability and security in retirement (assuming
the mortgage has been paid off), to increased commitment to the locality – and even (it was argued by some,
when council houses were originally sold off under Mrs
Thatcher's first administration) a greater commitment to
the stability of society.

Even if one accepts that these enormous benefits exist,
they do have costs. One is the very sharp increase in the
total amount of debt in society. Second, an indirect consequence has been a significant slowing in the building
of new houses once local authorities were less directly
involved. Those that are built are now far more market driven than planned for social purposes. Most of
all, the ever growing demand for housing for purchase,

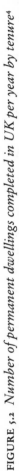

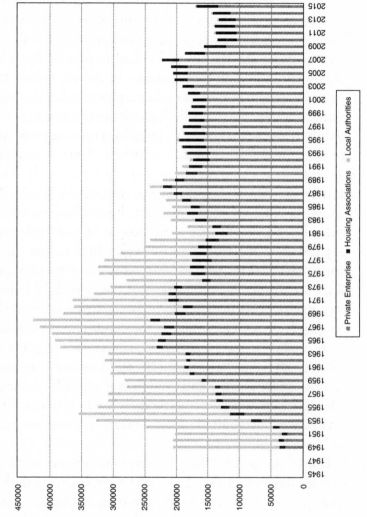

FIGURE 5.2 *Number of permanent dwellings completed in UK per year by tenure*[4]

[4]Data from 'Table 241: Permanent Dwellings Completed, By Tenure, United Kingdom, Historical Calendar Year Series' (Department for Communities and Local Government, 23 February 2017). Available at https://www.gov.uk/government/statistical-data-sets/live-tables-on-house-building. Accessed 2 March 2017.

which has outrun supply, has raised prices of housing so dramatically that a house has become as much, or even more, a store of value than a home. This, in turn, drives the attraction of a second/third home purely for investment purposes and, worse still, the concept of 'buy to hold' (where the owner has no intention of either living in or renting out the property), which has been seen to some extent in London. Conversely, the encouragement of a large liquid rental market at reasonable prices would allow house prices to stabilize and return a home to being principally a good shelter in a safe and convenient location.

The most difficult problem has been that although all house prices have risen significantly (with a very few exceptions in areas of depopulation), the differentials around the UK have increased even more rapidly. Thus today the average price of a family house in London is £483,803, in the south-east more widely is £316,026 and in the north-east is £128,631.[5] There is effectively no longer one housing market but several, only loosely connected. Figure 5.3 shows that Scotland, Wales and Northern Ireland, together with the North of England, are the areas where the ratio of house prices to gross earnings of first-time buyers has not changed dramatically in over 30 years.

How we build and what we build for is the practice that provides a basic sign of our values. Cheap and temporary accommodation or huge differentials in housing standards make a clear statement about our lack of solidarity. The move from a home as a haven to a home as

[5]'UK House Price Index Summary: December 2016' (Land Registry, 14 February 2017), https://www.gov.uk/government/publications/uk-house-price-index-summary-december-2016/uk-house-price-index-summary-december-2016. Accessed 2 March 2017.

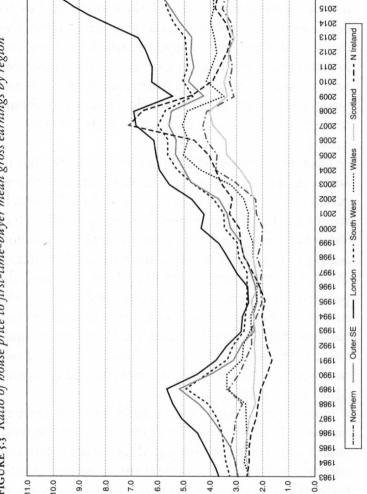

FIGURE 5.3   *Ratio of house price to first-time-buyer mean gross earnings by region*[6]

[6] Data from 'First Time Buyer Gross House Price to Earnings Ratios' (Nationwide, 2017). Available at http://www.nationwide.co.uk/about/house-price-index/download-data#~. Accessed 2 March 2017.

an investment implies a reduced value for community. Sustained effort to renew housing stock is both a generator of economic activity and also a foundation for the creation of new communities. Yet, by itself it is only one part of the solution. Where housing is treated as the whole answer, the value it symbolizes changes from being solidarity and creativity to paternalistic materialism.

It is well understood that the UK has seen a growing problem with housing supply over many years, and the result has been a very sharp increase in the cost of housing in many parts of the country.

Rising housing cost is a symptom of growing wealth, not a cause. To live in a house which is growing in value only brings an increase in a household's wealth if you are planning to move to a cheaper area or a smaller house, if your home is one of a small minority of houses in the areas which are seeing growth in value, or if you inherited it, intend to sell and will have no need to replace it. To put it more simply, there is no point in being in a property growing in value unless you wish to get off the housing ladder partly or entirely. Arguably therefore, rising property prices only benefit those who need their house as an investment.

That is not the case for the majority of people needing to buy a house, who thus find all that is happening, if they choose to move, is that they pay proportionately more as well as receive more. If they are trying to move to an area of greater wealth, housing is likely to prove an often insuperable obstacle. Concerning London, if you move out, it will be hard to move back.

Building a house is only the first challenge. Any prospective purchaser will also need to be able to fund running costs and maintenance, income for which depends on employment. Without a rising economic tide, new

housing will deteriorate and potentially become a problem area. In some cities, the problem has become critical.
Many streets in Liverpool declined first in population
as people moved away to find work, and then in care
and maintenance before being finally abandoned.[7] The
city has worked to tackle this problem with a mixture
of incentives for redevelopment or simply by knocking
down housing stock that is never likely to be needed
again. Even good housing, although necessary, is not by
itself sufficient for regeneration. Liverpool has plenty of
housing, but not enough jobs to sustain the lives of the
people who would live in the houses.

So, in the owner-occupier market, if the UK is to
build communities rather than simply build houses, we
need to address the dysfunctions caused by ever-rising
house prices and the consequent drive to own a house
as an investment. We need also to ensure that houses are
built and communities developed in such a way as to
cause local economies to thrive and thus local communities to thrive also.

It should be the responsibility of democratically
elected local governments to ensure that communities
are created as well as houses built in the areas for which
they have responsibility.[8]

---

[7]A number of years ago, Liverpool Council attempted to reverse this situation by
putting abandoned and derelict properties on the market for £1 (http://www.bbc.
co.uk/news/uk-england-merseyside-34474378).

[8]Although the Social Value Act 2012 applies generally to social housing, social
value ought to be an objective of local government with 'Section 106 payments'
(the contribution by private developers to social needs) encouraged right across an
area and not only in the specific development to which they relate. Local authorities could create something that might be called a Community Transformation
Board with a responsibility for development of social value. But how we measure social value needs developing if the Act is to have bite, and not just to be
bid candy.

There is a parallel problem in social housing. The key performance indicators for housing associations (HAs) are all about the maintenance of housing, and neglect entirely the creation of community or the development of a local economy. HAs were originally set up to alleviate poverty – and housing was seen as a key driver of that. Now, instead, housing has become an end in itself, as an examination of many HAs' annual reports will show, and its core purpose has been forgotten. When the government cut rents in June 2016, insights from interviews in the sector suggest that many HAs cut their community programmes to save money – after all, the government wanted more houses built.[9] A significant number of housing associations are seeking to square the circle by developing private sector homes, the profit from which can go to support their historic core business.

This issue is not helped by successive governments' failure to recognize the 'soft' values and practices HAs contribute (jobs, clubs, street wardens, etc.) – in part because models for demonstrating their financial value are not yet fully developed. Intuitively, we know that breaking the cycle of recidivism has financial value, but to whom and by how much? If the value accrues to, say, the prison service and not to the HA, is it worth an HA getting involved? The support of ex-offenders is a classic 'silo' management problem. A recently released ex-offender will often have needs relating to mental health (NHS), housing (housing association), education (FE or other) and probation, and potentially be at risk of reoffending (police). No single agency is responsible for

[9]I am grateful to Charles Arbuthnot for his advice on this chapter, and for sharing his experience from interviews with many HAs.

bringing all these together. Yet HAs are among the most entrepreneurial of intermediate institutions, as their survival over the last 50 years of changing ideas demonstrates very adequately.

Instead of creating social value, there is ever more pressure on HAs to build more and more houses to solve the housing crisis. When this pressure is combined with reductions in grants, there is almost literally an obligation to make bricks without straw. If you are to build more with less, you naturally cut everything that doesn't increase the output of houses, especially the prioritization of community, and the economic regeneration necessary in many of the areas in which HAs are especially active. We need to be aware that 63 per cent of HA tenants were receiving housing benefit in 2015, compared with private sector levels of 28 per cent.[10] HAs are at the cutting edge of the need for reimagining Britain, not only in values, but also in economic regeneration. Expanding their role and responsibilities (with proper funding formulas and incentives to work in partnerships for economic regeneration, education and public health) could mobilize already effective and imaginative bodies to a far greater degree than has been imagined. There is the possibility of creating communities with aspiration and courage as well as resilience and stability, even in areas of currently greatest deprivation.

Housing is thus one of those foundational areas in which failures to set clear values and practices lead to disasters in policies that damage many other aspects of life. Policies without clear practices to underpin them will be blown

[10]Data from 'Annex Table 2.4' of 'English Housing Survey 2014 to 2015: Social Rented Sector Report' (Department for Communities and Local Government under Crown Copyright, 21 July 2016). Available at https://www.gov.uk/government/statistics/english-housing-survey-2014-to-2015-social-rented-sector-report.

by the wind. The practices should not only be guided by but embody the values. Our addiction to increasing the proportion of home ownership, and to making money on houses as investments, has become a practice that demonstrates the shallowness of our underlying values.

Since 1945, the housing challenge has become both more complex and more difficult. A market fractured into sub-markets operating in radically different ways, as for example the distinction between London and Scotland or Wales, has a profoundly limiting impact on the economy, and causes much damage to the family and to local communities.

In a hypothetical housing market where 100 per cent of properties were rented, and where rents did not vary much from differentials in pay in different parts of the country and different areas of each town, moving house would be quite simple. The opportunity of work elsewhere would involve no more than changing rented accommodation and the higher rent would be matched by higher pay. Equally, in a market where 100 per cent of properties were owner-occupied, but the multiple of local earnings required to buy was broadly similar for similar sorts of houses in similar areas, then although the need for large capital transfers would remain, there would be a level of liquidity which would make looking for new work potentially affordable. The same applies to a mixed economy of rented and owner-occupied housing, provided the mix was equivalent in equivalent areas and there was an adequate and easily traded source of both sorts of housing in each part of the country.

Tragically, none of this is true. Housing in London is illiquid, in desperate over-demand, and requires wild multiples of salary to buy compared with the rest of the country. In other areas (for example, Cornwall), second homes have pushed up prices beyond the reach of local, permanent inhabitants. The London effect slowly diminishes but continues on all good commuting routes into London, and is still felt up to two hours' journey away. The second-home effect is widespread.

The result is a constraint on the capacity of businesses and other employers in London to employ people on 'ordinary' salaries, typically those of teachers, public sector employees, charities, or routine clerical jobs in large companies. At the same time, very high levels of pay suck resources into London, draining centres elsewhere in the country and constraining diversification of employment and decentralization of senior positions in major forces within the economy.

To reimagine Britain we must thus reimagine housing.

The first form of reimagining is to reclaim the purpose of housing. Housing exists as a basis for community and community exists for human flourishing. Building new housing without clear community values and aims will lead to the same problems being repeated again in the future. Although there will never be such a thing as a perfect community, and human fallibility and sin will always put paid to utopian schemes, there can be communities which provide incentives and means for gathering people together and for the development of hope and expectations of good social behaviour.

Reimagined core values and practices in any housing development will be linked to health in many forms. Good communities build financial, physical, mental, spiritual and relational health. In Southern Africa, the concept of *ubuntu*, 'I am what I am because of who we all are', locks together community and personal identity. At the heart of Christian and Jewish understanding of being human is the great summary of the law, a summary common in Jesus' time among the rabbis: 'love God with all your heart, soul, strength and mind' and 'love your neighbour as yourself'. Jesus' own use of this summary carried this understanding of being human in Christian thinking. Once again, the question of identity is bound together with the reality of community. We live in a society which does not easily accept the idea of loving God, but still recognizes the rule of loving neighbour as something of at least theoretical benefit. The creation of communities that facilitate neighbourliness, and which show the signs of health just mentioned, is partly based in building plans and the design of buildings in relationship with one another. High walls, lack of common space, poor lighting, restricted local economies and poor healthcare and education will all contribute to failing communities and thus to isolation and despair.

So far, so easy. As always the problems in any society are not in setting goals but in implementation. The search for the Holy Grail of effective and socially beneficial housing communities is one that has defeated generation after generation since 1945. Whether it was the era of tower blocks and Corbusier-style brutalism, or relocation into endless estates without community centres, and whether development has been private or public, there has always been a complaint about the absence of true community.

Of course, part of this is nostalgia. Communities were always under pressure, especially among the poor, and the images of the happy poor sitting cheerfully on doorsteps while chatting amiably with one another ignores the absence of sanitation or heating, the short life spans, the gross inequalities, the frequent violence and high levels of crime. An antidote to such images is to read the memoirs of those who grew up in areas of poverty in the 1950s; or, even more, to read some of Charles Dickens' descriptions of Victorian London, or look at William

Hogarth's pictures. But, whether communities have succeeded or failed in the past, it is without question true that we thrive in healthy community and thus we must pursue it and foster it at every opportunity.

The process of developing and maintaining community health depends heavily on values such as subsidiarity and solidarity, and developing patterns of very local government that have both a broad enough range of responsibilities and adequate access to financial resources to permit action that increases community well-being. To a large extent, especially in rural areas, such patterns of responsibility exist in the UK and across Europe in the form of parish councils and their equivalents. They are easily laughed at, discussing lack of mowing of verges, or arguing over street lighting, but their apparent vices of extreme detail and obsession with the particular are their real virtues. Through their efforts, paving stones are levelled, streets made safer, speed limits negotiated and local planning considered.

The problem with local government at the most local level is often that there is too little scope for local commitment. School availability is often far removed from their control or even influence (for example, over the total number of available places and their key locations), as is local healthcare at general practitioner level. Planning recommendations are easily appealed and overturned, and in urban areas these are frequently in danger of being both on a far larger scale and far more removed from the daily experience of local people. This is not an argument for simple localization; obviously there needs to be a place that holds the larger-scale pictures at regional or national level. Nevertheless, the absence of a local voice with persuasive force leads to the neglect of local communities, the absence of local ambition and the weakening of local resilience.

Within the assisted sector of rentals, through HAs, changes in objectives could lead to distinct differences in outcomes, once community development and not mere building became the primary aim. What then would an HA's basic purpose be? It would be to build bridges towards both personal and community health, using housing as their key asset to deliver this. This would be a fresh way of thinking, although, for many, a welcome one. Some HAs are already working from this premise despite the challenges. Bromford HA in Wolverhampton, for example, have developed a neighbourhood coaches scheme that breaks down silos and supports residents, especially those with multiple needs, by allocating a coach to a smaller area than usual for housing officers, enabling coaches to work more closely with residents. Another example comes from Trafford Housing; the box below shows Trafford's objectives in the service of the common good:

The Partnership's key objective is that 'partners and people work effectively together to improve outcomes for individuals, families, communities and localities'. Their priority outcomes are as follows:

- Local people are enabled and empowered to achieve their ambitions.
- Individuals and families in vulnerable situations are supported to improve and sustain their quality of life.
- Trafford has a thriving voluntary and community sector.
- Partners are supported and challenged.

Available at http://traffordpartnership.org.

There would need to be a new set of key performance indicators, not abandoning the importance of adequate management and maintenance, but drawing in, as primary aims, the requirements of a healthy community. They could include such things as a reduction in the number of active Anti-social Behaviour Orders, in crime and in reoffending, in untreated and uncontrolled mental illness and in loneliness, and an increase in normal life expectancy as a result of better diet and social involvement. All of these are becoming measurable as researchers are exploring well-being indices, social value indices and parallel soft means of surveying adequacy of life quality. Concentrated work in this area would be of immense benefit to society as a whole, not least as it is likely to show that investing in community is not a public sector cost but a significant public sector saving.

The question remains as to how such performance indicators could be met. In one sense, the means is also part of the outcome. It begins with connecting all the stakeholders, agreeing a plan for the community and seeing who can do what the best. Instead of looking inwards (how quickly did we fix the leaking roof?), housing managers would be members of the board and look outwards if they are to have any chance of hitting their indicators, by working collaboratively across what are currently well-siloed institutions. For example, they would have to ask the NHS and public health bodies what issues trigger ill health physically and mentally and how they, as an HA, could create partnerships to address the issues. They would have to ask the schools how they could partner to reduce young offending and truancy. They would have to visit the prisons to learn about reoffending and how to break the cycles. Of increasing importance in today's society, HAs would be able to partner with other providers to alleviate the alarming levels of loneliness among our elderly.

Additionally, they would find great advantage in having both the facilities and initiative to involve intermediate voluntary groups that provide activities (often free) which are themselves likely to contribute to value formation and to community solidarity. These vary from faith-based organizations to self-help and training groups for adults, and often have overlaps between different groups who share the provision of services and training to provide them. In other words, the HA becomes part of a network which has obligations, accountabilities and incentives to deliver healthy communities.

And what of the private market? The complexities of inequalities of housing value and the rights of property owners make equivalent community building more difficult but no less essential in predominantly private housing estates. It has been recognized for decades that the value of property, once allowance is made for the form of ownership, is driven by a combination of factors, the two most important of which have been location and the cost of the building itself.

The clearest example of the issue of location is London, which by its enormous size, its status as national capital, and the presence of the world's principal financial market, demonstrates the issues of property with remarkable clarity. Small London houses sell for far more than large properties in rural areas, or even city centre properties in the capitals of Northern Ireland, Wales or Scotland. Location value is both self-reinforcing and also linked to the wider economy. London has very high property values because huge numbers of people want to live and work there, because its economy is generally strong and the opportunities for employment combined with the pleasures of a London lifestyle create demand. Equally, because property in London seems to have its own micro-economy, many people want to buy there, even if not to live in their property more than occasionally; as a result, property prices continue to remain high, but communities suffer. It is becoming more and more difficult for anyone on an ordinary salary to find somewhere to live within easy commuting distance of work. The same is true to a lesser extent for a number of other cities, including Birmingham and Manchester. The latter has benefited from many years of good local leadership which has enabled it to become a very powerful force in the north-west of England.

Gross inequalities of housing value and thus of wealth within a community result in community disintegration. Those with property understandably want to protect the value of what they own, or better still see it rise. They are likely to resist encroachment by social housing, or even by necessary urban infrastructure, including bus routes, low-cost shopping and more major developments that have to go somewhere, such as prisons, hospitals and state schools.

The NIMBY (Not In My Back Yard) factor makes local forms of community government at parish level resistant to outsiders and reluctant to sponsor diversity if there is any possibility that it will diminish housing values or be perceived as a risk to the aesthetic of the community. Yet a community that is too expensive and exclusive becomes like a hedonistic version of ancient Sparta: only the elite live in it and it is surrounded by suburbs of what are effectively helots – serfs – whose job is to be there during the day and be away or invisible at other times. There is no diversity, no mixing, no valuing of difference, no sight of the poor; in all, a failure

of genuine and caring community. The values and practices increasingly implied by the balance of property
values and influence of location are those of materialistic
economic maximization with no account of justice or
equality. These are justified by saying that it is the work
of the market, not recognizing that markets that do not
serve the common good are dysfunctional, and like the
UK property market in the early 1990s and after 2008,
end up consuming themselves and those who are over-
extended in slavery to their demands.

Yet what can be done about it? HA estates and properties are to some extent discrete entities with a capacity to make policy, although it is essential that policies
are owned and designed by the communities which are
being created. Private property has a right and long tradition of being protected by law from undue interference.
Local government is able to engage with communities
and is democratically accountable for their decisions;
they should be the ones with responsibility for the management of social value and the creation of community.

As private property is part of a market, then to some
extent fiscal and planning guides must seek to establish
clear principles for the just and transparent operating
of the market. There can be supplementary taxes on
properties left empty for large proportions of the year.
Capital Gains tax should continue to apply to all properties where the beneficial owner is overseas, as vacant
properties weaken community. There is an argument
for attaching the same tax to all properties, perhaps on a
tapering basis for very long-term ownership. The idea of
a location tax, or wealth tax on the underlying value of
property, needs re-examining, although it is clear that the
problems of its implementation are huge, and possibly

the damage to personal liberty would be greater than the gain in societal equality.

Most of all, all legislation, and all permission or encouragements relevant to housing, and to new building, must include a strong element of community-enhancing aspects. It is critical that large numbers of new houses are built where they are needed, but building by itself is only a means to an end, the end being communities that are healthy in every way. With all the necessary relaxation of planning limits and opening of opportunities for development must come clear pre-conditions based on values and practices that will imagine health in every form from individual to environmental as the principal characteristic of new development.

No new estate should be built above a certain small size without the developer having to create areas for meeting, halls, space for shops and exercise, schools, clinics, centres of counselling and support, places of worship and other community facilities to ensure a clear community focus. There must continue to be a significant proportion of genuinely low-cost housing on all developments, especially in large urban centres like London and other major cities, so that there is genuine social diversity and mobility of population and thus the mixing of different groups in ways that enable the formation of relationships and communities. The issues of climate change and the environment must be faced, and the forms of energy generation and waste disposal future-proofed. Local community transformation boards could be tasked with overseeing these issues to ensure that responsibility is taken collectively. They would also ensure that private developers, public sector providers and voluntary groups are all lined up to facilitate its success, as well as large-scale landowners, including the Church of England.

The re-empowering of local government at its lowest level, capable of raising and spending money for local benefit and attentive to the details but not exclusive in its policies, is a cornerstone of community development with relationships that are based on equality and justice, not merely on the value of a plot of land. The need is for a top-to-bottom reimagining of almost every aspect of housing development in this country with a view to recapturing, through thriving communities, the vision of a new Britain, more equal, more healthy and with greater opportunity.

SUMMARY

- The principal aim of housing, both public and private, should be the creation of community.

- This is dependent upon the values of community, especially solidarity and subsidiarity, but also courage and ambition, and stability and resilience.

- Good housing and the ability to move are essential to equality and justice.

- More responsibility needs to be given to local management of housing.

- There is not one but many housing markets in the UK, and their differences create deep inflexibilities and even injustices.

6

Economics and Finance – Serving and Inspiring

In 2016, Ken Loach directed and produced *I, Daniel Blake*, which may well become a seminal film, setting out the experiences of ordinary people excluded from full participation in the economy and caught in the morass of the benefits system. There are thousands of lessons to be drawn, and a deep sense of repentance needed for allowing such an iniquitous and depersonalized way of facing the economic challenges of the post-Great Recession years. As portrayed in many other books and films of recent times, and as can be seen in so many parts of this country (and indeed across Europe), 'austerity' is not merely an economic term. It is a word that almost invariably conceals the crushing of the weak, the unlucky, the ill and a million others. Austerity is a theory for the rich, and a reality of suffering for the poor. It hits the least well-off areas disproportionately, randomly and without mercy. Unless the economy is built on foundations of justice, the common good and solidarity, words like aspiration are utterly meaningless and stability is a dream.

We need to recognize that the economy either enables an agenda, blocks it, or sets it. However much we may wish to resist the power of economics (and I wish it a lot), we are constrained in what we do by the state of the economy and by the international influences on it. When it is going well, possibilities of human flourishing abound. When it is going badly, all our best-laid plans founder. However, despite that reality, there is a good deal of room for justice, for the common good, for setting priorities within the economy that put the human being and human dignity at the centre – for all human beings.

The market is not efficient: it does not indiscriminately produce the best outcomes for everyone; and that needs to be recognized so that the market is not treated as a deity whose whims cannot be challenged.

The values of a reimagined Britain will be seen in the way the economy works. Economics (and in our country the place of finance) is values expressed in numbers.

To pay attention to economics as part of our values is to ensure that we express in action what we say in theory. For most people, the economy is what conditions the flourishing of life. As Charles Dickens' Mister Micawber said in *David Copperfield*: 'Annual income twenty pounds, annual expenditure nineteen pounds nineteen and six, result happiness. Annual income twenty pounds, annual expenditure twenty pounds nought and six, result misery.'[1] The reality and certainty of the income and the control of the expenditure are only partly within our control. When times are hard, to quote a user of a food bank whom I met, 'the month is just a little longer than the pay'.

---

[1]Charles Dickens, *The Personal History of David Copperfield* (London: Bradbury and Evans, 1850), pp. 125–6. The figures in decimal money translate into income £20.00, expenditure either £20.025 or £19.975.

To speak of values without looking at the nature of the economy is incoherent. Countries are not built through imagination alone but with visible elements which express the reimagined values. The Britain of the Victorian era was magicked into our sight at the opening of the 2012 London Olympics. Kenneth Branagh played the great engineer Brunel, and the set recalled that Victorian Britain was called the workshop of the world. Its values were expressed globally and visibly in steel, iron, ships, coal and construction.

To reimagine Britain, there must be a sense of what our infrastructure should look like, what we will see when we travel through the land. That visible expression of values and hopes requires attention to economics and finance. As I have written elsewhere, either economics or finance set our values, or they are the subject of our values.[2] For the latter to happen takes concentration and deliberate action.

There is some sort of myth that the attitude of Jesus (or of the Church or Christians generally) to money is uniformly negative. Jesus spoke a great deal about money, conscious of its power over the behaviour and aspirations of all those listening, from the very rich to the very poor. The parables about money are especially dangerous when taken out of context, and they have historically been used to prove whatever the reader wanted. Jesus has been shown, to the satisfaction at least of the person doing the showing, to be everything from out-and-out capitalist to committed Marxist.

The reality is that the politics of Jesus, and thus God, who is revealed by Jesus, do not fall into any human

[2]*Dethroning Mammon* (London: Bloomsbury, 2016).

categories. God is neither left wing nor right wing, but stands above all such forms of political or economic ideology. God relates to human beings, loves the poor, the widow and the orphan, endows the earth richly with goods and fruitfulness enough to satisfy every human need, and judges our selfishness and self-seeking.

Individuals are therefore expected to use and develop what they have received, living in relationship with God and with each other, so that when they face God's judgement they are prepared in every way, with a good account of life and nothing wasted. They are to live in expectation of the return of Christ, trusting his mercy and grace shown to them, captured by his love so that they may live in love with their neighbours.

Jesus was remarkably practical about the day-to-day living out of such an attitude. Towards the end of Matthew's Gospel, there is a stream of parables about being 'ready'. They follow a passage in which Jesus prophesies the Last Judgement; each parable has a judgement in it. At the end of Matthew chapter 25, there is a description, not in parable form, of the judgement itself, which has already been discussed.

One of the parables speaks very straightforwardly about handling money, or to put it more grandly, about the economy and finance. Of course, its application is far wider, but the setting is one of business and responsibility for it. It is often called the parable of the talents, and it tells the story of a very wealthy ruler who is going on a journey. He calls three trusted servants and puts them in charge of parts of his property, giving the first servant five 'talents' (a large sum of money), the second servant two talents, and the last servant just one. The master goes away leaving them to trade. The first two double their money; the last, who is afraid of the master, buries his talent. When the master returns he asks for an account of their stewardship. The first two servants are richly rewarded, but the third is castigated for being lazy and wicked, having not even put the money on deposit to earn interest. The servant tries all kinds of excuses about the toughness of the master, but to no avail. He is thrown into outer darkness.

We need to remember that the context of this section of Matthew's Gospel is judgement: the final judgement of God over all humanity. Thus this parable is also in one sense about that judgement. Rich or poor, abundant in our gifts or with many handicaps and difficulties, what have we done with our lives? Are they treated as responsibilities, thus as being part of a community, or are they simply our own concern? The sense of radical autonomy which so easily undermines our culture and values fights against any sense of value-laden responsibility for others. Yet our history and our future depend on working in communities of love-in-action.

The parable has a number of contrasts between the repeated stories of the first two servants and the story of the third. First, they know and understand the master and are quick and active in his service. It is easy for us to hear the third servant and believe him, but he is either wrong or deceitful. With the first two, the master speaks of joy, and rewards commitment. With the third it is clear that the servant is unaware of the true nature of the master. He is fearful when he should be brave, and foolish when he could be wise.

Second, the servant is self-regarding, not aware of the accountability for what he has been given. His whole action is about preserving his own safety, and he answers with a statement of his own perceptions, not the realities of being given a significant amount of wealth.

As we see in other parables in this section, and in the Last Judgement description, Jesus seeks a response which is outward looking, courageous and generous. This is where it applies to reimagining Britain.

The 'what ifs' of the next few years may easily overwhelm. What if a huge number of foreign students stay on after they have studied here? What if immigration drives down living standards? What if terrorism returns to our streets again and again? What if the world out there is so threatening that it feels safer to retreat into our bunker?

No country is always right, nor have our actions ever lacked strong elements of self-interest. Yet our values, of community, courage and stability, acknowledge that we have received much and are greatly gifted. As a result, like those with the talents, we have used our skills to make more than we started with. That has not always been done well, but when it is, and when our better instincts prevail, as with the generous and predominantly efficient supply of development and emergency aid, with the development of many industries, based in science and technology, with skills in law and finance, then we demonstrate our sense of solidarity and the common good.

The first two servants showed courage, creativity and aspiration. They took what they had and treated the obligation to make something with it as a duty of stewardship for what they had been given. The result was not only joy, but also greater responsibility. They demonstrated that stability, a capacity to be resilient and to produce sustainable results, was also part of who they were and what their master wanted.

Our identity is demonstrated as much or even more by our actions on finance and the economy as it is by the expression of moral virtues. The immense complexity and competitiveness of global markets calls for enormous reserves of courage and stability in order to overcome the tendency of markets to short-termism, unsustainability and panic, all leading to gross injustices against the poor and weak. The pressures to achieve may easily lead to success pursued by ruthless self-interest in which our solidarity as individuals and nations is forgotten, and we seek only our own gain. Jesus deals with this temptation in the description of judgement coming to those above all who failed to see or recognize the needy as those loved by, and indeed representing, God.

Society as community requires a reasonable level of equality, and equality is always undermined by asymmetries of power. This is a problem of human nature more than one of economics as a mathematical question. Human beings are flawed; Christians call the flaw sin. We seek to protect what we have unless there is a conscious effort to do the opposite, and a genuine incentive to behave differently. The slave who hides his money neither contributes to the common good nor demonstrates gratitude for the gifts and talents that he has by using them. Sin leads to monopoly behaviour in economics and those in positions of power exercise it by reducing competition, which holds down prices and threatens their comfortable enjoyment of low-risk returns on their investment.

The existence of monopoly suppliers of goods has always been seen as dangerous. At best it has been used as a tool of favouring one aspect of the economy, through patents and granted monopolies in return for government or powerful figures receiving the benefits. At worst it has emerged from the scheming of small groups or the determination of one person seeking to dominate an industry and force up prices. The Scottish economist and father of modern economics Adam Smith wrote: 'People of the same trade seldom meet together, even for merriment and diversion, but the conversation ends in a conspiracy against the public, or in some contrivance to raise prices.'[3]

The capacity to conspire against the public, as he put it, has been a subject of government for many centuries. In recent history, it was United States President Theodore Roosevelt, a Republican and Progressive, who pursued the fight against Trusts and Monopolies shortly after 1900. His initiative led to the break-up of Standard Oil, which gave birth to Mobil, Esso and numerous other companies, but which had controlled, under John D. Rockefeller, most of the transportation of crude oil and petroleum products in the USA. Today, there is a debate about the reach of the major technology companies and whether they hold enough undue influence over their consumers to warrant being broken up under anti-trust legislation, particularly in the United States and Europe. Market failure is behind the differentials, for example in anti-cancer drugs where in the USA prices of old drugs are raised by colossal multiples when there is no alternative. For example, in America the median monthly price for patented cancer medicines in mid-2017 was $8,694 as against $2,587 for the same eight drugs in the UK.[4] That has nothing to do with differentials in costs of production; it is merely taking advantage of an inefficient market, for there is no other kind – it is merely a question of degree.

[3]Adam Smith, *An Inquiry into the Nature and Causes of the Wealth of Nations* (London: The Electric Book Company, 1998), p. 183.
[4]'The Big Read: Cancer Pill Costs Soar as Drug Companies Retain Pricing Power' (*Financial Times*, 30 April 2017).

The economy should exist to provide just, responsible and sustainable growth. Finance is a key component. In the last 30 years it has become over-dominant, a sector of the economy in its own right rather than a facilitator of the market – indeed, often its master, rather than its servant.

The transformation of finance from servant to master has been a feature of economic life in Europe since the Reformation, once markets in modern form began to develop. There have been waves of financial activity in which the volume of financial transactions which did not relate directly to the real economy of services and production grew disproportionately in volume. The result has always in the end led to a crash, as the tower of financial activity became over-confident in its own inherent stability and lost sight of its fundamental dependence on the day-to-day workings of every human being in an economy.

Markets are a benefit when they facilitate trade and economic activity. As places of meeting and exchanging they go back as far as human beings have had settled and agricultural occupations. Ideas such as futures markets (the ability to set the price today for goods to be purchased or delivered at a given future date) are an obvious aid to farmers and can be dated back to ancient Egypt.

The Reformation marked a turning-point, after which the morality of making money from money became more acceptable than it had been previously. Thereafter, markets grew in everything from commodities to company stock, but enthusiasms and what has been called 'the madness of crowds' has led to moments when the price of the financial contract lost all real contact with the underlying commodity. In 1637, the first well-known economic bubble was in tulip bulbs in Holland. In 1720, the South Sea Bubble in London led to insane valuations of company stock and large-scale fraud, followed by market collapse, ruining many. In the mid-nineteenth century in the UK an especially active rise in railway shares ended in a crash that destroyed the wealth of large numbers of investors (including the family of the woman who was to become the wife of the Archbishop of Canterbury, Edward Benson). The devastating 1929 crash has been brilliantly and amusingly documented by J. K. Galbraith,[5] who recounts (possibly apocryphally) that Joseph Kennedy (father of President Kennedy and former ambassador to the United Kingdom) sold out at the height of the boom in New York when he heard a shoe-shine boy discussing the price of US Steel shares, on the grounds that if the shoe-shine boy was in the market it was too risky.

The 'Great' Crash of 2008 was thus merely the latest in a long series, and like all previous financial crashes its effects are far more severe than a normal economic downturn because it subdues confidence, or what John Maynard Keynes called the 'animal spirits'[6] of economic activity. A powerful analysis of the causes of the crash showed that a high proportion of growth in the Western economies from 1992 to 2008 was the result of growing levels of debt. Debt, in fact, rose faster than the economy as a whole, becoming necessarily a larger and larger proportion of the economy. Much of it, especially in later years, was used by consumers for consumption, and

[5]John Kenneth Galbraith, *The Great Crash 1929* (Boston: Houghton Mifflin Company, 1954).
[6]*The General Theory of Employment, Interest and Money* (Cambridge: Cambridge University Press for the Royal Economic Society, 1936), p. 161.

less and less for investment.[7] Many years ago a cynical and rather unpleasant dealer explained to me why markets worked: 'It's the "one more mug" theory – there is always one more mug' (I had just proved to be one such). In 2008, the mugs ran out.

In addition to the figures shown in the graph below, the financial sector's GVA (Gross Value Added, a sort of calculation of its own GDP) rose 103 per cent between 1997 and 2007 – much higher than the 57 per cent for all other sectors. Employment in the sector only rose 6 per cent in that period, however, compared to 11 per cent overall.[8]

The underlying impact of the long years of debt-fuelled growth of the economy in the UK was also a growth in inequality. Inequality leads to asymmetries of power, and asymmetries of power lead to more inequality. The capacity of those in positions of power to protect their interests becomes more and more entrenched, until there is a reversal of some kind – either forced, or voluntarily because of a change in culture.

Between 1979 and 2007, the top 10 per cent of earners in the UK increased their share of total income from 28.4 per cent to 42.6 per cent. Two-thirds of those gains went to the top 1 per cent, and of the 1 per cent's gains, 60 per cent went to bankers, even though financial sector workers only comprise one-fifth of 1 per cent of workers. All of these gains have been through bonuses.[9]

If we take the three categories of historic and culturally embedded values suggested in Chapter 1 – community, courage and stability – it is clear that disciplined

---

[7]Adair Turner, *Between Debt and the Devil: Money, Credit, and Fixing Global Finance* (Princeton: Princeton University Press, 2015).
[8]Brian D. Bell and John Van Reenen, 'Extreme Wage Inequality: Evidence and Policy Responses,' *American Economic Review* 103 (3) (2013), pp. 153–7.
[9]Ibid.

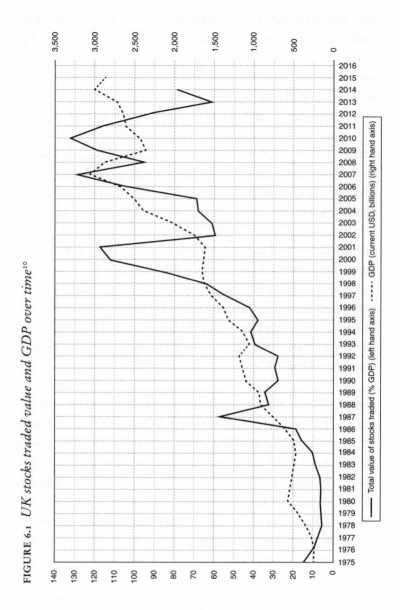

FIGURE 6.1 *UK stocks traded value and GDP over time*[10]

[10]Data from 'United Kingdom' (The World Bank Group, 2016), http://data.
worldbank.org/country/united-kingdom. Accessed 10 April 2017.

and properly behaving markets and economies should make a significant contribution.

Finance serves community because it is a common need of all people. Where it is well distributed and open to everyone according to reasonable and equitable criteria, it sustains subsidiarity, as decisions are made on the economy not entirely or even principally by governments and regulators but by the billions of individual economic choices made in the economy every day. The common good is served by mutual compassion and generosity. Gratuity is seen as a virtue. The power of money to ration some goods which are seen as common, such as healthcare and education, is limited by social convention, regulation and taxation.

Courage is enabled by the possibilities inherent in well-regulated but free markets. There is scope for new business and aspiration, for risk taking and creativity. One of the reasons for the failure of the centralized economies of the Soviet Union was that the vast majority of creative effort and aspiration went into beating or gaming the system. The more than a billion people lifted out of the most extreme poverty in the world in the last 30 years[11] have benefited from – among many other things – reduced control of previously over-regulated and over-centralized economies. It is not the whole story, nor the whole reason for the absolute improvement in living standards in many places (this book cannot deal with something that requires volumes of its own), but it has played a considerable role.

---

[11]'Poverty and Shared Prosperity 2016: Taking on Inequality' (Washington, DC: World Bank, 2016), https://openknowledge.worldbank.org/bitstream/handle/10986/25078/9781464809583.pdf. Published under Creative Commons Attribution CC 3.0 by IGO.

Stability in development will require free markets and fair trade in order to enable the poor to grow while the rich pay the cost of historic unsustainable economic development that has damaged the natural environment, and often been based on trade barriers and 'new colonialist' resistance to open markets. Stability needs a price for carbon, and needs incentives and market forces that encourage good development and inhibit bad. The complexity of such a global endeavour is so great that it is inconceivable that it can be handled by regulation alone. Regulation is invariably backward looking, and can never cope with fast-moving global changes. There needs to be a combination of international agreement on principles and aims of development (which requires a significant culture shift), combined with properly regulated but relatively free markets.

However, the words 'free markets' are not an incantation which magics prosperity or justice into being. The parable of judgement (discussed earlier in this chapter), the words of Adam Smith and the history of crashes speak to the need for a realistic view of the nature of human beings that will enable markets to be kept free and fair, not only from state interference (for honest or corrupt reasons), but also from the human proclivity to what the Bible calls sin. You cannot regulate the human heart.

Free markets are only truly free for the powerful. In the UK, the USA and across Europe the advent of the gig economy and zero-hour contracts is a product of free markets. In its form it is the same approach as would have been seen in Liverpool in the 1930s, where dockworkers queued to see if they had work that day. They had to be there, were not guaranteed work, and any work they did was only secure for one day. The legacy of the injustice and oppression this represented has been a powerful cause of social division ever since.

A truly free market would apply principles of zero hours or a gig economy between people who were equally powerful. Where there are asymmetries of power the market is never free. It is for this reason that workers not only need protection by law, but also require collective bargaining capacity, adapted to the conditions of the twenty-first century.

A reimagined Britain will always be constrained by the influences of the huge trading blocs of the world. It will invariably be affected by flows of finance. Its own financial systems need to be both sufficiently strong in some parts to be effective internationally and also sufficiently local to ensure that creativity and aspiration are financed effectively at the micro as well as the macro levels. Jesus' parable deliberately speaks to different levels of wealth and of entrusted responsibility by the master who goes away. Without a range of opportunity, all that happens is the embedding of asymmetries of power, the encouragement of rent-seeking[12] by elites and by those who can corner access to resources, and the abuse of the poor and marginalized.

The period since the reopening of international financial markets on a grand scale, especially through the international bond markets, in the early 1960s has seen a vast concentration of banking services and capacity, at a global and also at a British level. Through skill, traditions, accidents of language and geography and the errors of alternative potential centres, the City of London (for these purposes I include Canary Wharf, though that is geographically inaccurate) has become

[12] Low-risk unearned returns.

the dominant force in international finance. The City is the largest global centre for currency and derivatives trading. It is dominant in international commercial law and accounts for 19 per cent of international bank lending. It was the major place of large-scale marketing and developments (although not invention) in new forms of financial instruments, of risk-management tools such as options, swaps and futures. It became the dominant force for employment in southern Britain, with over 300,000 people working there or as a result of City activity, and is the largest regional contributor to exports. The spin-off from the enormous wealth generated was seen in property prices, school fees for private schools, the re-emergence of domestic staff as a category of employment, restaurants, hotels and many other activities. It has drawn in many of the best and brightest of British graduates, from all disciplines, making it harder for engineering companies to recruit engineers, or for other parts of the country to attract those of the highest skill; most are unable to resist the 'streets paved with gold' syndrome which has made London a draw, fictional or not, since Dick Whittington and his cat. The number of banks in the City increased sharply, to over 500, yet the vast majority were occupied only in international business, and the number of banks on the high street became more concentrated. After 2008, the number shrank even more dramatically, as the demutualized Building Societies merged with banks for survival, and two of the largest UK banks, Royal Bank of Scotland and Lloyds, were taken into public ownership in order to prevent them failing.

The result is that the UK has the most concentrated retail banking sector of all the richest economies. Headquarters are for practical purposes in London, even if legally elsewhere. There are very few really local regional banks. Power is concentrated and thus the interests of the powerful dominate. While the vision was not ultimately realized, it was in response to such issues that a consortium which included the Church Commissioners sought unsuccessfully to open a new bank (under the name of Williams & Glyn), with the aim of running it on 'good banking' principles[13] – as an institution for the common good, not seeking to be overly complex in its responsibilities, but delivering fair banking for all at the local level. It is these principles that should be undergirding our banking system, to be part of preventing the repetition of what happened in the 50 years leading to the 2008 crash.

The economy is unbalanced. In a powerful 2009 article in the *Financial Times*,[14] Martin Wolf described the UK as a 'mono-crop economy', with the crop being finance. He compared it to countries that rely on a natural resource for the vast bulk of their income. The protection of the mono-crop distorts politics, changes political priorities, rewards those close to the crop and deprives those further away, and starves other sectors of talent and investment. In the work of the Parliamentary Commission on Banking Standards that took place between 2012 and 2014 (on which I sat), I argued unsuccessfully for a proper review of the net benefit of the banking industry to the UK since 1945. I suggested it should take into account the hard factors of tax paid,

[13]Specifically, these principles are a focus on public purpose, treatment of customers, financial education, community contribution, pay and rewards, and transparency.
[14]Martin Wolf, 'Britain's dismal choice: sharing the losses' (*Financial Times*, 15 December 2009), https://www.ft.com/content/f693b6a4-e9af-11de-9f1f-00144 feab49a. Accessed 10 April 2017.

employment created and exports delivered as against the cost of the bailouts and rescues, and subsidies from an implied government guarantee of bank indebtedness, known as 'too big to fail'. It should have also considered the soft factors of increased global influence against over-concentration of the economy. A major reason for the lack of success in persuading the Commission to undertake such work was neither its complexity nor its cost, but rather its potential political embarrassment.

The theory of free markets is one that enhances values and virtues. The reality is very often of concentration and misallocation of resources in a way that ends by eliminating the very values on which it feeds.[15]

Any reimagining of values must move away from the unnatural domination of financial services, corrupting in their cause of inequality, distorting all possibility of a fair and open economy at a national level and depriving the vast majority of the population and of the economically active of real opportunities for community, courage and stability.

At the very least, while the City in its international activity is essential, and has potential for enormous contributions to the UK, a reimagined Britain will have to include other areas. It must be considered whether it should break up the over-concentrated domestic banking and finance sector, creating local finance for local economies, and enabling smaller units to focus on the common good of specific regions. One or two great national banks operating at an international scale are sufficient for an economy of our size. More becomes a threat.

Within the UK there is a need for a complete reimagining of the architecture of our financial institutions.

[15]See Martin Sandbu, *Financial Times*, 16 August 2017.

There has been some progress. The appalling spread of ultra-high interest loans for short periods (payday lenders) was reduced through proper and efficient regulation. The credit union movement of locally based community banks is expanding quite steadily. In Northern Ireland it is a very much larger part of the personal finance sector than in Scotland, Wales and England. However, the need for major changes, to ensure that finance is as concerned with the local as with the global, is more and more evident.

The implications of reimagining the common good across the country, rather than assessing the general good on average for the country, would be to eliminate the gross inequalities hidden by averages. The huge change coming as the impact of leaving the EU works through the economy over a generation or so will require an economy that is exceptionally flexible and balanced on several points of strength. Relying on the grossly unequal drawing power of one sector is like harnessing a carriage with one elephant and a series of horses. They are unlikely to go in a straight line, or be able to turn well.

An economy that represents values embedded in our history and culture will be balanced across the nations and regions, and across income groups. It will provide a wide range of opportunities for all levels of ability to realize their potential, with firms and businesses that apply for government contracts being required to sponsor students at university and apprentices in highly skilled jobs. It will be supremely flexible, able to adapt rapidly to the fourth industrial revolution of robotics, driverless vehicles, the development of ever more renewable energy, and a thousand other changes that are as yet unforeseeable.

Above all, it has to be an economy that as well as being open to courage, aspiration, competition and creativity, is able to welcome the alien and stranger through a sense of confidence and equality of opportunity. In this way it is sustainable and protects community, simultaneously developing the traditions of the country alongside the base and strength of the economy.

The practical implications of such an economy are very significant. They require a consensus on the nature and purpose of taxation, to ensure that equality is supported through the wealthiest paying the heaviest burden; that tax is paid where the money is earned and the profits are not held in tax 'havens' out of the reach of officials; and that there are incentives for creativity and courage economically, and discouragements for playing safe like the third slave in the parable. Such a tax system would require extensive simplifications and reform. It requires a clear social and moral purpose in spending by government in all areas. Above all, in today's world it requires transparency in the way the economy works. The greatest danger to community is the sense that some people can game the system while others are bound by it or indeed held back by it. It is the sense of asymmetrical risk and unfair advantage that led to the justifiable anger against the banks.

The next two generations will face many threats and dangers. There is nothing new about that, and the threats are no greater than in the last few hundred years. Yet the fact that Britain has prospered before does not guarantee that it will do so again. In the last ten years, the rate of growth of international trade has slowed remarkably[16]

[16]Martin Wolf, 'Sluggish global trade growth is here to stay' (*Financial Times*, 25 October 2016), https://www.ft.com/content/4efcd174-99d3-11e6-b8c6-568a43813464. Accessed 10 April 2017.

and the outlook remains very doubtful. There is a significant group of economists forecasting a very long period of 'secular stagnation',[17] low and very unequal growth lasting more than a generation. Secular stagnation, with only a small minority sharing the sparse rewards, is a great threat. The lack of growth in international trade encourages one-off deals and preference to favourites, always something that is at the cost of the poor. The rise of religiously motivated violence, renewed nationalisms, and resurgent threats of power grabbing and war all add to a sense that it would be better to raise the drawbridges. Yet economies cannot live by themselves, except in siege conditions and even then some international links are essential. Preferring ourselves in the end destroys ourselves.

The consumer-driven society – shown by Adair Turner to have been a major factor in the Great Recession – has re-emerged as the sole driver of the economy, with the non-financial sector still failing to show up with investment of its enormous cash holdings. The absence of the value of courage and aspiration is greater and more reprehensible in big corporations than in individuals mired in poverty and the victims of a globally changing economy.

By contrast, a moral and value-laden society will demonstrate flexibility with justice, and in so doing gains the capacity of sustainable stability. The economy may be dangerous but should be an ultimately benevolent part of life, to serve the common good. As in a number of prosperous countries today, inequality is accepted within reasonable limits, but it is expected that

[17]See, for example, Larry Summers, 'The Age of Secular Stagnation: What It Is and What to Do About It', *Foreign Affairs* (March 2016), https://www.foreignaf-fairs.com/articles/united-states/2016-02-15/age-secular-stagnation/. Accessed 10 April 2017.

the vast majority of people will live in ways that demonstrate the common good and mutual care. There will be justification for the intuitive approach to differentials of reward that says that those who care for other people in their jobs should not be paid vastly less than those who seek to trade in finance and commodities without direct participation in the underlying assets. At the same time, the entrepreneurs who create employment, develop new industries and risk all in their creativity will gain a reward for their skills.

None of it is anything less than obvious. Yet we do not and have not seen it in many years, even generations, and the tolerance of its absence is deeply troubling and deeply divisive. Economics in the end has the penultimate word. (As might be expected, I trust that the last word is with God).

Raising drawbridges is economic suicide for the common good, and human flourishing. It denies our history of generosity and gratuity. It inhibits and even prevents creativity. It is not sustainable. For all that, it is tempting, because an open, flexible and flourishing economy doing well for Britain and the world requires courage.

Brexit poses both opportunities and threats, but underlying them is the reality of a British economy that has underperformed for many years;[18] Brexit brings the need for new imagining into sharper focus.

There is thus a challenge posed by the economy that must cause Britain to ask questions about values, for values lead strategy and strategy sets policy. A flexible, creative, generous, just, well-balanced and sustainable economy has implications for every other sector

---

[18]Martin Wolf, 'The economic ills of the UK stretch well beyond Brexit' (*Financial Times*, 29 September 2016).

of life, both those which consume resources, and those which need investment to generate resources. In all that is discussed in this book, it has to be assumed that the funding comes from a well-regulated and well-balanced economy which is suspicious of over-mighty sectors, and cautious about trusting in them.

A clear example of this healthy suspicion is Norway. It is a country that has more resources in the oil and gas sector than the UK, and yet only one-tenth of the population. Norway was cautious about the effect of the wealth produced by oil and gas, and thus put government revenue into an offshore sovereign wealth fund, for use once the oil and gas are exhausted, or their value collapses. Time will tell whether this has been a good strategy, but it has enabled other sectors of the economy to continue to flourish, skills to be developed, and Norway to play a major role in the international political scene, especially as a peace negotiator.

By contrast, the UK has spent most of its oil and gas wealth and has little to show for it. For some time the sector dominated the economy, competing with financial services; we were a 'duo-crop' economy. Now it has gone, and like a squandered lottery win, we are faced with all the same problems, and less capacity to manage them. While the numbers may to some extent add up, to rely on valuing only what we can easily measure is to be dragged into the 'general interest' approach to the economy, ignoring the common good, which leaves vast numbers in the position of suffering and injustice portrayed in *I, Daniel Blake*.

SUMMARY

- Economic injustice has always been a reason for reimagining our future.

- The economy is not naturally just, nor does it serve the interests of human communities, without deliberate policies to that effect.

- There is a grave danger that the 'success' of the UK is measured economically, simply because it is measurable, rather than because it is right.

- We cannot pretend that we are able to make decisions without taking account of global factors, and the interaction of economic and finance-based values (or their absence) can lead to a sense of economic fatalism.

- There is a profound need for a recovery of economic courage, especially within UK-based companies.

PART THREE

Values amid Global Change

7

The World Around Us

In 2018 – the centenary of the end of the First World War – the countries of Europe and even the USA find themselves in a world wholly different from November 1918. Empires have more or less ceased to exist; former imperial possessions (or countries once dominated by the so-called Great Powers) like India and China are now themselves international forces of immense and growing importance. The USA has passed through isolationism to global dominance and is once more looking inwards, perhaps temporarily. The UK has changed its policy towards Europe and, with politicians and Parliament having to spend so much time on Brexit, risks giving an impression of being turned inwards, with less influence internationally.

At the same time, the sense of the interconnectedness of the world has grown enormously since the 1950s, first with mass ownership of televisions, and then dramatically accelerated since the development of the internet and now of social media. The results are images of a reality that we cannot experience. We see on our screens the shadows cast by the fierce light of struggles and suffering far away. From time to time there are especially harrowing or powerful images, such as those of a refugee child drowned on a beach, or a small boy dug out of a bombed building, or a girl running naked from a napalm attack. The cry goes up that 'something must be done', but once the reality sets in, resistance grows to the 'something', if it means that the shadows on the screen become a physical reality in front of us.

Thus in 2015, as the number of refugees crowding to the outskirts of the European Union grew, and with the Mediterranean and Sahara becoming places of mass death from drowning or thirst as migrants sought to cross to Europe, the German government opened its borders. At railway stations, Germans stood with signs saying 'welcome'. In that year, about 890,000 people entered Germany.[1] One or two other countries took similar, or only slightly more limited, approaches. The UK offered only 20,000 places over five years. Other countries such as Poland refused point blank to take anyone at all, even after initially saying that they would only take Christians. The mix of people coming was complicated. A significant number were from Syria, as refugees of war. Very large numbers came from Iraq and Afghanistan. Some came from Libya, again a country torn by war and a failed post-conflict settlement. Some were from countries like Eritrea, where a tyrannical government made the risks of travel less unattractive than remaining. Many were from Nigeria, fleeing war, poverty, civil instability or hunger. The list goes on and on.

A world in which someone in the poorest of towns can go into an internet cafe and window-shop in London's Knightsbridge, New York's Fifth Avenue or Paris's Boulevard Haussmann is a world which reveals

---

[1]'Migration Report 2015: Central Conclusions' (Bundesamt für Migration und Flüchtlinge, 2016). Available in English and German at http://www.bamf.de/SharedDocs/Anlagen/DE/Publikationen/Migrationsberichte/migrationsbericht-2015-zentrale-ergebnisse.html.

inequalities on an unimaginable scale and confronts them with the image of what they do not and never could have. The notion of 'you stick where you were born', whether by choice or by compulsion, has gone (aided, in the case of our own country, by two hundred years of promoting and sacralizing our structures and institutions through colonial rule). This has changed patterns of migration. It is also true that displacement, exile and asylum seeking have occurred throughout history. Differentiating between economic migration and forced migration is important, as is acknowledging that the advent of mass communications has blurred the boundaries between those two to a degree – but it has not collapsed them completely. Figures here are difficult to interpret – they reflect population growth, and possibly the result of the collapse of centralizing world powers. The number of migrants, Internally Displaced Persons (IDPs, refugees in their own country) and refugees (international) is around 65 million as opposed to 20–30 million in 1945, at the end of the most devastating war in human history. The sheer numbers, and their visibility, and the capacity to travel, and the deadly and horrific fate so many suffer, of which we are now aware, have changed the nature of what it means for most countries to relate to the rest of the world.

Whereas when we last reimagined the nature of the UK in 1945 it was possible, and indeed probable, to have a largely isolated economy, that is no longer practicable. With the exception of a very few hermit states such as North Korea, globalization has become a preponderant if often unwelcome part of daily life and of political decision making in most countries.

The result is that the question of 'who is our neighbour?', the ethical challenge to our generosity, is far

more wide ranging than at any time in history. The idea
of caring for our neighbour is, in our culture, rooted in
one of Jesus' parables to the extent that the phrase 'to be
a Good Samaritan' is proverbial even among those who
do not know the story.

Jesus tells the parable (as so often in the Gospel of
Luke) in answer to a challenge, this time from a lawyer. He is asked by a lawyer what the lawyer must do
to have eternal life, to be in heaven. Jesus replies by
getting him to quote the best-known summary of the
Jewish Law – love God, love your neighbour – and tells
the lawyer to live it out. The lawyer, wanting to demonstrate that he is righteous, asks, 'who is my neighbour?', and Jesus tells the story. It would have been
a familiar tale of banditry and bad luck, with aspects
of dark humour. As with the other extracts from the
Bible, it is a passage about love-in-action, and, like the
others, one that has passed into our culture as a definition of values.

Just then a lawyer stood up to test Jesus. 'Teacher,'
he said, 'what must I do to inherit eternal life?' He
said to him, 'What is written in the law? What do you
read there?' He answered, 'You shall love the Lord
your God with all your heart, and with all your soul,
and with all your strength, and with all your mind;
and your neighbour as yourself.' And he said to him,
'You have given the right answer; do this, and you
will live.'

But wanting to justify himself, he asked Jesus, 'And
who is my neighbour?' Jesus replied, 'A man was going
down from Jerusalem to Jericho, and fell into the hands
of robbers, who stripped him, beat him, and went
away, leaving him half dead. Now by chance a priest

was going down that road; and when he saw him, he passed by on the other side. So likewise a Levite, when he came to the place and saw him, passed by on the other side. But a Samaritan while travelling came near him; and when he saw him, he was moved with pity. He went to him and bandaged his wounds, having poured oil and wine on them. Then he put him on his own animal, brought him to an inn, and took care of him. The next day he took out two denarii, gave them to the innkeeper, and said, "Take care of him; and when I come back, I will repay you whatever more you spend." Which of these three, do you think, was a neighbour to the man who fell into the hands of the robbers?' He said, 'The one who showed him mercy.' Jesus said to him, 'Go and do likewise.'[2]

Like the parable of the prodigal son, it is a story of endless depth. It speaks of power and weakness, the powerful caring nothing for the weak, until a stranger comes to help. In that sense it is a parable of liberation, of the universality of the human spirit. It speaks of legal and moral obligation; that the lawyer is seeking the first and Jesus confronts him with the second. It had a different sting for the early church reading it, as Luke's Gospel circulated fewer than 50 years after the resurrection. For them it spoke among other things of a church that was to be welcoming and open even to historic enemies, a church in which the power of God overcame human and political traditions and barriers, and made of love a universal language.

For us it is also a story with bite. In addition to the other lessons, it tells us that where we see need we

[2]Luke 10:25–37.

are to respond. We are not to be those who walk by on the other side; at the very least we must give what we can. The Samaritan gave perhaps a week's average wages or less: probably in the UK today about £250–£500. The point is that he responded to need and gave to a man from a race that was historically the enemy of his own.

More than that, he worked in partnership, on a business basis. He takes the man to an inn and pays the innkeeper to look after him. The Samaritan needs to get his business done; he cannot stay forever with the man, and knows both what is necessary and what is possible. The innkeeper is an often unsung hero of this passage (innkeepers in the Bible are mainly known at Christmas nativity services in primary schools for saying 'full up, go away', shyly and inaudibly). It is implied that he takes on the injured man and nurses him back to health, trusting the return of the Samaritan, again an enemy. He too cares for the neighbour.

When the world is composed of the village in which one lives and more or less that alone, such a sense of obligation may be revolutionary, but it is achievable. What are we to do when we know of the vast levels of need and suffering all over the world? Such knowledge is new to us. In the days of Empire there was a good deal of disregard for the suffering of those caught up in famine. During the roughly 160 years of British rule in India, there were regular famines in the areas controlled, and famine relief was sporadic. The last, and among the worst, was the Bengal famine of 1943. These failures, those in other parts of the Empire, and the infamous reaction of the British government to the Irish famines of the 1840s, continue to cast a dark shadow over the myths of the unsullied benevolence of Empire.

The greatest difference between then and now is not the level of suffering but our awareness of it. Before the advent of television, reporting was often late, frequently limited in its reach, and seldom as vivid as the sights of the starving, of the refugees and of the other victims of natural disaster or war we see today. The privilege of knowledge and sight brings duty and responsibility. We cannot walk past without a rightful sense of facing judgement for so doing. Whichever way we look at it, the idea that the actions taken should – to paraphrase the Golden Rule – be those we would wish to be applied to us if we were the victims, is one that can only be ignored by a hardening of heart.

There is, however, another, equally important tradition in the Bible, which is that of wisdom. What the Samaritan did was fairly obvious, as it would be to most people today. If you come across an accident, or the victim of crime, you stop and seek to get help that is qualified and equipped. You are a Good Samaritan.

What do we do when the problem is not of one victim but of scores of millions? How do we find help when all the resources of a nation will be drained? How do we compare the needs of those closer with those of the far away? What the Bible calls wisdom requires action that is obedient to God in the light of our known obligations by acting in the right way in the circumstances. Wisdom is both value driven and contextual. The sharp-edged challenges of the prophetic voice call for radical action based in righteousness, while the pragmatic approach of the wise takes account of what is realistic as well as what is right; holding the tension between the two is at the heart of political leadership. Within the Old Testament, that struggle, first in the Kingdom of Israel and subsequently in Judah, is found in the prophets and in the books of wisdom. Especially when Judah is caught between warring empires, the question arises as to which to support. There is nothing new in hard political choices, and today as always the task of politicians is to be righteously wise. (That steep challenge is why believers should pray for all of them!)

The last few years have seen a renewal of the dramatic voices first of the fringes of politics and more and more of large numbers of voters standing up to established elites, especially over the speed of societal change and, above all, the question of immigration. Throughout Europe, centrist parties have found themselves squeezed. Voting opportunities like the referendum on EU membership gave an opportunity to express strongly held views through the ballot box in a way that was not softened by the packaging of policies that emerge from general elections. The issue is not *whether* 'something must be done' in response; clearly it must. The question is 'what?' We are all aware of the ancient danger that when 'something must be done', we see any 'something' and do it, however counterproductive.

In 1945, Britain's role in the world, as for roughly the previous 160 years, was more or less clear. There was still an Empire, and although its government and range would have to change with independence for India, Pakistan (1947) and what are now Myanmar and Sri Lanka (1948), it was clear that the UK was still a global power and would remain so for many years. The same is still true today, at least potentially, although in a very different way. The assets retained by the UK are mostly intangible. Hard-power projection still exists, but is very limited, normally requiring alliances and partnerships. There has to be reality about both our limited capacity to act alone, and even more so, about the effectiveness of hard power by itself.[3] Our experiences in Iraq and Afghanistan have demonstrated that even the utmost bravery and skill, and the commitment by NATO of large forces, cannot always produce the results we seek.

By contrast, the last few years have seen considerable success where power is used in combinations of alliance and with partnerships bringing different skills. Above all, such efforts have borne fruit in places in which a tipping point is identifiable and thus dramatic change is achievable. A good example is Sierra Leone. The intervention in Sierra Leone at the turn of the twenty-first century was based deeply in our history. The country was founded in the nineteenth century as a home for rescued slaves, and the founders were much influenced and aided by British statesmen such as William Wilberforce. It is a small country, with significant natural resources. In May 2000, British forces intervened in the civil war raging in the country as rebel forces advanced on Freetown, the capital. At first, the British acted as observers and trainers, as well as preparing the way for evacuation of foreign residents. However, the mission developed to the point where it tipped the balance in the country and enabled what has, up to 2017, become a fairly stable government to emerge. The use of force was combined with training, relief, the setting up of reconciliation projects and many other forms of support. Most recently, when the country was struck by the Ebola virus, British troops and aid were again deployed to great effect.

Sierra Leone has been a good example of the application of the ideal of the Good Samaritan to foreign

---

[3]General Sir Rupert Smith discusses this question with great insight in his book *The Utility of Force* (London: Penguin Books, 2010).

policy. The 2000 intervention was measured, minimized violence to ensure that the use of force was essentially a quasi-police action, was limited in time and effective in result. The second intervention, against Ebola, was again clearly focused and with achievable objectives.

In 2018, the UK plays host to the Commonwealth Summit. Brexit is leading to fresh concentration on the Commonwealth, but if that is simply in pursuit of our own interests, especially those of trade, then it will lead nowhere. The Commonwealth grew out of Empire, as a symbol both of a shared history (for good and ill) and of an intention to reach across great differentials of wealth and culture. It potentially sets a pattern of some kind of common interest, which should lead to shared actions. The question is whether such actions, let alone interventions, are a mark of an 'ethical' foreign policy, or are simply the result of pursuing our interests, the deployment of realpolitik ultimately for our own benefit.

Lord Palmerston, in the House of Commons in August 1844, said, 'We have no eternal allies, and we have no perpetual enemies. Our interests are eternal and perpetual, and those interests it is our duty to follow …' It is the most succinct and confident expression of realpolitik. By contrast, Robin Cook, on 12 May 1997, early in the new Labour government as newly appointed Foreign Secretary, said, 'Our foreign policy must have an ethical dimension.' The two statements were not as contradictory as they appear, or are often made to seem. Cook went on to argue at length and with great sophistication for the reality of an overlap between interests and morality in a world of profound interdependence in everything from human rights, through economic growth to climate change. Palmerston developed his arguments by claiming that it was in our interests to be ethical.

The reality is that we are interdependent (it is certainly strongly arguable that this has always been the case, but it is made more obvious by technology and social media), and any attempt to shut ourselves off from the rest of the world has both terrible practical consequences and immense moral difficulties. The parable of the Good Samaritan, however, calls not merely for interdependence with those who are our temporary allies in the quest to protect our eternal interests, but for a leap of imagination to see that active love in pursuit of our common humanity is achievable and transformative.

The argument will come back that this is all right for the individual but clearly absurd for a nation with its own complex needs and vulnerabilities. That is a powerful point, but it omits any consideration of the context of mass migration and of us possessing a deep awareness of what is happening elsewhere in the world.

Migration is something that has both push and pull factors. It is often said that no one chooses exile, but that is not the case. The tense and crushing grief of living in countries which may not be involved in civil or foreign wars, but where the rule of law is at best intermittent and usually corrupted and non-existent, is one of the most powerful push factors. Combine that with the sense that this is how one's country has always been and always will be, and thus that the children for which one hopes, or which one has and loves, will be no better off, and possibly worse, and the push factor becomes enormous.

Push is more important than pull. There is a myth that a nation can control immigration. For Britain (as an island) it is easier than for many, but it is still impossible.

Immigration will come overtly through legitimate arrivals that overstay, or through students. It will come ille-
gitimately through trafficking and people smuggling. It
will come irresistibly when a disaster or civil war in some
part of the world that was part of the Empire results in
thousands of refugees, and pictures of their suffering. In
some places, large numbers of people have a legal right
to come to the UK because they have UK passports. In
others, there are close family members who are resident
in the UK.

Chapter 8 will deal more closely with the issues of
immigration and integration. The issue for this chapter is: how can the UK develop a foreign policy that is
both values and interests driven? The question assumes
that pretending the rest of the world does not exist is
not a sustainable policy. Splendid isolation did not even
work for the USA in the 1920s and 1930s, when the
world was far less connected, the total of US trade was
a far smaller proportion of its economy than that of
the UK today, information was less visual and readily
accessible, and the events of Europe or Japan appeared
far away. Today, a foreign policy that is true to values
is bound to be directly and deliberately a proactive foreign policy.

To return to the Good Samaritan: the wounded
Jewish man was none of the Samaritan's business. The
risk of intervention was high. The costs were significant. Yet his action showed that he was a neighbour
to the victim and thus, according to the Jewish law, to
be loved. Note the remarkable reversal of the passage.
The lawyer asking the questions quotes the law about
loving one's neighbour as oneself. Jesus ends his story
with a question. Surprisingly, it is not 'Who then was the

Samaritan's neighbour?' – answer expected, 'The help-less and wounded man' – but 'Which of these three, do you think, was a neighbour to the man who fell into the hands of the robbers?'

The answer is 'The one who showed him mercy'. Jesus in his answer immensely widens the nature of the concept of neighbour from those who are close by, or are within our group, to anyone who offers us friend-ship, or needs our help. 'Go and do likewise' covers both recognizing that the Samaritan, the lawyer's bit-ter enemy, is the lawyer's neighbour, and that mercy is a grace which reaches beyond ethnic, national or reli-gious boundaries.

In our own society and state structures, since 1948 we have recognized the grace of caring for neighbours through the provision of a National Health Service, free at the point of care. The size of the commitment is enor-mous, well over £100 billion each year. The budget for pensions and for benefits is also vast. It is not true that the grace of loving neighbours falls only to the indi-vidual. We have institutionalized Good Samaritanism because it is deeply embedded in our values. Practices and values meet in our health and benefits systems, at least in theory.

The parable of the Good Samaritan speaks of unity. The rescuer is bound to the victim by a common human-ity, and recognizes that they are of one kind, not two. In solidarity he reaches out, and in generosity he ensures that there is resilience in the rescue; the victim will be cared for as long as he needs help. It is a courageous act, risking rejection. Because it is active, innovative, boundary-breaking, clear and quick, it speaks deeply to our sense of what is right.

Applying our values to foreign policy has to take account of our interests. Robin Cook spoke of an ethical dimension to foreign policy, not an ethical foreign policy.[4] Actions have to seek to protect our safety and enhance our effective working in a world of competing and often hostile interests.

The greatest change in the last 20 years in the development of British overseas power has been in the quality and quantity of development assistance and foreign aid. It has grown steadily, both as a percentage of GNI and in absolute terms.[5] Equally importantly, it has ceased to be tied to trade, but has become one of the best-run aid programmes in the world, operating on the basis of need.[6] Our top three areas of aid expenditure are disaster relief, health and education. We are saving lives, tackling global inequalities and leading the way in the creation of a more just world.[7] The result has been a maintaining of British global influence in a period first where our military effort was closely focused on the wars in Iraq and Afghanistan.

[4]As previously mentioned, Lord Palmerston's own view is also more nuanced than the oft-cited quote used earlier in the chapter. In the speech from which I quoted, he also said this: 'I hold that the real policy of England – apart from questions which involve her own particular interests, political or commercial – is to be the champion of justice and right; pursuing that course with moderation and prudence, not becoming the Quixote of the world, but giving the weight of her moral sanction and support wherever she thinks that justice is, and wherever she thinks that wrong has been done ... and as long as she sympathises with right and justice, she never will find herself altogether alone. She is sure to find some other State, of sufficient power, influence, and weight, to support and aid her in the course she may think fit to pursue.'
[5]'Net ODA (indicator)' (OECD, 2017), https://data.oecd.org/oda/net-oda.htm. Accessed 15 February 2017.
[6]The Development Assistance Committee Peer Review of UK Development Aid (OECD, 2010) spoke highly of the UK as a global leader in development. Available at http://www.oecd.org/development/peer-reviews/45519815.pdf.
[7]'Follow how the UK invests in developing countries', DfID Development Tracker (Crown Copyright, 2017), https://devtracker.dfid.gov.uk/. Accessed 16 February 2017.

The hard and soft threats to the UK remain. Terrorism is a constant menace: despite numerous plots having been foiled in recent years, in the first half of 2017 there were three attacks in London and one in Manchester. There is a need for extensive cooperation with European neighbours, the US and further afield. Terrorism is not only or even mainly a domestic problem. Attacks on British citizens or interests are at least as likely outside the UK as within. The nature and causes of hard threats are complicated. Terrorism is nowadays often linked to religion, and is thus ideological, global and generational. To cut off the causes requires simultaneous action, abroad and in the UK. Soft threats are perceived in the form of the wave of migration, and specifically the worry it causes in fragile communities. The fear is unjustified if immigration is handled rightly, but in areas of need fear is understandable. As we approach Brexit, soft power threats also come in terms of a worsening of our terms of trade or of the loss of ability to export without a significant fall in the value of the pound. This in turn would generate inflation, and limit UK domestic spending power.

The problems raised by vast movements of peoples involve recognizing the questions of the capacity of the UK to play its part in receiving the millions fleeing war and extreme poverty. We can only respond in three ways. The first is to refuse all access. The second is to open our borders to some or a large extent. The third is to do one or two, but also act so that over the long term the need for immigration is reduced.

The Good Samaritan is the one who does not solve every problem but does the best with what he has. In the parable he does not solve the crime problem on the Jericho road, or set up a system for ambulances and recovery units. The UK cannot solve every, or even any, global problem, but it is both right and in our interests to have a foreign policy that is committed to peace, stability and development – three essential foundations for giving hope to those affected by poverty and war – and thus to reducing the pressure to move or the necessity of armed intervention. In so doing we practise our values of the common good, of courage and of resilience over the long term.

Our recent history is excellent. Apart from the achievement of the UN target of 0.7 per cent of GNI in foreign aid, other examples of high-profile effectiveness to set against bad impacts of foreign policy include a leading role in tackling human trafficking and modern slavery, and campaigning against sexual violence in conflict and against female genital mutilation. They are all headline contributions to the global common good and development. If we are to be committed to doing what we can with what we know, then in the same way as these campaigns have focused on the areas of greatest need, so must our future efforts. It is essential not to be precious or naive. Fair and just trade is better than aid. It creates sustainable development more probably and more effectively, and increases self-respect and independence in countries receiving aid. It is clear that a challenge is to enable development to diminish the need for aid. In terms of values, this is all about sustainability.

Such ideas require the practical application of policies that stabilize countries and liberate human potential. We are called to solidarity, but also to subsidiarity. Rescuing people caught up in famines and disasters is absolutely essential. By itself, however, it creates a cycle of dependency.

By contrast, foreign policies that engage realistically and wisely at the site of problems may increase subsidiarity, develop intermediate institutions and civil society, and then promote subsidiarity. Dependency is reduced, and the courage to develop is encouraged. There is scope for entrepreneurial activity, creativity and competition that is suitable to local circumstances. Most of all, the efforts on populations are more likely to be sustainable, based around the common good at a global level.

That is, of course, all very well in theory, but somewhat utopian in practice without a clear-eyed and sacrificial view of the requirements of applied policy. The most important building block is a stable society capable of dealing with disputes without civil disorder, and of disagreeing vehemently but well. That is a rare gift. In the UK we undervalue the benefits of established means of disagreement, and of the well-founded assumption that votes are decisive and that freedoms are to be protected. By contrast, the Freedom in the World 2016 report[8] from Freedom House classes 109 of 195 countries as 'not free' or only 'partly free' based on compliance with the Universal Declaration of Human Rights' protection of political and civil liberties.

Reconciliation is a portfolio word that has within it many approaches to building peace and sustainable security. It covers mediation, restorative justice, the tackling of impunity, the restoration of relationships, and above all, developing a capacity for non-destructive disagreement.

Tackling instability abroad is in the interests of the UK because it is protection against uncontrolled movements of people and it potentially opens up foreign markets and cultures to fair and free trade to the benefit of all. Yet the requirement which follows of a proactive foreign

[8]Arch Puddington and Tyler Roylance, 'Anxious Dictators, Wavering Democracies: Global Freedom under Pressure' (Freedom House, 2016), www.freedomhouse.org/report/freedom-world/freedom-world-2016. Accessed 20 April 2017.

policy is immensely demanding of our own courage and resilience. Reconciliation in areas of war is the work of generations, not months. It will involve creating stability, occasionally with the use of armed force – so long as it is capable of achieving its ends, has a clear objective, has a pre-determined exit strategy, and above all is proportionate, legally authorized internationally, and part of a long-term plan for peace and reconciliation. Recent interventions in Libya, Iraq and Afghanistan all failed some of these tests. The last is the most demanding. Armed force by itself, however powerful, will almost always fail (and within the Christian tradition is held to either be highly morally dubious or simply morally wrong). It must bring in very strong partnerships locally, have grassroots acceptance, and involve partnerships that avoid all aspects of colonialism but run with the grain of local culture.

Reconciliation in areas riven by conflict starts with building local knowledge, requires extensive relationships, relieves physical deprivation, is always risky, and must be resourced over many years until it is embedded.

A proactive foreign policy is expensive in its own terms, when looked at in a silo. If it is part of an overall approach to the handling of external threats and to a sense of commitment to values that seek to see all parts of the world in one way or another as our neighbours, it is not only virtuous, but meets both the Cook and Palmerston tests. The next chapter looks more closely at the issues surrounding immigration and integration.

SUMMARY

- Brexit necessitates a re-examination of our foreign policy. This is neither a necessary duty, nor a luxury when all is going well, but a profound expression of our values.

- Our history, language and interests bind us internationally to large parts of the globe.

- The interactions between countries, and our need for partnerships in facing external dangers or opportunities, mean that we have both a global responsibility and an opportunity to influence the fate of billions of people, as well as protecting ourselves by developing international engagements.

- We need a proactive foreign policy that diminishes threats by tackling them abroad, and increases our opportunities by the use of soft power.

8

Immigration and Integration

Of all the great challenges to any society or culture, among the most difficult and dangerous but also the most potentially rewarding with which to deal is great movements of people. The emergence of new powers in the world and the development of ancient empires very often related to large-scale migration. The fall of empires or the change of dynasties has often been linked to invasion not by mere armies but by whole people groups. There is nothing new about great people movements.

In modern times, many societies have sought either to prevent migration within their borders or to create a 'melting pot' culture that brings all those entering into an acceptance of the prevailing values and cultural norms. Three major examples of the latter are France, Germany and the USA. The last is often called a country of immigrants.[1] Successive waves of immigration have occurred since the late sixteenth and early seventeenth centuries, and only the descendants of the cruelly treated original inhabitants can trace their ancestry further back. There

[1] During a visit to the United States in March 2017, Irish Taoiseach Enda Kenny gave a remarkable speech that summed up this sense of it being a 'country of immigrants': http://www.taoiseach.gov.ie/eng/News/Taoiseach's_Speeches/Remarks_by_An_Taoiseach_Enda_Kenny_TD_White_House_Reception_16th_March_2017.html.

has been a very strong and well-established legal, moral and cultural pressure to become American, which has generally worked, albeit with significant struggles from time to time. France has a strong and well-established tradition which has been put to the test with large-scale immigration from many places, including the former French Empire in North and West Africa. Germany has set the pace in the recent wave of European immigration.

The fact that in the USA there have been struggles and difficulties in the past, very severe at times, makes it hard to comment on what is happening in the current age without knowing what the outcome will be, which may be many years from now. However, whatever the difficulties of the past, there was a common assumption that the white majority were in charge, both before and after the Civil War and the Civil Rights movement. That assumption enabled large numbers of people to be admitted from Europe and Ireland (albeit with significant controversy initially), because they reflected the appearance and sometimes the assumptions of that majority. It is striking that, as human equality has at last become a more generally accepted fact, an African American has been elected and re-elected as President; and Indian or Hispanic Americans, or other persons of colour, or those of Islamic faith, are seen in all respects to be as American as anyone else. Despite that, the strains of integration now seem to be more acute, with a revival of alt-right movements with links to racist ideology, as seen in Virginia in August 2017.

It is very easy for so-called 'elites' to perceive immigration and integration as a simple process, with the latter following on automatically from the former, ignoring the enormous strains that are imposed when immigration grows and integration has not yet taken place. Very often the signs of these strains are dismissed as racism, rather than recognized as the costs on usually quite concentrated communities of learning to live with rapid change.[2] The European Union is deeply divided for the very reason that some areas have refused to bear these pressures whereas others have shown extraordinary courage and generosity in doing so. Germany's acceptance of over a million refugees in the 2015–16 period compares with the refusal of countries like Poland to take any meaningful number. The reasons behind particular cases may be historic, but from a European perspective there is a striking inequality of burden-bearing.

To reimagine our future we must take account of the differences between immigration and integration, and have a clear sense of the values that apply to each. The previous chapter argued in part in favour of the established UK foreign policy – which seeks to reduce the push factor of immigration through support for the quality of life and the levels of hopefulness in countries from which people come – as well arguing for a far more generous policy towards refugees (a consistent policy of the Church of England and other Christian and faith groups for many decades).

Events will always ensure that there is some immigration. Wars drive helpless families out of their homes, without a safe place nearby. Climate change will make some areas far less able to support populations than they are today. Further, our own demographic problems, with an ever increasing population of the dependent elderly, and the need for a highly flexible and skilled economy,

---

[2] J. D. Vance, *Hillbilly Elegy* (London: William Collins, 2016), is a remarkable testimony to the pain of changing culture and identity, set in the Appalachian Mountains in the USA.

especially after Brexit, all act as pull factors. To this we add the great national advantages of significant global standing via our universities, major companies and also in the financial services sector, all of which attract large numbers of people to study and develop skills in this country. Immigration has strengthened our nation and many others.

Immigration and integration have been issues in these islands for centuries. Hadrian's Wall was built to keep people out at the beginning of the second century AD. The Roman civilization of Britain vanished under successive waves of immigration in the centuries after the withdrawal of the Roman Legions in the early fifth century. Jewish immigration fluctuated, the prohibition against it finally relaxed under Cromwell in the 1650s. The religious wars in Europe in the sixteenth and seventeenth centuries brought large-scale immigration from Protestant groups, especially the Huguenots. In the nineteenth century there was German, Polish and Jewish immigration, especially in major cities. Areas like Brick Lane in east London were seen as the home of foreigners, often thought in the past to be politically dangerous. Dock areas were often places of large-scale immigration, in cities like Liverpool and Glasgow as well as London. In the 1970s the UK received significant numbers of Asian refugees fleeing Uganda.

The values underpinning the historic British reception of foreigners are beautifully set out in some words by the nineteenth-century English writer Samuel Smiles inscribed outside the chapel in Canterbury Cathedral which was granted temporarily to the Huguenot refugees fleeing persecution in sixteenth-century France. The chapel is still in use by the Huguenots today; around the time of its 300th anniversary, Smiles wrote:

It is a remarkable circumstance that the original French Calvinist church still continues to exist in Canterbury Cathedral. Three hundred years have passed since the first body of exiled Walloons met to worship there – three hundred years during which generations have come and gone, and revolutions have swept over Europe; and still that eloquent memorial of the religious history of the middle ages survives, bearing testimony alike to the rancour of the persecutions abroad, the heroic steadfastness of the foreign Protestants, the large and liberal spirit of the English church, and *the glorious asylum which England has in all times given to foreigners flying for refuge against oppression and tyranny*. (Emphasis added.)

While Smiles was writing specifically about the English, the reception and integration of refugees has long been understood in the UK as both a duty and a pride. In all times, the question has not been whether, but how?

In the last chapter we looked at the Good Samaritan, who could have intervened in a number of ways; the only option that would not have been ethical was to walk by on the other side. It is deeply embedded in our culture, especially in the last 100 years, that turning our back is not what we do. It is easy to talk of migrants as a group, to distinguish between economic and political immigration, and to speak of the increased pressures on the social needs of the population. The Good Samaritan saw not a category called 'victim', but a person bleeding and dying. Our historically Christian culture values the individual human being as of infinite dignity, and thus, whatever our response, as someone who must be treated as we would wish to be treated ourselves. That we have often failed in this task is not a reason to give up, but rather to do better in the future. The need will continue to be there: with greater mobility, increased communication and visibility of foreign suffering, and the push and pull factors already discussed, this is a political question that will not go away. It has never been possible to solve it by barring the doors, nor is it feasible or wise to leave them wide open to all comers. Making distinctions between levels of suffering is immensely difficult and often ethically questionable. We must therefore imagine a country which is faithful to its values of hospitality and refuge, but purposeful in its intentions around immigration, as those arriving will often come from very different cultures, and the challenges of absorption are on a different scale to the past.

The huge complexities of immigration and integration go back into the depths of history and prehistory, and are deeply embedded in our values. In the Old Testament, war and hunger drove populations hither and thither. Within the books of the Old Testament one sees a constant tension between those who wanted Israel to be a light drawing all the nations to the worship of the God of Israel, and those who were deeply concerned about purity, holiness and the dilution of the people of God, and therefore resisted foreign incomers.

The most beautiful story setting out the difficulties of immigration and integration is found in the book of Ruth. It is a love story, wonderfully told, a mixture of tragedy and light romantic comedy. Above all it is about the nature of love expressed in communities dealing with outsiders. It is a short and simple story that captures much in a few pages. A Jewish couple from Bethlehem, Naomi and her husband, with two sons, flee Israel at a time of famine. They find a place to stay in Moab, a neighbouring area in long-term enmity with Israel. Both sons marry Moabites, which for many in Israel was a serious sin. Subsequently, Naomi's husband and both her sons die, without children. Naomi decides to return to Bethlehem; one daughter-in-law, full of tears and sadness, leaves her and goes back to her Moabite family. The other, Ruth, in a most moving scene, says:

> Do not press me to leave you
>   or to turn back from following you!
> Where you go, I will go;
>   where you lodge, I will lodge;
> your people shall be my people,
>   and your God my God.
> Where you die, I will die –
>   there will I be buried.
> May the Lord do thus and so to me,
>   and more as well,
> if even death parts me from you![3]

They return, impoverished and alone, to Bethlehem. Ruth goes into the fields to glean for the leftovers from the harvest (it was the law in Israel not to harvest right to the edge of a field so as to leave something for the poor to collect), and is seen and protected by Boaz, a cousin of Naomi's. After the harvest, Ruth offers herself to Boaz, who is unmarried, and so becomes his wife. He accepts at some cost to himself, while a nearer relative refuses because Ruth is from Moab. The story ends with Ruth giving birth to a child, who is to be the grandfather of King David, the greatest leader among the kings of Israel.

It is a story worth reading, as the colours in it change from the grey despair of being a refugee, the deep

[3]Ruth 1:16–17.

darkness of bereavement and absolute poverty, to the first colours of day as the two women are helped by the God-fearing Boaz, and to full and bright rejoicing at the end.

The family that returns are economic migrants. They have no 'well-founded fear of persecution'. They are not being hunted. In today's terms, Ruth is not eligible for asylum. They take welfare benefits in the primitive form of gleaning. They are protected by the rich and powerful Boaz, who from his first words ('The Lord be with you')[4] demonstrates his faith and obedience to God. Fed and kept at the expense of the community, they are welcomed and loved, and in the providence of God, Ruth becomes crucial to the story of Israel, making a contribution to the history of the nation that is remembered to this day.

The story of Ruth sets principles which have gone deep into our values and culture and which echo the values set out in Chapter 1 of this book. First, the community in Bethlehem is united, despite the time of hardship in which Israel is repeatedly raided by foreign enemies, including Moab. The unity holds up even in the presence of a hereditary enemy, Ruth, from a current oppressor. The story is even more poignant if one takes into account it is set 'in the time of the Judges' – where the book of Judges has just ended with the atrocious treatment of a woman from Bethlehem and the complete breakdown of a nation. The story thus shows hospitality to the stranger, but even more profoundly so at a time when everything would cry out against such hospitality, the kind of time when nations traditionally turn in on themselves. In the story of Ruth, the goods

[4]Ruth 2:4.

of the earth are treated as being there for the common good, while the right of private property is not abrogated. Generosity in allowing gleaning (essentially a sort of social security of the time) goes with good husbandry and stewardship. There is solidarity with the widows and the stranger. God's embrace is portrayed as reaching beyond immediate neighbours to those who come seeking help and will live by the rules. In this story, values overcome fear and selfishness.

Second, Boaz demonstrates courage. He protects Ruth from sexual harassment or even rape at the hands of the labourers. He stands in the town gate to proclaim his willingness to buy the land that Naomi has inherited, and in the course of doing so also takes Ruth, a foreigner, into a mixed marriage. The outcome is stability in the terms of the time. Inheritance and the family name are preserved. Naomi sees her grandchild. There is gratitude to God. There is resilience as a result of keeping God's law not only in letter but, more importantly, in spirit, through attitudes and through faith that results in glory to God.

The issues around immigration are seldom tidy and neat. The division of people into economic or political refugees is often artificial since severe political instability leads to economic hardship. Yet immigration by itself alone is never a solution, unless it is accompanied by integration that has some of the qualities of Ruth's beautiful vow to her mother-in-law, which in a few words encompasses presence, loyalty, care and identity. In the Israel of that time, faith and identity were closely aligned.

The difficulty we face today is finding equivalents that ensure that values are shared and that the structure of society is not torn by the pressures of immigration,

while at the same time retaining not only active involvement to reduce the push factors, but also commitment
to 'the glorious asylum which England has in all times
given to foreigners flying for refuge against oppression
and tyranny', in Smiles's words. We also have to find
forms of integration that neither overwhelm our own
practices and values, nor require those arriving to lose
their previous identities or to be unable to contribute the
values that they bring. The art – and the potential – lies
in the mixing.

It is far easier to see what it is necessary to oppose than
those things which it is necessary to support. Integration
is undermined by ghettoization, by an inability to speak
the language of the host country, by separate schooling,
by inequality, racism and exclusion. It is undermined by
cultural attitudes, by unchallenged assumptions about
each other. There are thousands more things of which
one could write. They are all things to stop, to prevent
and to avoid. What is it that contributes positively? The
answer is love that melts suspicion, and is expressed in
generosity that takes risks. There are no short cuts, there
are no levers, no magic wands. There needs to be a confidence from within Britain that enables a liberal and generous openheartedness, or, to put it simply in a phrase
from the Bible, love for the alien and the stranger.

Have another look at Ruth. Remember that she was
from Moab, an ethnic group at war with Israel for generations. Remember that she was needy and poor, a drain
on the economy. Remember that she married one of the
richer people in Bethlehem, an older man, full of virtue and faith, with land. That may well not have been
seen as ideal by some ambitious families with unmarried daughters. Boaz married Ruth because he was what
was called in Hebrew the *goel*, the kinsman redeemer.

As the nearest male relative willing to do so, he married to preserve the blood line of Naomi's dead husband. It could have been mere duty. Marry, conceive a child and move on, perhaps marrying someone else; it was, after all, a polygamous society. The story is clear: this is a love match, an ending of surpassing happiness.

The values that are in our history encourage our solidarity, our generosity and risk taking in accepting the aliens and strangers, and allowing their culture to nudge and develop ours so that the resulting stream is deeper and richer than either of the two before they were integrated. Yet there is always the question, what does it look like in practice? Our own history gives us examples of the working together of stories from different parts of the UK for the common good. The UK's national identity is both fractured and shifting dynamically and positively through new aspects of the story.

An important aspect of facilitating integration effectively is to recognize that it is neither easy nor automatic. Widespread struggles with integration in many countries illustrate that the approach today will necessarily be different from that of the past. There is no war or clash of civilizations, but there is the unprecedented impact in peacetime societies of powerful and culturally distinct multiplicities of statements of value and purpose.

Integration must be a purposeful and conscious effort, resourced well, at every level of government and civil society, with both boundaries (the necessary negatives mentioned above) but more importantly also with positive and compelling inducements and advantages. The alternatives are ghettoes and fear. The All Party Parliamentary Group on Social Integration published a powerful and thoughtful report in January 2017, with six principles for integration, which overlap with many of those set out below.[5]

Integration requires the resourcing not only of those coming in, but also of the communities and areas that received immigrants. Integration is deeply threatened where shortage of resources leads to new arrivals being seen as competitors for housing, school places, medical care and other social resources. It has been true for some time that refugees often find themselves sent to the poorer parts of the UK, to live in communities that are already under threat. Resources large enough to strengthen receiving communities must accompany those arriving.

The major inducement for integration will always be the opportunity to play a role in an exciting and vibrant society. There must be hope of an improved life for the first generation and, even more importantly, for second and third generations, for it is in a lack of identity, belonging and hope that we find disillusion which leads to searches for meaning that can end in radicalization.

Language learning is the *sine qua non* of integration, the key to all possibility of progress.[6] This means not only attaining high levels of literacy, both verbally and written, but also taking on board the culture and nuanced meanings implied in the language. Integration is founded in language, and thus in a conscious policy of training and recruiting adequate numbers of teachers of English as a Foreign Language.

In the UK it is not only English that is formative but also Welsh, Scots and Irish Gaelic, depending on where

[5]All Party Parliamentary Group (APPG) Report, p. 5, January 2017, http://d3n8a8pro7vhmx.cloudfront.net/themes/570513f1b504f500db000001/attachments/original/1483958173/TC0012_AAPG_Interim_Report_Screen.pdf?1483958173.
[6]APPG Report, Principle 4.

people live. English itself is a major source of integration in many other countries (for example, India, Pakistan, Nigeria and Kenya) and indeed it is often found in particularly dynamic forms in countries where it has been adopted as the national language. This makes it even more of an obvious foundation for identity than it might have been had it been confined to the UK.

Second, an understanding of culture relies on history and anecdote, and this invariably includes religion, art, music, drama and their influences on how we see ourselves. In other words, successful integration requires that people should hear the story of these islands, both good and bad, and be familiar with the myths and legends, true and untrue, that shape attitudes and understanding. The BBC, both in the UK and internationally, has played an essential role in disseminating these stories.

The Roman occupation, the Dark Ages, the Anglo-Saxon settlements, the Norman Conquest, the Wars of the Roses, the Hundred Years War, the development and abolition of the feudal system, the Black Death, the development of democratic government, the wars and conflicts around religion, the Spanish Armada, Trafalgar, Waterloo, the Great War, Dunkirk and D-Day are only a very few of the aspects of history in England. Wales has its own powerful heroes, and narratives around the mining and steel industries, or such people as Owain Glyndŵr. To speak of Scotland without mentioning the Scottish Enlightenment in the modern era, or Robert the Bruce, Mary Queen of Scots, the great engineering traditions, the Highland Clearances and many other stories is to miss out on the foundations of Scottish identity. Northern Ireland is probably the part of the UK with the most, and most competing, narratives that give rise to identity at numerous levels, often contradictory.

Politics is shaped by conquest of the English and by the English, Reformation in different forms in all the various parts of the UK, the Acts of Union, partitions, civil wars, the Glorious Revolution, the nineteenth-century reforms, empires and their losses, and so on. We do not have to rewrite Our Island Story,[7] but there does need to be a set of stories that contribute to shaping national thinking, both those of the component parts of the UK and those of general application. In their interaction is the richness of the whole country.

Of course, culture is not learned chiefly from books but in relationships, and the role of groups that form intermediate institutions is thus especially important. A very good example is the Near Neighbours projects, funded by the government and implemented through an agency of the Church of England; they work very effectively at a local level in bringing together members of different faiths and ethnic groups.

Discussion of religion and religious belief is something from which many people (including the APPG) shy away. To teach about it seems to imply proselytism, or state favour. However, it is impossible to be neutral in matters of religious belief. By their nature they are meta-narratives, all-encompassing explanations or ways of thinking that provide a framework for thought and action. Failures of integration relate very often and in large measure to the increasingly diverse counternarratives emerging in each country as immigration has brought very diverse cultures together. The impact of immigration, when combined with economic and social dislocation since 2008 at least, easily leads to loss of

[7]H. E. Marshall, Our Island Story, originally published for children in 1905, with an idealized view of British history.

confidence in the historically dominant story of a nation, and thus loss of confidence in its purpose and meaning.

A recent example quite puzzling to many non-Americans is the USA. In the autumn of 2016, much of the US electoral campaign was fought around slogans such as 'Make America Great Again', as though America had lost its predominance. The reality from outside the USA was of a country that remains among the richest and most powerful (militarily and in other ways) in the world. In the nineteenth century, the British Empire worked on a two-power naval strategy: that the Royal Navy should be as strong as the next two navies combined. In the twenty-first century the US Navy is more powerful than the rest of the world combined. Yet despite these huge advantages and objective realities of dominance, even near-hegemony, the narrative in the USA had failed to convince a very large proportion of the population that the USA was indeed powerful.

Historians will debate the reasons for centuries. Doubtless the rise of other powerful nations such as China, and the advent of international terrorism on home territory, led to a sense of unease. At the same time, changes in the technology of automation, such as robotics, meant that the underlying ideal of being American – the capacity to make what one could of life – was increasingly seen as hampered and even undermined by inequality of opportunity. The result of domestic discontent, and changes internationally, has been a diminution in confidence in the American story, making integration more of a challenge. Immigration without integration is a threat in any nation. Immigration remains manageable when all is going well. When the only beneficiaries are the super-rich, and there is a suspicion that someone is holding back the rest, then the threat of immigration is transformed (especially by those using such issues to gain power) into 'them' and 'us'. The strength of values well put into practice is essential to enable integration to be a draw, rather than simply a menace to the identity of the immigrant. Loss of identity is always linked to some extent to moving into a different culture. It is a deeply felt bereavement, especially when it is observed by the first generation in second and third generations. Good integration holds up a new culture that is both attractive in and of itself, but which also seems to flex and adapt to benefit from the best that comes in with immigration. Where there is suspected or real injustice and inequality, integration becomes a painful loss of identity without corresponding and greater benefits.

There is a mirror effect on local communities into which there is large-scale immigration. They too may feel a loss of identity, as well as resenting the pressure on local services such as housing, health and education. To live on an estate that has historically had a very strong sense of local identity and then to find that a high proportion of families at the school gate have English as a second language (if at all) is an experience that leads to anxiety. If the anxiety is combined with the economic pressure of great change, this can turn into fear of the newcomers, and even outright hostility. The response to these sorts of resentments must begin by recognising their origins, rather than designating them as racist. Local communities must be resourced sufficiently to be able to accommodate immigration without pressure on local services. There is also a requirement for very good community work at the very local level.

Third, successful integration requires an acceptance of an established moral framework with which to understand society and to make essential ethical judgements. The increasing diversity of such frameworks in Britain and much of Europe and North America makes ethics ever more confusing to those seeking integration.

By contrast values in family life have changed enormously. Attitudes to sex outside marriage, cohabitation and sexual identity and orientation have already been discussed. For those coming to a new country who are immigrants from societies with very strong codes in these areas, it seems that there is an abandonment of good values. In fact, what we are seeing is a diversity of values in different areas of life. For example, in Northern Europe, financial probity in public life or institutional leadership has become more and more important. Insider trading was only made illegal in the UK in 1980. Many politicians before the 1970s would have been thought hopelessly corrupt, accepting gifts from rich friends, whose interests they supported with legislation.

Our social history has many stories that illustrate improvements in values, especially, as discussed already, in the great reimaginings of the mid-nineteenth and mid-twentieth centuries. The care for the sick, the unemployed or the elderly may not always be as we would wish, but the change has been that we recognize it as necessary. On the whole Britain values kindness and inclusion far more than it did in the past.

Trying to convey a sense of values in support of a process of integration and assimilation is far more complex than simply parroting them. It has led to banalities about 'fairness', without saying who decides what fairness means, and which are easily disproved by appeal to history.

Many coming to the UK from former parts of the British Empire will have a clear sense that the Empire was only fair for the rulers, which will tinge with suspicion their gratitude for being here. Seeking to impose manifestly hypocritical values in pursuit of integration is doomed to failure. For someone coming from a country where the folk memory is still of colonization, a British value of fairness can seem simply to be a cloak for an assumption of a right to power. Such errors as setting very high costs for applications for citizenship make a symbolic and value-driven statement to the effect that integration is an economic asset rather than a social obligation.

Values must be coherent with and learn from our history if immigration's threat is to be turned into opportunity and the Britain of the future is to be enriched by the different cultures within it, rather than divided. When held within a story of our past that is transparent about failures, the values of community, of courage and of resilience, worked out by policies that are directed towards the common good, creativity and innovation and sustainability, provide a story for our future which makes room for rich diversity as a blessing, not a threat.

SUMMARY

- Immigration has always been part of our country's history, and the granting of asylum one of our most valuable contributions to the world.

- Immigration is inescapably linked to integration, and the challenges posed today are greater than in the past because of the vast numbers of people on the move around the world, and the very large differences in culture. It thus needs a clear and positive policy.

- Local communities receiving immigrants need support so that they do not feel that resources are becoming overstretched.

- Integration depends above all on fluency in English (as a common language).

- Integration must be a two-way process in which the richness of other cultures and identities is not lost, but reacts with the host culture for the common good.

9

For Those As Yet Unborn –
Solidarity with the Future

The issue of climate change merits specific attention because it is in many ways the most important issue facing us. As is widely accepted by the vast majority of the scientific community, climate change is an existential danger to the planet and to its human occupants; it is therefore of pre-eminent importance to incorporate it into the application of our values. The small minority who disagree consider it as either not serious, or not caused by human activity. They would therefore relegate environmental concerns to a lower priority. The question of climate change and environmental justice tests our system of wisdom.

There are many ways of looking at the subject, but two interdependent perspectives stand out. One is with the planet and its ecosystem at the centre of the argument, and the other is about human flourishing, with humanity and its future at the centre.

Both are rooted for many people in Christian thinking, from the book of Genesis onwards, but the former has grown in public perception more recently as understanding of climate-change science has led to growing concern about the impact of climate change not just on human beings but on biodiversity, and on the very nature of the world about us. Frequent reminders of the rapid extinction of species, the disintegration of ice caps, the loss of glaciers and many other aspects are seen not just as bad for people, but as evils in and of themselves.

Pope Francis demonstrates the growing value put by Christians on the gift of creation in his encyclical *Laudato Si'*, which had a major effect on the outcome of the 2015 Paris climate summit, where a new set of global agreements on climate change were agreed by the vast majority of countries. The Pope wrote:

> Authentic human development has a moral character. It presumes full respect for the human person, but it must also be concerned for the world around us and 'take into account the nature of each being and of its mutual connection in an ordered system'. Accordingly, our human ability to transform reality must proceed in line with God's original gift of all that is.[1]

St Francis himself in the twelfth century saw the created order as ranking alongside human beings – as their brothers and sisters.

Care for creation as having an intrinsic value is deeply rooted in the whole of Scripture. It starts with Genesis, and the portrayal of an intimately interconnected world, where everything that happens in the human realm has consequences in the natural and animal realms. Human beings are tasked with responsibility for caring for creation and, later, in the story of the flood, with giving account for the 'lifeblood' of every animal. The legal system of the

---

[1]Pope Francis, '*Laudato Si'*: On Care for Our Common Home' (Vatican Press, 2015), p. 6. Within this extract, Pope Francis also cites two encyclicals written by Pope John Paul II. http://w2.vatican.va/content/francesco/en/encyclicals/documents/papa-francesco_20150524_enciclica-laudato-si.html#_ftn8.

Old Testament provides for rest for the land as much as for its people, and the well-being of the nation is always linked to that of the land itself. In the New Testament, the picture of renewal and new life brought by Christ is not limited to humans, but reaches the whole of creation, groaning for renewal in Romans 8, and finding fulfilment, healing and salvation in the imagery of Colossians 1.

This chapter, however, will focus on the great danger to human beings from climate change. It is the principal example in which our historic values, applied in the twenty-first century, have significant bite not only for our generation but also for those as yet unborn, including our responsibilities and obligations towards them.

The issue of climate change in its application to human flourishing is a combination of the scientific, the economic and the moral, with the added dimension of time in a way that is unusual. It is the combination of these disciplines that makes discussion of the issue so toxic. I shall deal with each in turn.

The dominant thinking in our global economy – focused on contemporary interests and problems – suggests that we ought to minimize the constraints on what happens today because it is in the interest of the living to ensure that there is a stable and flourishing economy. Some argue that the as yet unconceived have no existence which gives them the right to hinder the rapid improvement in world economic standards that has occurred since the late 1970s. During that time, more than one billion people have been lifted from the most extreme levels of poverty (albeit still into places of great hardship and vulnerability).[2] Key

---

[2]'Poverty and Shared Prosperity 2016: Taking on Inequality' (Washington, DC: World Bank, 2016), https://openknowledge.worldbank.org/bitstream/handle/10986/25078/9781464809583.pdf. Published under Creative Commons Attribution CC 3.0 by IGO.

elements in the improvement in the lives of such a large proportion of humanity have been some aspects of globalization, transport of goods, cheaper energy (especially in the generation of electricity), and food prices kept low yet with improvements in diet.

Infant mortality has dropped, populations have risen sharply and have moved into the safer or at least less dangerous environments (as regards food and water security) of the big cities. More than half the population of the world now dwell in urban areas. Yet urban living consumes more resources. Food (produced outside cities) needs transporting, houses are likely to be better heated or cooled. Rising living standards increase the demand for vehicles, for electricity and gas, and for natural resources for building materials.

In other words, burning things and consuming things has made life better for many in some countries. On the basis of this success, many argue that to restrict the use of carbon-generating fuels potentially threatens further advances in reducing poverty, improving diet and developing transport in a way that would deprive a large part of the poorest people on the earth of the hope of escaping extreme poverty. Those arguing against drastic action now suggest that human solidarity demands that having climbed the ladder of prosperity[3] ourselves, we do not then deny it to others.

The abuse of the environment has also been deeply rooted in our historic value systems, driven in the Christian parts of the globe by a cultural or religious commitment to an exploitative understanding of creation set out in the apparent meaning of Genesis 1:26–31.

[3]But see my book *Dethroning Mammon* on the deceptions of measuring prosperity.

Then God said, 'Let us make humankind in our image,
according to our likeness; and let them have dominion over the fish of the sea, and over the birds of the
air, and over the cattle, and over all the wild animals
of the earth, and over every creeping thing that creeps
upon the earth.'

So God created humankind in his image, in the
image of God he created them; male and female he
created them.

God blessed them, and God said to them, 'Be
fruitful and multiply, and fill the earth and subdue it;
and have dominion over the fish of the sea and over
the birds of the air and over every living thing that
moves upon the earth.' God said, 'See, I have given
you every plant yielding seed that is upon the face
of all the earth, and every tree with seed in its fruit;
you shall have them for food. And to every beast of
the earth, and to every bird of the air, and to everything that creeps on the earth, everything that has the
breath of life, I have given every green plant for food.'
And it was so. God saw everything that he had made,
and indeed, it was very good. And there was evening
and there was morning, the sixth day.

The command to subdue was, until the end of the 1960s,
interpreted very literally, to rule and dominate as a king
may dominate his subjects.[4] Among religiously conservative groups in, for example, the USA it continues
to be seen as justification for resisting climate-change
mitigation, combining an indifference as to the effects

[4] I am indebted in my comments on this passage to Dr Paula Gooder's magnificent
presentation to the General Synod of the Church of England in York in July 2015.
She herself drew on a number of sources, including some very interesting work
by Professor Richard Burroughs.

and a sense that God will sort out the consequences. A US Senator has suggested that it is arrogant to think people could have any impact on God's earth[5] and infamously brought a snowball before the Senate in an attempt to disprove global warming.[6] Yet this passage is one that sets out basic principles of the call to human beings to reflect God's creative love for the whole of the earth, and to exercise that responsibility in the context of love.

As is well known, our own standards of living depend heavily on the use of carbon-generating materials, with currently only 7.1 per cent of our energy generation coming from renewables[7] (although at points in 2017 it was more than 50%). Given it is clear that our economic prosperity in the UK at present depends to a large extent on fuels and materials which are considered to contribute to climate change, and thus that the investment required and the cost of moving to renewables is often thought to be high and very demanding in terms of national effort and policy, the subject has been controversial on economic grounds alone. Two prominent contributors to the debate (among many on both sides) have been Lord (Nicholas) Stern[8] and

[5]James Tashman, 'James Inhofe Says the Bible Refutes Climate Change', Right Wing Watch, http://www.rightwingwatch.org/post/james-inhofe-says-the-bible-refutes-climate-change/ (8 March 2012).

[6]Nicky Woolf, 'Republican Senate environment chief uses snowball as prop in climate rant' (*Guardian*, 26 February 2015), https://www.theguardian.com/us-news/2015/feb/26/senate-james-inhofe-snowball-climate-change.

[7]In 2014, excluding nuclear power and imports. Data downloaded from 'Statistical Bulletin: UK Environmental Accounts: 2016' (Office for National Statistics, 5 July 2016), https://www.ons.gov.uk/economy/environmentalaccounts/bulletins/ukenvironmentalaccounts/2016. Accessed 3 April 2017.

[8]Nicholas Stern, Baron Stern of Brentford, is an economist and academic, and was knighted for services to economics in 2004. He chairs multiple research centres on climate change and until July 2017 was President of the British Academy. See, for example, Nicholas Stern, *Why Are We Waiting? The Logic, Urgency and Promise of Tackling Climate Change* (Cambridge, MA: MIT Press, 2015).

Lord (Nigel) Lawson.[9] While both have written books that accept the general assumption of climate change as being caused largely by human activity, they take very different approaches. (I should note here that far more than 97 per cent of climate scientists agree that global warming is real and man-made. Whilst the arguments are scientifically conclusive, they have not moved the majority of people to modify their lifestyles or expectations; the debate should therefore be less about the fact of climate change and more about how we respond to it. Although the debate is to a large extent over, the passages below illustrate two different views, reflecting the need to see the values-based judgements that each demands.)

Lord Stern argues with a sense of urgency for very significant changes in the structures of the global economy, notably putting forward an argument that the opportunities offered by the technological and economic renewal required will significantly outweigh the costs to the existing global system and open a much brighter future for human beings. He is also very clear about the immense economic threat of climate change, which would be on a scale that has never been seen before. Among the dangers are vast movements of people, dwarfing even that experienced today, as parts of the world with high populations become uninhabitable, or incapable of supporting existing populations. His fall-back argument is that even if one accepts that the outcomes of human activity will result in less serious change than anticipated by the vast majority of scientists in the field, a precautionary

[9]Nigel Lawson, Baron Lawson of Blaby, is a politician and journalist. He has served as Secretary of State for Energy and Chancellor of the Exchequer, and co-founded the Global Warming Policy Foundation think-tank. See, for example, Nigel Lawson, *An Appeal to Reason: A Cool Look at Global Warming* (London: Duckworth Overlook, 2008).

principle should cause us to act now prophylactically, since, if the prediction is proved to be correct, it will be far too late to act effectively; in fact, he argues, it is close to being too late already.

Lord Stern, together with an increasing number of advocates of radical action to combat climate change, adds a very important element to his argument. He suggests that the economic opportunities arising from the necessary investment to decarbonize the economy provide extraordinary scope for the creation of new industries, services, jobs and revenues at individual, company, national and global levels. In other words, he contradicts the suggestion with which the eco-movements are often associated: that the response to climate change is to deindustrialize and put up with worse lives, lower life expectancy and high levels of economic inactivity.

The evidence is anecdotally supportive of his view, and economically rational. New forms of power generation will demand new technologies to be developed and implemented. The manufacturing and construction of wind farms, solar arrays or even (controversially included as part of the green process) nuclear power stations creates tens of thousands of jobs. Innovative projects that are already being developed or considered, such as the world's first tidal lagoon power plant at Swansea Bay, add yet more.

Lord Stern suggests that power generation is only the beginning of the problem. The development of transport networks, new forms of car, better communications and the support of all the new technologies, and many other areas, offer the chance for the market leaders to be at the forefront of a new industrial revolution.

Lord Lawson accepts the premise of human-caused climate change for the purposes of his book, although he has in the past questioned the degree to which the science is proven. However, even if it is accepted, he argues for a slower and more cautious approach, and for aiming for adaptation rather than radical change. He expresses the view clearly that generations yet unborn have no right to determine our actions now, especially when the discounted cost of what will be saved in the future is compared to the actual cost of what we will lose today, not least potentially in removing more people from absolute poverty.

The science of climate change is accepted by the vast majority of scientists working on the subject.[10] The figures for rises in global average temperatures seem clear, with 2015 passing the level of one degree Celsius above the level of 1850, an enormous change by historic standards. Equally, the rise in levels of greenhouse gases and especially carbon dioxide in the atmosphere also seems established, with measurement at the South Pole reaching 400 parts per million in 2016, a far higher level than any recognizable from ice-core samples, which establish figures for thousands of years. Discussion of climate change is often vituperative, with those who deny its existence held to have no regard for the consequences for biodiversity, the value of the earth and human survival. The debate is further fuelled by politicization.

This is particularly potent in countries like the United States when traditional (and environmentally dirty) sources of energy such as coal or tar sands are criticized, to which some on the political right respond by

[10]John Cook, *et al.* note that a range of studies have shown that more than 90 per cent of scientists agree on climate science. 'Consensus on Consensus: A Synthesis of Consensus Estimates on Human-caused Global Warming', *Environmental Letters* XII (4) (13 April 2016), http://iopscience.iop.org/article/10.1088/1748-9326/11/4/048002.

suggesting everything from doubt about the science to conspiracy theories involving a plot to reduce the strength of the nation.

In the UK there is less polarization, and scepticism about human-caused climate change has failed to capture any significant political momentum. However, neither is there a passionate and deeply held commitment to change, despite the considerable progress there has been in making the issue mainstream politically and the dedicated campaigning of activists. The result has been that the voice of advocates for change is only very effective in times of economic and budgetary strength, and then only when the necessary steps do not have negative and proximate effects.

On an international scale, the interests of the UK would also be greatly affected by climate change that leads to a significant rise in global temperatures. The most significant impact would be on land availability and related immigration. There would be small but significant movements of people from islands in the Pacific or Indian Oceans as sea levels rose. This is already happening, and although marginal in terms of the world population, it is obviously very significant for those having to abandon ancestral homes and islands. More significant in terms of numbers and proximity to the UK would be increased desertification and reduced land access across Africa. This in turn would increase the pressure on people to move as large numbers sought to live in areas where food supplies were secure. Even before such a catastrophe, shortage of water would increase civil instability and low-level and local conflicts, always a major push factor for the migration of people.

For these and many other reasons, climate change is a major aspect of the UN Sustainable Development Goals.

Goal 13 is entitled 'Take urgent action to combat climate change and its impacts' and begins by saying: 'Climate change presents the single biggest threat to development, and its widespread, unprecedented impacts dispro-portionately burden the poorest and most vulnerable. Urgent action to combat climate change and minimize its disruptions is integral to the successful implementa-tion of the Sustainable Development Goals.'[11]

And yet, and yet ... Climate change and the environ-ment are almost never seen as core issues in public opin-ion polls and have very little impact on elections or the fortunes of parties. In the UK, the Green Party has not yet managed to get more than one seat at Westminster, far fewer than its equivalents in Germany or elsewhere in Europe. In terms of the UK's own targets for decar-bonizing the economy, we are steadily falling further behind (see fig 9.1 overleaf).

There is good reason to be nervous about the future of the climate and our planet. Outcomes may not be cer-tain, but if the predicted negative impacts happen, they will be irreversible for many centuries and will pose a life- and prosperity- threatening danger not only to those being born today but also to those yet to be born.

The questions around the future cost of climate change are unquantifiable. A materialistic approach to measur-ing them will come up with an approximation of a future value or cost, combined with a discount rate that is mere estimation, to arrive at a figure for today that is as likely to be accurate as it is to be next week's winning lottery numbers.

[11]'Sustainable Development Goal 13: Taking Urgent Action to Combat Climate Change and Its Impacts' (United Nations, 2016), https://sustainabledevelopment. un.org/sdg13.

FIGURE 9.1 *UK's actual and projected energy consumption*[12]

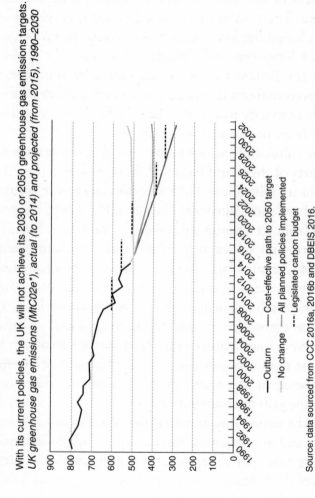

With its current policies, the UK will not achieve its 2030 or 2050 greenhouse gas emissions targets.
UK greenhouse gas emissions (MtCO2e), actual (to 2014) and projected (from 2015), 1990–2030*

Source: data sourced from CCC 2016a, 2016b and DBEIS 2016.
* Note: 'MtCO2e' = 'Million tonnes of carbon dioxide equivalent'.

[12]From Matthew Jacobs, Alfie Stirling and Catherine Colebrook, 'Out of Shape: Taking the Pulse of the UK Economy' (IPPR, 2016). Available at http://www.ippr.org/publications/out-of-shape.

The third element of the debate, in addition to the scientific and economic, is the moral. On top of Burke's dictum that we have a contract with those yet to be born, we have historic values established by long-standing practices of sustainability in our politics, economy and culture. These values have given us great resilience to huge change and have enabled us to enjoy the rare blessings of long-term stability. Resilience must be a basic value for Britain in the future, especially post-Brexit (but even without it), facing a world of rapid change in which a capacity to adapt without losing identity will be at the heart of national flourishing.

The culture into which most of the economically richest parts of the world have drifted is no worse than the past in its selfishness, but seems to have fewer natural brakes and more illusions. The natural brakes of the past came from a common adherence, in the UK at least, to the form and values, if not the reality lived and exhibited, of Christian faith. Yet even the form gave sufficient weight to ideas of solidarity, the common good and the universal destination of goods for those ideas to become embedded within European political culture. They were foundational in the formation of what was to become the European Union, as well as in the drive for the liberation of Eastern Europe – especially Poland – from the grip of communism.

At the same time, moral virtues of creativity in commerce and industry grew more powerful within Europe, finding many of their roots in Protestantism on both sides of the Atlantic. For much of the post-Second World War era, these two groups of values – the ones that hold us together and the ones that drive growth and entrepreneurial activity – have been set against each other. The French speak dismissively of the Anglo-Saxon

model of the economy. Germany holds up a combination of Christian or Social Democracy, against the perceived 'red in tooth and claw' capitalism of the USA
imitated to some extent by the UK of the Thatcher and
post-Thatcher years.

Much of it is polemical exaggeration and stereotyp-
ing. In both variants, economic growth has been the
dominant definition and validation of 'successful' government, and the aim of full employment and a somewhat mercantilist approach to international flows of
trade and capital has been a more or less implicit objective of policy. The emphasis on regional or national
economic success has gained more traction with the
breakdown of the World Trade Organization's Doha
trade negotiation round, the rapid growth first in Japan
and then in the last 30 years in China and India, and
the obvious need for economic development in parts
of the world overlooked until recently, especially sub-
Saharan Africa.

In this context, the success of the Paris COP21 climate talks was astonishing, building on many years
of effort and recovering from severe setbacks such as
that of Copenhagen in 2009. The agreement reached at
Paris, achieved in December 2015, came into effect on
5 October 2016, only ten months later, when 132 countries had ratified it. Within five weeks, the election of
President Trump cast doubt on the continuation of the
process. His campaign had included much doubt about
the reality of human-generated climate change, and set
as a higher priority the protection of American jobs
in the coal industry and the development of American
continental sources of oil and gas through new technologies and the exploitation of tar sands in Canada. In
June 2017 he announced that the USA was withdrawing

from the agreement, yet the reaction of most of the rest of the world has been to restate its commitment.

Economic development since 1945 and recent changes in the mood of the USA, the world's most economically and militarily powerful democracy, provide the context for the moral challenge to issues around the environment. This context produces practices that illustrate the moral dilemmas faced.

The most important dilemma is the question of the limit of solidarity. In discussing the issue of foreign policy as well as immigration and integration, I have argued that solidarity is essentially a global demand, and that our Christian heritage requires us to see our neighbours not only in geographical terms but also through the fact that we are aware of their plight, and should thus be moved to appropriate action.

We have already seen in this chapter that the arguments over climate change are profoundly complicated by time and consequent uncertainty. Lord Lawson argues that the levels of uncertainty make immediate drastic action wrong in that it damages those around us, who are living now, relative to the uncertain benefit for those yet to be born, whose very existence is not yet assured. Lord Stern not only presents a 'green economy' as a huge economic opportunity to create wealth in the present (on the very large assumption that the world buys into the necessity of a green economy now) but also argues forcefully for the need to protect future generations from our past and present actions, despite there being a level of uncertainty as to the exact impact of climate change (if not its gravity).

Resilience and sustainability are values which are implicit in our national history, albeit not in environmental terms. They combine with solidarity and the common good to make a powerful political and moral argument for the demands of climate-change mitigation to be built into all our practices. Resilience and sustainability redraw the answer to 'who is my neighbour' in terms of time, demanding that our neighbour includes those who will need our help now for their lives in the future to be assuredly endurable.

Resilience is the value which seeks to ensure that a given system or society is able to withstand shocks and changes in conditions. It consists of stability and surplus capacity. No one builds a structure to cope with precisely the maximum strain that it will endure, but a degree of redundancy of strength is incorporated. The greater the level of uncertainty as to the strains to be endured, the larger the level of redundancy that is required to cope with miscalculation or failure.

Two examples illustrate this point. Durham Cathedral is one of the greatest of the Norman cathedrals; indeed, to many it is the greatest of all cathedrals. In the nave during choral evensong in winter the massive pillars, beautifully carved, soar into the darkness of the roof, drawing the sound of choir and congregation and returning a deep sense of the mystery and majesty of God. The cathedral was described by Sir Walter Scott as 'half church of God, half castle 'gainst the Scot'. A modern engineer would mutter 'over-engineered', and nearly a millennium after its building the result is clear. It has resilience. There is a huge redundancy of stonework, of strength, because the builders in the twelfth century had no means of calculating the exact stresses and thus of knowing what was required. To compensate, they put in enough strength to be sure for all circumstances.

Sustainability is the value of being able to keep going, to maintain direction, life and energy. Contrast the design of Durham Cathedral with the brilliant *Solar*

Impulse, a solar-powered aircraft which completed a series of round-the-world flights in 2016. The aircraft had a vast wingspan and tiny cockpit, with everything possible done to reduce weight. Bad weather grounded it, and damage sustained in unexpected squalls delayed some stages. Yet it accomplished its purpose. Here the calculation of tolerance was precise, and extra resilience which could cope with the unexpected was minimal.

Apart from the enormous differences in the capacity of the mathematics, engineering skills and computing power available to the constructors of *Solar Impulse* and Durham Cathedral, two other assumptions shaped the way in which the engineering was done. First, the time horizon was utterly different. *Solar Impulse* was required for one series of flights once; Durham Cathedral was expected to stand as a declaration of the grandeur and eternity of God for centuries.

Second, the sense of solidarity was different. The cathedral was for all people who might come; the aircraft, for its two pilots alone. Resilience and sustainability in combination are dependent on purpose, but also on uncertainty, on the range of solidarity and the common good; in other words, on the scope of sense of responsibility and time duration for which the object is required.

A life in a century's time is worth exactly what a life is worth today, unless one reduces humanity to mere economic calculation. The grave error of those resisting measures to be taken now in order to protect the earth and its population after the deaths of all those currently alive is that they reach for what is calculable, and apply methods of use only in the short term to areas that are so uncertain that no discounting makes sense.

If one starts with the idea of the intrinsic worth of the human being – an infinite value which is not susceptible to calculation – then that value is the same today, however far in the future one looks. The uncertainty is over whether people will exist in a hundred years, and we have a moral obligation to do what we can to ensure that they will. More than that, we are as bound to them as we are to those alive today.

Combine that extension of the time range of the common good and solidarity with the uncertainty of exactly what is happening or will happen in climate change (although we know *something* is certainly happening) and the infinite value of each human being alive today or in the future, and the requirements of values of resilience and sustainability, even at a cost today, become clear. The required creation is a Durham Cathedral where it is better to over-engineer and avoid collapse, rather than a *Solar Impulse*.

Christians are starting to recover a better understanding of the Genesis creation story. Paula Gooder argues that it must be remembered that the command to dominate is given to human beings created in the image of God (within the Christian approach, a root cause of the sense of each human being's value as far greater than any calculation of economics or social use). That sense of the mark of God leads to a revision of the understanding of Genesis 1 to see that the creation is to be nurtured as God would nurture it. It is not a possession for disposal but a trust to be cared for. In her argument, Gooder draws together the human-centred approach which has dominated this chapter, and the whole system, planet-centred approach to which I referred at the beginning.

Uncertainty, the current value of future human beings, a religiously based call for stewardship: all these call for costs to be paid today to ensure that the climate is resilient and sustainable, so that we see ourselves in solidarity with the as yet unborn, seeking their good in common with ours. Lord Stern sets out an optimistic and aspirational challenge to be at the forefront of the new economies that are required to express solidarity without kicking away the developmental ladder for the billions alive today. If we respond to that challenge with courage, as well as through community and sustainability, we have a chance almost literally to build a different future.

Of course, Christian re-thinking of environmental priorities has mirrored the huge steps being taken in wider society. Basic personal steps like recycling have become more normal. There is massive investment in renewable energy. The Church (through the investment policy of the Church Commissioners) is progressively greening its portfolio. As individuals we are able to put pressure on our pension funds, or savings holders, in the same way, and consciously to look for green alternatives for vehicles and in other aspects of daily life.

Most of all, there are huge opportunities for energy production in many parts of the country and in ways which will create employment. This is especially true for western-facing coasts and for areas of significant tidal activity, such as Scotland, Northern Ireland and Wales. Research, development and production of suitable technology should continue to be a high priority in our fiscal structures and in employment strategy.

There are many more ways in which all of us, individually and collectively, can begin to address the issue of climate change. And there are grounds for hope, in the human creativity demonstrated in response to the challenge, and in the ability to consider wisely and courageously how we live together, today, and in solidarity with the future we deliver to those as yet unborn.

SUMMARY

- Issues relating to climate change (largely accepted as proven) and the environment are economic and moral as well as scientific.

- Human activity, which has contributed significantly to current problems, is out of step with faith-based understandings of responsibility for the planet, and needs to change.

- The combination of economic, scientific and moral issues, as well as the need for global partnerships in response to climate change, help to explain the incendiary nature of the subject.

- We have an economic interest in helping to lead the development of a 'greener' economic system, which need not be a threat to our own well-being nor to that of other human beings.

- We have a moral responsibility to those as yet unborn, as well as a duty to the whole of creation, to address our stewardship of the planet.

10

The Key Actors

A friend wrote to me in early 2017, after we had been on a visit to Auschwitz/Birkenau.[1] He was mulling over Edmund Burke's observation that 'for evil to triumph all that is necessary is for good men to do nothing'. He had looked it up and found that what Burke was saying was that the evil-intentioned combine well, and all we need for evil to triumph is for those of goodwill to do nothing, not to combine, not to resist in any way. He ended by commenting:

> Popular images of desultory social forces today focus on unpleasant soundbites, demeaning remarks, outrageous tweets, intolerant attitudes. But the Holocaust was about exhaustive planning, painstaking detail, astonishing organization. There was nothing reckless, narcissistic, or cavalier about it. Edmund Burke's words could be sent to anyone who thinks you can be a Christian without the church, a right-thinker without political association, a Christmas-letter-lamenter without sustained combination and coalition-building with friend and stranger. For the triumph

[1] Reverend Dr Sam Wells, personal communication, 13 January 2017: Sam is author of a number of superb books on ethics and modern life.

over evil, it is necessary that the good never under-
estimate the energy of their enemies, and prevail not
by the rightness of their cause but by the faithfulness
of their implementation and the relentlessness of their
detailed planning.

I quote the letter because the argument of this chapter is
that for the common good – for solidarity, for community, courage and stability in a reimagined Britain – we
need a common effort: courageous coalition, cohesive
and generous working, patience, endurance and stability among the actors who are crucial to the future of our
country. There are potential foundations for hope, but
they rely on builders. The culture of dependency that
is so often part of human nature is the principal bar-
rier to building onto the foundations. We cannot rely
on 'them' doing the work, where 'they' is someone or
something else, be it government or the 'invisible hand'
of the market.

The common good – and all of the values and practices it encompasses – is not something legislated or
mandated, but is the sum of innumerable small and large
actions by every participant in society. It requires every
part of local and national government, businesses, other
intermediate institutions and individuals. It assumes
a certain amount of abuse and free riding within society, because within the concepts of the common good,
and community specifically, is the understanding that
human beings are by nature prone to failure, illegality,
selfishness and what the Bible calls sin, the centring of
the world on oneself or even on the world around us,
rather than other people and God.

For example, the nature of each human being, and
above all human beings *en masse*, in anything from a

company to a whole nation let alone the world, is that the sense of moral responsibility diminishes in proportion to the size of the group. In conditions of stress, those closest to us are those who matter most.

To the extent that this is true, it sets a pattern of conflict within society – observable today – that leads eventually but inexorably to disaster. Most people will struggle for their own advantage. Many will give everything for the advantage of their household. Patronage networks, tribes, social groups or local communities exert a powerful hold. Political parties are a tool of power on a collective basis. Companies engage loyalties to some extent, but as each grows, the sense of responsibility diminishes. In the market state in which we live in the UK there is a fear (I suggest unjustified) that the loyalty of people is limited by the extent to which they think they will gain some advantage from that loyalty.

The seventeenth-century British philosopher Thomas Hobbes, quoted earlier in this book, wrote in *Leviathan*, 'in the first place, I put for a general inclination of all mankind, a perpetual and restless desire of power after power, that ceaseth only in death'.[2] He lived through the period of the English Civil War and the Commonwealth (1649–60) and saw clearly the natural impetus to power, and the fear of anarchy.

The influential Christian Realist Reinhold Niebuhr[3] looked at the conditions for virtue in a society, analysing the possibilities of a just society, and concluded that at the heart of the issue is a power struggle. The historical circumstances of his time, with the rise of Hitler in

[2]Chapter 4, *Leviathan: Or the Matter, Forme, & Power of a Common-wealth Ecclesiasticall and Civill* (1651), http://www.bartleby.com/34/5/13.html.
[3]See *inter alia, Moral Man and Immoral Society* (New York: Charles Scribner's Sons, 1932).

Germany, and the newly founded Soviet Union seeming to be the main countervailing force, means that such a view was not surprising. Karl Marx's own theories have at their core, among other assumptions, the principle that power is only surrendered to greater power. Human selfishness means that elites resist the loss of influence and position, and thus the loss of wealth and security, to which influence is inextricably linked.

Many would argue that this remains true as much in the twenty-first century as in the 1930s when Niebuhr was writing. It is easy to make the argument, and to some extent it underpinned the case made by those advocating Brexit, by the so-called populist movements across Europe and by President Trump during his election campaign. Expressions such as 'drain the swamp' (referring to reversing the lobbyist-dominated political culture of Washington, DC), and similar attacks on lobbying in Brussels and other EU centres, played on a sense that 'the system' was rigged. It is felt by many that power and wealth and security can only be acquired by underhand means, by being in the loop and at the centre. There is no sense of justice, fairness and equal opportunity. Thus the Brexit campaign focused, apart from immigration, on returning power to the UK, taking back control.

Manifest and noticeable inequality of treatment feeds these suspicions of an unfair system. In 2008, at the height of the banking crisis, the then-Chancellor of the Exchequer found himself compelled to commit approximately £250 billion to support the banking industry. Even those banks which needed rescuing with taxpayers' money seemed to be able to continue to pay large salaries and bonuses and to argue strongly against the tighter regulation that followed the crisis. By 2017, and the inauguration of President Trump, the new administration (heavily staffed from Wall Street at the most senior level) began planning to roll back much of the regulatory system. In the EU, there was a similar process.

By contrast, in the north-east of England, the valleys of Wales, in Greece, in Portugal, in the 'Rust Belt' states of the USA, and elsewhere it was obvious that a fraction of the same commitment of funds at various times in the last 35 years would have saved whole economies, or, for example, major industries such as steel, coal and heavy manufacturing. They, too, employed hundreds of thousands of people, but those people had less voice and influence.

Such an argument can be presented as tendentious, populist and quite simple to attack by counterclaims. Those who disagree reply that banks are not merely basic to employment in the City of London, or Paris, or New York, but that the health of the banking system provides the means for the rest of the economy to work. To let the banks and bankers suffer the consequences of their own conscious and unconscious actions and attitudes would condemn a society at best to economic depression and quite possibly to total breakdown and anarchy as the concept of money as a store of wealth and means of exchange is thrown into doubt.

Yet it feels unfair, and that sense of unfairness, of free riders being not just a small proportion of the system, but at its heart, indeed controlling it, leads to the breakdown of community, courage and stability, of those things that hold us together, drive us forward and keep us going.

There is nothing new about this problem, nor anything new in it leading to breakdown and collapse. In the Old Testament there is a story of the division of the Jewish Kingdom of Israel, established as a regional great power under the powerful military leadership of King David, and the wise, but finally corrupt, kingship of

King Solomon. When Solomon died, he was succeeded
by King Rehoboam.

> … all the assembly of Israel came and said to
> Rehoboam, 'Your father made our yoke heavy. Now
> therefore lighten the hard service of your father and
> his heavy yoke that he placed on us, and we will
> serve you.'
> … Then King Rehoboam took counsel with the
> older men who had attended his father Solomon while
> he was still alive, saying, 'How do you advise me to
> answer this people?' They answered him, 'If you will
> be a servant to this people today and serve them, and
> speak good words to them when you answer them,
> then they will be your servants forever.' … The young
> men who had grown up with him said to him, 'Thus
> you should say to this people who spoke to you,
> "Your father made our yoke heavy, but you must
> lighten it for us"; thus you should say to them, "My
> little finger is thicker than my father's loins. Now,
> whereas my father laid on you a heavy yoke, I will
> add to your yoke. My father disciplined you with
> whips, but I will discipline you with scorpions."'
> … The king answered the people harshly. He disre-
> garded the advice that the older men had given him and
> spoke to them according to the advice of the young
> men, 'My father made your yoke heavy, but I will add
> to your yoke; my father disciplined you with whips,
> but I will discipline you with scorpions.' …
> When all Israel saw that the king would not listen
> to them, the people answered the king,
>
> > 'What share do we have in David?
> > We have no inheritance in the son of Jesse.

To your tents, O Israel!
Look now to your own house, O David.'[4]

The story is a classic example of the failure of an out-of-touch elite. The Kingdom of Israel had twelve tribes, held together by a common history but with a deep sense of tribal identity and among the majority some resentment against the ruling family. At the heart of the history writer's theological and social vision was that Israel should be united, and in all respects have its first loyalty to God, demonstrating such loyalty in justice and mercy, and in obedience to the Torah, the Law of Moses, so fulfilling the covenant with God. Put simply, Israel should love God in the same way that God loved Israel. If there had to be a king, then the king should love Israel in the same way God did. Much of the history of the Old Testament is the constant pattern of obedience, disobedience, crisis, repentance, obedience that was the life of the people of Israel. Community, courage and stability were the virtues that created the possibility for a flourishing society, and the influence of this pattern of societal virtue has remained with us ever since, universalized through the Christian story.

The story of Rehoboam tells of the archetypal pattern of youth against wisdom, 'strong' leadership against compromise, arrogance against humility. It reveals that there was a party within the state that had been uncomfortable with the government of Solomon, recalling that the first duty of the king was to maintain the covenant with God, and thus the kingdom, because God would be faithful to Israel if Israel was faithful to God.

[4] 1 Kings 12:1–16.

The story is easily translated into our times. The first duty of the state is to maintain security. Security requires community, courage and stability; it is not a natural order of things.

Finding the common good can only be achieved with justice and with limits to the free riding of the unscrupulous and to the general inequality of society. Suppression of legitimate demands for equality and justice leads to the eventual breakdown of community, and without great and tyrannical repression, is followed by the break-up of the state, and the loss of security. The answer to the problem in Ancient Israel was the same as it is today around the world. Those in power and with influence need to see their calling as service and not control.

Within the UK (and indeed the USA and many democracies) the majority of those in office seek power in order to achieve clearly articulated aims based on a commitment to public service. It is easy to be cynical, and there is no such thing as an entirely pure motive, not least because the nature of electoral politics means that politicians must bear in mind the impact on those who are likely to be voting for them. Former Prime Minister Margaret Thatcher is reputed often to have asked, 'what will this do for *our* people?' when considering a new policy proposal. In a democracy, power can also be curtailed by electoral cycles. Yet, despite many people's cynicism about politics, most politicians are striving for a better society.

Influence is more corrosive to justice than power because it is less transparent. It may be the result of patronage, support for electoral costs, friendship or kinship, or simply the 'rational' decision to support the group that supports the interests of those with influence. It is almost invariably linked to wealth.

The delusion of influence is that it is based on a view of the world as zero-sum in which the advantage of any group can only be matched by an equal disadvantage to another. The reality of community, courage and stability is that it leads to a structure in society that opens the most opportunity to the most people. It is striking that a number of European countries such as Switzerland, Germany and the Nordic states have both lower inequality and a generally stronger sense of the common good.

The young advisers to King Rehoboam had influence over him, and sought to replace the experienced and wise advisers of his father. They were keen to establish power rather than to serve the kingdom. At the creation of the office of king, before King Saul was chosen, God had warned the people of Israel that if they replaced divine authority with human it would lead to abuse of the kind recounted in this story. The young group saw any concession by the king as a loss of authority, not an acceptance of moral virtue by the sovereign power.

The older advisers, those who had lived through roughly forty years of the golden age of Israel, had kept their ability to see the reality of the politics. They knew that kingship was a means of ensuring community, but only if it was a rule of service, not domination and self-seeking. When the king lost support among the tribes that were not linked to his family, then the common good and solidarity were replaced by mere power seeking and advantage hunting. The result was a disastrous weakening and ultimate collapse of the kingdom.

There is a very clear understanding of human beings in this story. They require the visible signs of authority, but authority will always seek to gain power and increase its own security of position. In the story of Rehoboam, the old and the young represent respectively those who have a first loyalty to God, and who remember God's ways and warnings, and those whose first loyalty is to the king. The former saw a society with the potential for abundance and grace; the latter saw only a zero-sum competition of equivalence and exchange.

Yet, as we all know, it is more complicated than that. Even in the days of Rehoboam, society was made up of more layers than at first seemed obvious. Below the king were the tribal leaders, each relating to clans and families. The army was immensely important. Advisers played a key role. The symbol of the kingdom's unity was the temple at Jerusalem, built by Solomon, from which a priestly tribe exercised significant power and influence. The question then, as now, was how to ensure that the overall systems of society functioned for the common good, and were not captured by sectional groups, whether of the powerful and rich or by populist movements. As with many ancient societies, the problem in Israel was that the mechanisms of control at the centre were not efficient; they could not exert more power than the centrifugal forces of clan and tribe. The challenge for reimagining the impact of our historic values is to ensure that the equivalent voices of wisdom draw the country together for the benefit of all. How do we overcome the tendency of those with influence to exercise power to their own exclusive advantage, and how do we ensure that the weakest are as well served, loved and protected as the strongest? One part of the answer is the encouragement and development of these practices and values in intermediate institutions.

The players in society today are vastly more complex than in the past. The British habit has been not to simplify a complex system with elemental principles, but to seek to make it work in practice, even if in theory it is incomprehensible. This approach is one that distinguishes the British system from many on the continent of Europe. There is an implied social contract that says that, provided intermediate groups work to the furthering of good practices, they will be welcomed and encouraged. We have seen this in such cases as church schools and heritage societies, the British Medical Association and other quasi-private regulatory bodies, as well as many more examples. Social capital is seen as important. This attitude leads to odd structures, but good results – although, as now, it requires reimagining at times of major change.

Reimagining is happening at all levels, especially in terms of values and practices. For it to work well, however, there is a need for the natural tendency to seek power, especially in times of change, to be disciplined by a seeking of the common good and solidarity, by examples of courage, and by practices that are sustainable. In other words, the bias towards oneself and accumulation needs setting aside. What is good for me, or good for us, or the company and its shareholders, or the members of the association or the trades union, has to be sought in the context of what is good for all, and what protects the vulnerable and poor ahead of all else.

In recent years, working out the relationships between intermediate institutions and the rest of society has very often ended up in the courts, or had to be addressed through legislation. Yet neither of these are effective means of building foundations for hope. The key issue is not top down or even bottom up or middle out, but a solid understanding of the demands of being part of society, and a rejection of attitudes of exchange and equivalence, of zero-sum games, while accepting the vision of mutual flourishing being possible in an atmosphere of abundance and grace.

It is at this point that an understanding of values drives the evolution of practices. Within the structures of government, the greatest deceit springs from an age of information. Benchmarks, standards and expectations are both necessary and valuable, but they cannot be substitutes for responsibility and relationship. As discussed earlier there is a profound tendency to believe that once it is theoretically possible to centralize and control through the use of sophisticated systems, government has the obligation to do so. Thus in the first years of this century, when I was chairing an NHS General Hospital Trust, I was introduced to the 136 priorities that had been set centrally. They were monitored through sophisticated systems. Those systems did not work well other than as collectors of information. The power to know is not the same as the capacity to make change.

Government should establish, as a driving principle, that subsidiarity applies to all levels of its activity. The assumption should be that everything will be done at the lowest efficient level. The implications of this principle are especially powerful in the structures of finance, and the practice of financial devolution should match the aspiration of subsidiarity. Those who do not control the money flow are less likely to feel responsible for outcomes and will reasonably argue with the electorate that the fault for failure lies with those who control the purse strings. The recent development of elected mayors and significant devolution of services to areas under their authority is a brave experiment with this principle.

An instant result would be more devolution to the four nations of the United Kingdom and local government at every level, and at local government level a target that the majority of spending comes from a council's own fund-raising, with an appropriate formula to even out resources and deal with large and unjust inequalities which exist for long-standing social and historical reasons. Furthermore, obligations should be put on local government only if there is a guaranteed income stream to pay for it, with independent monitoring of the resources and outcomes. From 2010 to 2020, cities like Liverpool will have experienced cuts in revenue of more than 50 per cent, without an equivalent shift in the obligations they are meant to meet. The crisis in local government funding in the UK is essentially one of philosophy and values. Local government structures are treated as departments of state, not locally elected and accountable bodies. The reason for such treatment is that the vast majority of their funding has for many years come from the centre.

The business sector, including nationalized or heavily regulated industries, must recognize that funds allocated for community engagement or corporate social responsibility are not a substitute for being *with* and part of the community.

In the story of Rehoboam, one crucial element of the failure of the kingdom is that the king sees the demands of the majority of his people as a question of the monarchy doing something *to* them. He had no sense of 'with'; he ignored an opportunity to generate a sense of partnership between the king and his people. We should not ignore our opportunities for partnership today. Intermediate institutions create social capital by being *with* their communities, at every level and in every place. The reality of being *with* is shown in what they experience at local level, what responsibility they feel and how they respond. It is love-in-action.

Many UK companies are extremely good in this regard. Branches are encouraged to be good community citizens, not merely handing out money (which is too often a means of doing something *to* a community) but making time for staff to volunteer where they live or where they work, making the effort to live out the terms of the military covenant by paying special attention to veterans, giving time for employees for community service as magistrates or similar roles. The result is that the joys and pains of a local community are the joys and pains of its businesses, even if they are the local face of a major company with a headquarters far away.

However, it is often less true that the local experience of pain or joy is felt by the whole body of the company. A supermarket chain that specializes in opening out-of-town shopping centres may have branches that are very much 'with' the community, although at a global level its policies lead to the closing of town-centre commercial life. There is pain felt locally, but it is not transmitted and heard other than locally.

A good example of a commercially based business which acts as an effective intermediate institution is the Post Office. Its 11,600 branches are at the heart of communities across the UK. Research by government during 2016 calculated the Post Office's annual social value to its customers, to communities and small businesses, at up to £9 billion. The Post Office network is accessible: almost 93 per cent of the UK population live within a mile of a post office and 99.7 per cent within three miles. 95% of the population say they use the post office at least once a year, and one third of all small businesses visit the post office weekly.

Half of all post offices are in rural areas, and in more than 3,000 locations they represent 'the last shop in the village'. In remote locations, services are provided through innovative solutions such as mobile services and post offices in community shops, as well as in village halls, pharmacies, pubs and churches. Through its benefits distribution role, bill payment, budget cards and access to basic banking accounts, the Post Office helps to promote financial inclusion; it also runs a number of initiatives to protect vulnerable and elderly customers through its 'Adopt a Post Office' scheme, Crimestoppers 'Stamping Out Scams' campaigns, and the Banking Protocol Initiative.[5] In all these ways the Post Office demonstrates values of community, courage and sustainability.

The greatest contribution to the common good, to community, will be found by the business sector taking its share of responsibility for skills and productivity, in partnership with schools. The fourth industrial revolution has been discussed in the chapter on education. It is a period of high risk, but potentially very high reward, not only economically but also in social life. To reap the rewards will require businesses to develop much better training for people of all levels of ability. Relying only on schools, Further Education (FE) colleges and universities to produce 'ready to work' employees has always been a myth and will remain so. The need for skills that produce very high levels of added value is well understood to require lifelong training. Only employers can lead in such a process, and it requires much more investment than at present. Patriotism as a UK company is not found only in paying a reasonable amount of tax, but in participating actively in developing a vision for the workforce of the country and the common good of its citizens.

[5] Correspondence with the Post Office, September 2017.

The investment required springs from the second of the groups of values: courage, aspiration and competition, which cannot be dictated by potential return to shareholders alone, however essential that may be. Nor does the tired term 'stakeholder' help a great deal, as the vague boundaries of stakeholders and the different interests involved limit its usefulness. Historically, companies and businesses did not count as intermediate institutions. They were seen as something else: the corporate sector. Yet as Pope St John Paul II commented: 'A business cannot be considered only as a "society of capital goods"; it is also a "society of persons" in which people participate in different ways and with specific responsibilities, whether they supply the necessary capital for the company's activities or take part in such activities through their labour.'[6]

A society of persons is a society based in relationships, which must be geared to the flourishing of the whole person and not only to the ends for which it is formed. If it becomes utterly task-focused, the persons within it are mere means to an end, instrumentalized for the greater good – a demonic approach to the sacredness of the human person.

Companies and businesses must therefore rise to the calling of human flourishing. Not only have their societal responsibilities developed, but the last 30 years have also shown that it is in such bodies of all sizes that much development happens. They are places of learning about relationships, about creativity and courage, about sustainability and community in a changing and diverse world.

[6]*Centesimus Annus* (Vatican, 1991), paragraph 43.

Taking seriously intermediate institutions requires thought and planning in order that they may be encouraged. Much has been accomplished. Schools, clinics, hospitals, charities, churches and clubs are often the glue that holds local communities together. Yet much more is needed, for they are frequently staffed by volunteers, and are far less robust than they may appear. Above all, their nurture requires space in which regulation is minimized to the essentials (for example, the protection of children and vulnerable adults) and the weight of administration is kept manageable. Anyone who has tried to maintain charitable accounts knows the irritation of changing statements of practice and increased demands on reporting, often with little perceived result.

The basic principle is that intermediate institutions, including business, are essential to a society's capacity to reinvent itself. They require a benevolent ecosystem of regulation and encouragement. They interact with every level of government, which itself, if it is to be virtuous in its values, must be committed to subsidiarity in ways that strengthen the local, enabling accountability, close relationships with the communities they serve and a sense of the local driving its own agenda.

SUMMARY

- The key players in determining the practices, principles and values which form the basis of reimagining, and establishing new foundations, necessarily include government at all levels.

- They must also include intermediate institutions, from families or households to companies, schools, hospitals, societies and all the communities in which values are learned and practised.

- Such institutions need significant support and encouragement, and their importance should be recognised in our tax, regulatory and grant-making systems. The health of such institutions should be assessed on the values they embody.

11

The Churches and Other Faith Groups – Healthy Disruptors

The UK today has a huge variety of faith groups, in a way that was impossible to imagine in 1945. The vast majority of adherents have only arrived in large numbers since the 1960s, and the effort of seeking to work out how to live with such diversity is one of our greatest challenges. Sometimes they are all bracketed together, and at other times treated as the indigenous (Christian) and the foreign-and-strange (the rest). Both approaches are inadequate and often, in the latter case, also wrong. This chapter focuses principally on the Church of England, but in doing so recognizes that the contribution of Christian churches is an effort often done cooperatively, overcoming centuries of difference, and frequently led by non-Anglican churches.

Additionally, other faith groups play a huge role in many communities, and the vast majority of relationships with the Christian churches are healthy and mutually respectful. Thus, to some extent, what is said about the churches' contribution applies equally in different ways to other faith groups.

As a last preliminary comment, for Christians the principal role of the churches is to be witnesses to the truth of Jesus Christ. As such, they are to seek to draw

those who do not know the love of God who created all
people and things into confident experience of that love.
They do that by their prayers, their speaking, and their
own love expressed in action. If the churches are not
witnesses to Christ they are nothing, but as witnesses
they are called to speak about the daily lives and experience of the society in which they find themselves. Faith
cannot be sealed off from daily life.

Contrary to many myths, it is a very long time indeed
since the churches had a dominant or even significant
level of power in either England or the UK. There was a
period of days during the so-called 'Glorious Revolution'
of 1688 when – in the absence of any legal government –
Archbishop Sancroft acted, after King James II had fled
before the advancing armies of William of Orange (having first thrown the Great Seal into the Thames). Sancroft
played a large part in summoning Parliament. Dramatic
as the occasion was, it is not likely to repeat itself, and if
it did, better remedies would be found!

Parliament itself felt that Archbishop Laud was worth
executing in 1645, as one of the main advisers to Charles
I. Before that, Cardinal Pole was influential under Queen
Mary between 1553 and 1558 (they died on the same day),
and before him was Archbishop Thomas Cranmer (whom
Pole sent to the stake), one of the main architects of the
Reformation in England under Henry VIII and Edward VI.

Reading Shakespeare's histories it is noticeable that a
number of bishops appear, from Canterbury to Carlisle,
but their function is almost always incidental, and their
best roles are not as movers and shakers but as useful
walk-ons to add a bit of clout or commentary. That, of
course, tells us more about the perception of the Church
around the beginning of the seventeenth century than
about the historical reality.

To see the Church exercising significant influence, one has to go back to the medieval period. In 1170 Archbishop Thomas Becket was considered a sufficient problem for Henry II to encourage, if not plot, his murder. In 1215 Archbishop Stephen Langton led both the design and the negotiation of Magna Carta. His successor in the late fourteenth century, Simon of Sudbury, was also in charge of collecting the nation's taxes – a role which cost him his life in the Peasants' Revolt.

Yet by the late eighteenth century, although fabulously rich, archbishops were in political terms relatively unimportant. Together with the bishops, they had a significant number of votes in the House of Lords, and thus, in those unreformed days, they counted in that sense, but they could not set government policy and on the whole voted with considerable and often vain conservatism.

The reality came from the relative lack of military force. Soft power was considerable, but was no substitute for the hard variety. During the Civil War in the 1640s, although it was clear that the Church of England was under institutional threat, and despite it having an unrivalled network through parishes and dioceses, there was no capacity to alter the course of the war. On the one hand, the Church was deeply divided politically and theologically, and its happy historic tradition of independently minded clergy meant that it could not speak with one voice; on the other, it had no army, nor the means or will to raise one.

Yet as Edward Gibbon famously wrote in his introduction to *The Decline and Fall of the Roman Empire*, 'the various religions of the Roman Empire were to the people all equally true, to the philosophers all equally false and to the magistrates all equally useful'.[1] Even

[1] Volume I (London: Everyman, 1993), p. xxvi.

in the twentieth century – that age of mass conscription and total war, when Stalin could ask sarcastically how many divisions the Pope possessed, and Marx's phrase about religion as the opium of the people was common parlance – in many countries faith was seen as sufficiently subversive to warrant the effort of persecution; and, for that matter, still is. In England today, the Church of England is on the one hand mocked as being declining and powerless, while on the other the position of the bishops of the Church of England – or of the institutional church in education, in its chaplaincies or even in the day-to-day work of church communities – is opposed by various groups on the grounds of being dangerously powerful.

All of this seems a paradox, and not a new one either. As far back as 1941, Archbishop Temple felt obliged to justify writing *Christianity and Social Order*, by including a chapter called 'What Right has the Church to Interfere?' It remains the case that there is a habit of paying attention (although not obedient attention) to what churches say, especially in the case of the Pope in Rome, or to some very limited extent in this country, to the Church of England in its various forms. The same is true in other countries that have taken a more deliberate approach to abolishing the rights of churches or institutionalized religion, such as the USA with a rigorous separation of Church and State enshrined in its Constitution, or France, with its law on *laïcité*, which dates from 1905.

In 2017, 41 per cent of the UK population described themselves as Christians.[2] There is ample evidence of the positive role that the Church in England plays in terms of social capital, and of its significance in terms of numbers of people involved in Christian or other faith groups.

[2] http://www.natcen.ac.uk/media/1469605/BSA-religion.pdf.

Research on the volunteering contributions of Christians in England[3]

According to the last Citizenship Survey, in 2011 58 per cent of all Christians in England were involved in some form of civic engagement or volunteering, around the same as those of no religion. The Cabinet Office has found that across all faith groups, those who are active in their religion are more likely to volunteer (67 per cent) than those who are not (55 per cent).

A 2014 National Church and Social Action survey estimates that Christians contribute over 100 million volunteer hours and nearly £400 million to social action per annum. The top ten areas of benefit are:

- Food distribution
- Parents and toddlers groups
- Schools assemblies/RE work
- Festivals/fun days
- Under-12s non-church children's clubs
- Caring for non-church elderly
- Debt counselling
- Non-church youth work, 12–18
- Cafe open to public
- Marriage counselling/courses

---

[3]Data downloaded from 'Citizenship Survey: April 2010–March 2011, England' (Department for Communities and Local Government under Crown Copyright, 22 September 2011), https://web.archive.org/web/20120107021528/ http:/www.communities.gov.uk/publications/corporate/statistics/citizenshipsurveyq4201011; from Natalie Low, *et al.*, 'Helping Out: A National Survey of Volunteering and Charitable Giving' (Cabinet Office under Crown Copyright, September 2007); Geoff Knott, 'Investing More for the Common Good' (Jubilee+, 2014), https://jubilee-plus.org/latest/modal-research.php?item_id=6. All accessed 17 April 2017.

Practices led by faith groups encourage social community, seek the common good, develop a sense of belonging and generosity, and have a sense of resilience and
sustainability since they rely on a narrative of the love
and compassion of God rather than government funding. They nurture implicit values that are designed to
carry over into working life or social activities. They
feel a sense of shame when they fail. They are seldom
authoritarian and most often are simply stores of grace
and love, neither manipulative nor instrumentalizing
people's need for their own purposes.

In their activity they create a series of meta-narratives
that run counter to the nihilism of much popular postmodernity, or the inward-looking and self-regarding
behaviour that is frequently portrayed as normal or
even right. This leads to opposition, because it is the
source both of their influence and of the hostility that
religious views often arouse, to all intents and purposes
irrationally.

The opposition is not so much a result of the so-called
'do-goodery', or 'God-bothering' (to use the mock-
ing term often applied to Christians in social action, at
prayer or worship). It arises from the implicit, and often
explicit, criticism of attitudes and standards proclaimed
outside religious faith. Sometimes this is the result of
harshly and hypocritically judgemental attitudes by religious believers, but frequently it is simply through the
way that their words and actions hold up a mirror to
others. The reflection is not as attractive or valuable as
those others might have hoped.

In other words, faith is fine when it is merely 'useful', in Gibbon's terms, but is often unwelcome when
it seeks to change the way society works. There is clear

incoherence in an approach that applies tests of utility about Christianity and other faiths to ideas that are not based in utility but in notions of absolute truth.

The theological heart of the work of faith communities is not a desire to be liked but rather an ambition to reflect in lived experience (what they often call 'incarnationally') their understanding of the nature of God or of the ultimate purpose of life.

It is at this point that talk of faith communities as a single group becomes incoherent, as there are wide variations of the understanding of God, or even as to whether there is a God. Some religious movements are essentially atheistic, while maintaining a sense of eternal purpose and value as well as strong commitments to community life, especially around monasticism or its equivalent.

However, to speak of the future of Britain without dealing with faith communities is also incoherent. The results of a 2011 YouGov poll suggest that around ten million people[4] had attended a place of worship in the previous month. We have already shown the contribution made to society as a whole.

Thus, any reimagining of Britain has to deal with the very modern problem of incommensurate worldviews. It must reflect the different visions of the numerous faiths in the UK. It must recognize the absence of participatory faith, as well as the rejection of faith. In many cases, all these perspectives have both great utility and compelling

---

[4]The poll, carried out on behalf of the British Humanist Association, found that while 61 per cent of those surveyed in England and Wales identified as belonging to a religion, only 15 per cent had been to a place of worship for religious reasons within the last month. Results downloaded from 'Religion and Belief: Some Surveys and Statistics', British Humanist Association website, https://humanism.org.uk/campaigns/religion-and-belief-some-surveys-and-statistics/ (n.d.).

power to motivate and lead people. Faith communities are sometimes put in a collective box, frequently labelled 'problem', only to be seen as useful – like old and valued but out-of-date toys – on occasions when they fit the circumstances. The result is confusion and dissension.

Two examples serve to demonstrate the point. First, assisted suicide is found by many opinion polls to be favoured by the majority of the population, yet is opposed vigorously by the majority of the official leaders and members of faith communities, as well as, incidentally, by many disability groups and the British Medical Council. The argument is put to the faith leaders that they ought to pay attention to democracy, and allow the country to have its way without seeking to oppose a change in the law. There are many flaws in this argument, not least that opinion polls are easily manipulated, and that in a democracy any person or group should be able to argue publicly for or against the vast majority of policies. Nonetheless, faith leaders are presented as obscurantist opponents of something that is portrayed as obviously fair and just. They are, it is said, welcome to act for themselves – no reputable person is yet saying that assisted suicide should be compulsory – but they should not seek to impose their views on others. Notions of radical personal autonomy, and implicit ideas of the lesser value and utility of lives once health is impaired, are in conflict with notions of absolute truth that claim to sustain a civilized society.

The controversies around sexuality and gender are even more contentious. Here, the prevailing views, amply evidenced (contrary to the example of assisted suicide) by votes in Parliament, are that gender equality and the equality of all people regardless of sexual orientation, are fundamental human rights. To deny them is seen as advancing injustice, not morality, and is considered to be the equivalent of racism.

Yet there are exceptions for religious groups. It is not compulsory for orthodox Jews to have women rabbis, for Muslims to have women imams or for the Roman Catholic Church to have women priests. No church or religious group is obliged to place people in same-sex relationships in positions of leadership, unless they choose to do so. Like other churches and religious groups, the Church of England may legally discriminate against marrying couples where one or both partners are divorced with a previous partner still living, or where the couple are of the same gender.

Some activists for LGBTIQ+ rights argue that such discrimination should never be permitted by law, and should simply be rendered illegal. Others are slightly less demanding, but still say that the obscurantism of religious groups means that they should have no privileges in the state, such as the right to oversee schools, sit in Parliament or crown the monarch.

A third group argues that it is incoherent but it works, more or less. The Church of England National Society, for example, has led the way within the state sector on providing for all schools educational materials of high quality against homophobic bullying, and like all groups involved in state schools in England, keeps to the National Curriculum.

The Church of England today is well aware that its schools are an expression of its mission to England but are not a means of proselytism. Acts of worship in school assemblies are never universally compulsory and always contain phrases like 'Christians believe …' rather than dogmatic expressions of what is true. Especial care is taken when other faith communities are present in large numbers. Chaplains from the Church of England[5] act for all, whether in hospitals, or prisons, or schools and universities, or in the armed forces. Invariably there is a genuine interchange in which chaplains from other churches and many other religious groups behave in the same way. It is not tidy, it is often theologically incoherent and institutionally best not examined too closely, but it works well. That pragmatic and reasonable approach thus takes one to the question of what should happen: it forces the question what the roles of the Church of England, together with other faith communities and churches, should be across the UK.

Counter-narratives, and the challenge to a liberal hegemony that is dominated by the rule that there are no absolutes except for the statement that there are no absolutes, are essential components of the future of Britain. The churches especially, as well as other faith communities, are at the centre of retaining a sense of legitimate diversity of view. The resulting conflict and confusion is healthy for all in society, because it tests assumptions and requires relativism to prove itself against the claims of revelation, and against the demands of a vision of life that has a teleology, a clear destination, and which is accountable not only in this world but thereafter.

Ideological hegemony is always a threat when it is combined with the lust for power and an intolerance of dissent, which is inescapably combined with being human. The dangers of monolithic understandings of right and wrong and of the purpose and worth of human

---

[5] I use the example of the Church of England only because it is the institution with which I am most familiar. There is no suggestion intended that other mainline groups behave differently or less well.

beings have been evident throughout history. Whether a system was the creation of the Church, of a political party, or of the state, it has never managed to tolerate challenge. The result has been, at best, marginalization of diverse views and, more often, oppression and tyranny.

The strength of the views of faith communities, seen most clearly in the UK through the churches, is that they are anchored in a totally different understanding from the prevailing, secularist view of all that there is in life. They begin, in the case of Christianity, with revelation: the acceptance that although there can be some awareness of God through the natural order and through reason, it is in Jesus Christ that God is fully revealed; and that has happened in history by God's sole choice.

Thankfully, the churches no longer impose their views as by right, but fall within the authority of the state and are subject to the state in terms of what they can and cannot do. The campaign associated historically with Thomas Becket, Archbishop of Canterbury, in the late twelfth century, to assert the independence of church courts when it came to the trials of clergy, was controversial even then, and the equivalent seeking of independence would be mere foolishness now. The claims of the Papacy to a universal spiritual and temporal jurisdiction, which included the setting up or throwing down of monarchs, ended in practice with the Peace of Westphalia in 1648. In modern Europe and the USA, truth claims by churches are vigorously contested, and attempts to protect historic rights and privileges for their own sake alone have no traction. Declarations of what law ought to be carry the same weight – no more and no less – whether they emanate from churches or from other groups in civil society. All this is right.

Yet it is also right that the faith communities – and, within the English historical context, especially the churches – should continue to argue their case, because otherwise there is no means of examining clearly what are often self-proclaimed claims of a particular course of action being 'obviously true'.

At the same time, the credibility of truth claims requires visible expression. The churches continue to educate children and young people, and on the whole they educate very well indeed. Faith groups speak about compassion and the needs of the poor, and they have parishes and clergy and communities in every part of the country, including the poorest. Churches and other faiths have local leaders who are resident in, and committed to, even the poorest communities, unlike many other professionals who work there but live elsewhere. Faith leaders send their children to local schools, use local shops, are registered at local GPs, and in every way live the ups and downs of the community. They advocate for refugees and they take them in and care for them; and the narrative of the Church starts with God who reaches out to the alien and the stranger. The other Abrahamic faiths, Islam and Judaism, have similar narratives deriving from the histories of their origins, which lead them to provide profound care for the weakest.

Incarnational ministry is not a way of winning converts, but a demonstration of the experience of received truth about God. Through incarnational activities the churches and other faith groups force their way out of the metaphorical ghettoes to which they are often consigned by the impact of secular societies, or which they have created for themselves by their own foolishness.

It is a tendency of most faith communities to become introspective. One can generalize further and say that many institutions find introspection easier and more rewarding than action. The latter takes effort, and involves negotiating a path in a world where the institution's worldview is not widely accepted. The result is often perceived as impurity – a dilution of the true beliefs of the inner core, or the founders.

Such introspection is understandable, whether in a political party struggling with the compromises of government or the frustrations of opposition, or in a religious group, or any other corporate body with a collective narrative. The issues of leadership, values or aims are perceived as the fruit of past struggles, or the result of divine revelation. Even countries become introspective from time to time, seeking to recover some mystical and invariably mythical golden age, rather than dealing with the extraordinary complexities of a changing world.

As a result, across both faith institutions and liberal societies there is a sense of collusion in the privatizing of religion. They say to each other, 'we will not overly challenge the values of society outside our adherents, and you will not interfere with what we do among ourselves'. It is institutional Millsian liberalism,[6] and looks ideal, but in reality it is entirely unsuitable to the twenty-first century. Far from encouraging the unchallenged liberalism in which faith groups keep their views to themselves, or colluding with the idea that they can simply be 'useful', it is greatly to the advantage of society to ensure that institutions are outward looking, ethically engaged and challenging, and seek the prospering of their society as well as their own advantage.

[6]See John Stuart Mill, *On Liberty*, 1859.

In the early sixth century BC, the city of Jerusalem – until then the capital of the Kingdom of Judah for about 300 years and, intermittently, of a small regional power – was twice captured by the Babylonians. It was a useful strongpoint on the route to Egypt, the El Dorado of the Middle East at the time, itself a fading but great empire, over which Babylon had designs. The second capture followed a three-year siege, the hardships of which are beautifully and pitifully set out in two books of the Bible, the prophecies of Jeremiah and the Lamentations of Jeremiah. Extracts from the latter are often sung in cathedrals in the week before Easter: the setting by the sixteenth-century English composer Thomas Tallis is heartbreakingly beautiful.

Jeremiah is thought to have survived the second siege, and been taken into Egypt by force with refugees. However, in the decade or so between the two captures of Jerusalem he was asked by exiles taken to Babylon what they should do. Their expectation was of imminent return: that God would bring them back. Jeremiah answers unexpectedly, but with an insight that has nurtured the best of Jewish and Christian religious activity ever since:

> Build houses and live in them; plant gardens and eat what they produce. Take wives and have sons and daughters; take wives for your sons, and give your daughters in marriage, that they may bear sons and daughters; multiply there, and do not decrease. But seek the welfare of the city where I have sent you into exile, and pray to the Lord on its behalf, for in its welfare you will find your welfare.[7]

[7]Jeremiah 29:5–7.

The instructions from Jeremiah fall into three parts. First, settle down permanently with houses. Second, be confident about having families. Third, seek the prosperity of the city to which you have gone, or in simpler terms, be good citizens. The exiles were not to plan for return but for residence. They had gone as refugees – worse than that, as captive slaves – and they were told to become immigrants who integrated. They obeyed, to such an extent that for 25 centuries until the last 70 years the region around what was then Babylon, now part of Iraq, had a significant and flourishing Jewish population. More than that, in virtually every community in which, over the centuries, a Jewish diaspora has been established, they have been a blessing. Yet all the time they have retained a sense of their own cultural identity and faith.

The role of faith communities should be to bless the society in which they live, not to circle the wagons and seek to retain purity through separation. Their vocation includes supporting a good society, and preserving and developing its character on the basis of incarnational activity that is an outworking of the commands and nature of God. Of course, in return they should be able to expect to be treated with justice and fairness, the same rights as, in modern understandings of human rights, are expected for every human being.

That is simple enough for a religious group, but makes considerable demands on the host society itself, especially when its prevailing culture is ambivalent or even hostile to religion. There is a strong temptation for people in power to feel that they do not mind religion when it is useful, or when it is neutral, just so long as it makes no difference to the prevailing belief system.

A truly confident society will not seek to protect itself from challenge in such a way, but with liberal hospitality will seek the blessing of religious groups, believing that, within very broad boundaries, a free market in world views and truths is better than state- or populist-imposed restrictions. In economic terms, the contribution of faith-based organizations to the UK is estimated to be around £3 billion a year.[8]

A free market must mean not only the right to think freely, but also the right to seek to persuade, and the right to bless and support those facing needs or hardship. The Church of early medieval Europe, after the fall of the Western Roman Empire, established schools, hospitals and eventually universities as a demonstration of its understanding of the nature of human beings and of the freely given love of God. The vast majorities of faith communities in the UK today are moved to action out of a sense of seeking to bless and love, rather than seeking to renew long-vanished privilege.

Given the intellectual and cultural turbulence of the present, it is very good policy to provide space for the expression of such blessing. That means, for example, within the education system and subject to the National Curriculum, allowing opportunity for schools of a faith confession. They should be places of lively interaction of beliefs, not of forced observance, nor of sectarian habits and cultures that would subvert a hospitable, generous, sustainable, aspirational society.

Making space for an untidy collection of conflicting worldviews is not merely pragmatic, since the internet and social media (among other things) make the imposition of a single view impossible. It is also an expression of values. Such space demands solidarity without

[8]Cinnamon Network, Faith Action Audit 2016, http://www.cinnamonnetwork. co.uk/cinnamon-faith-action-audit/.

imposing central control, and thus respects subsidiarity. It encourages communities as well as individuals to aspire to have an impact on society through the quality and abundance of the blessing they bring. It provides resilience, natural bulwarks against populist extremism and sectional domination.

Space for blessing means space that is relatively unregulated, in which faith communities may contribute as they always have. For the Church of England that includes education and chaplaincy in a vast range of public institutions, all the while accepting that expressions of value may be challenging and uncomfortable. It also includes on a far larger scale the remarkable contribution of hundreds of thousands of lay people in their daily lives in all sectors of society. It has always seemed to work well, unless or until the reality of views expressed contradict opinion or policy.

The greatest danger that faces a liberal society that is open to question is not subversion, but its own fear of challenge and contradiction.

SUMMARY

- Faith groups are essential to society: their meta-narratives contribute to the implied or explicit understandings we have of our purpose and future.

- They are disruptors, challenging all sorts of assumptions.

- They are not merely useful, but provide the main fuel for driving processes of value definition.

- Society should have the confidence to ensure freedom of religion and beliefs, and free expression even of controversial views.

Conclusion

In times of uncertainty, like the present, we often ask our-selves what we should do. Establishing distant goals of great value is a useful activity, but the harder question is what do we need to do *now*? Taking the first steps towards identified goals begins the process of actually implement-ing what would otherwise be 'castles in the air'.

The great periods of change and reform in the way we behave as a nation have come from a combination of huge events and overseas influences. We have never been just some islands off the north-west coast of main-land Europe. In the mid-nineteenth century, the ferment following the ending of the Napoleonic Wars (an exter-nal threat with some unifying effect) coincided with the industrial and agricultural revolutions. At the same time, victory over France, especially at sea, had led to the crea-tion of the second British Empire (the first having ended with the loss of the American War for Independence). As more and more of the Indian subcontinent fell under British suzerainty, the demands of Empire grew, for better and for worse. It was a very potent mix, and led in part to the reforms which began in 1832 and contin-ued until the Education Act of 1870 and to some extent beyond.

In the period after the Second World War there were again major internal and external forces at play. Internally, the memories of the Great Depression and the suffering of the 1930s, especially in the north of Britain, in agricultural areas and away from London, all led to a reforming of economic management along Keynesian lines, with a strong emphasis on state involvement and an explicit target of full employment, by which was meant unemployment of no more than around 3 per cent. Once again, external events also played an enormous role in the reimagining of Britain. This time it was the loss of Empire, beginning with India and Pakistan in August 1947, Myanmar (then Burma) and Sri Lanka (then Ceylon) in early 1948, and progressively by the mid-1960s almost all of the British Empire. At the same time, the relationships with what had been called the Dominions (Canada, Australia, New Zealand and to some extent South Africa) also changed as the first three began to trade more in their own regions, and immigration altered the sense of near-exclusive links with the UK. South Africa was a different and more complicated case as a result of the election of the National Party with its hideous doctrine of apartheid.

These vast external changes had a profound effect on the UK economy, especially once continental Europe began to recover rapidly from the effects of the war. There again, a new force came into being, first called the European Coal and Steel Community and then the Common Market, eventually developing into the European Union. As a result of internal and external changes, the UK reimagined itself as part of the European Union, withdrawing from far-flung overseas commitments and struggling to redefine its place in the world. There were further, less dramatic bumps in the road, with a certain economic recasting, especially in the period after 1973, when the first oil crisis coincided with the advent of large-scale production in the North Sea, both of oil and gas. After an initial period (shared with much of the economically developed world) of high inflation and market turbulence – including, in 1976, the near default on international debt by the UK requiring IMF assistance – there was a significant shift in economic policy. Although it was very important economically, and eventually culturally, it was less a reimagining than an adjustment. Unemployment ceased to be targeted and first rose very sharply before falling back very slowly. Financial services grew in importance and London, almost always the single most powerful part of the UK economy since the early Middle Ages, became completely dominant, while vast swathes of former industrial areas, or of those linked to mining, were left largely to their own devices, with very severe economic effects from which they and their local populations still suffer.

Abroad, after the Treaty on the Final Settlement with Respect to Germany in 1990, and the collapse of the Soviet Union, the European Union expanded into a market of around 500 million people, which dominated our trade; however, as we were already a member this did not have a huge impact on our foreign policy. The war in the South Atlantic to recapture the Falkland Islands, in 1982, was hugely important psychologically, as was the first war in Kuwait and Iraq, in 1991, but again they did not lead to a huge shift in policy. The UK remained more or less willingly part of the European Union, and our trade with Europe was of great significance. Financial services and the role of the City of London continued to grow, even as the significance of North Sea hydrocarbon production fell, so that by 2008 we had become a mono-crop economy (discussed earlier in the book).

The result was that the financial crisis and associated Great Recession of 2008 had a profound effect on the UK from which it has yet to recover. Although economic output is now above the previous peak, the cumulative forgone growth during the period of slowdown is enormous. The psychological effects are even greater. Non-financial companies continue to hoard cash. Short-term interest rates remain near to zero, as do long-term government bond yields, so that the UK government has been borrowing at the lowest interest rate in history. Investment outside the financial sector is depressed compared with some of our main competitor nations, although it is showing signs of recovery. Employment has fallen less than anticipated, in part owing to workers accepting cuts in pay in inflation-adjusted terms, or even in absolute amounts. However, as has already been seen in the chapter on the economy, there is a historically high level of inequality in terms of education, housing, health and wealth, and a continuing very high level of domination by London, with many parts of the country lagging seriously behind.

It is the combination of massive economic shock and huge external change that I suggest will make the next couple of decades or more a period of reimagination on the scale of post-1945, or in the mid-nineteenth century, rather than simply an adjustment as in the 1970s and 1980s. The external change is, of course, leaving the European Union. I use the words 'external change' rather than 'external shock' very deliberately. It is impossible to foresee the long- or even short-term effects of Brexit.

Some argue that it will be simply a period of opportunity, with boundless liberation, money for everyone, and to paraphrase Doctor Pangloss in Voltaire's *Candide*, all will be for the best in the best of all possible worlds. It is said that the negotiations are simple, the period of two years to complete them is ample, and the adjustment will be helpful. New trade treaties will be negotiated with all and sundry in the twinkling of an eye. The Commonwealth will become a major trading partner, and by the end of the process we will, like the Dodo in *Alice in Wonderland*, say 'EVERYBODY has won and everybody will have prizes.'

Others, on the 'Remain' side, are apocalyptic in their forecasts. They foresee the arrival of the Four Horsemen of the book of Revelation (death, hunger, war and conquest), or at the least the UK economy becoming like that of Greece, with massive rises in unemployment, a sharp fall in the value of the pound, consequent high inflation, the country turning in on itself and succumbing to extremism and xenophobia. They argue that the negotiators for the European Union, and after them the individual states and the Parliament, have no incentive to negotiate a good deal for the UK, as although the UK is a trading partner of importance for the bloc, for each country it is less essential. They think that the Union will need to punish the UK to deter subsequent attempts to leave. They think the time allowed for negotiation is hopelessly inadequate and that there is thus a high chance of an ultra-hard Brexit. They foresee years without good trade arrangements, a country ill-prepared to stand on its own outside the European Union and with little interest from those with whom we hope to trade. They forecast government utterly absorbed in negotiation and Parliament occupied for years in consequent legislation. If those wildly in favour sometimes seem to resemble Dr Pangloss, those who are most against risk giving the impression of channelling the depressed robot, Marvin, the Paranoid Android, in *The Hitchhiker's Guide to the Galaxy*.

This deliberately exaggerated description reflects the normal material of knockabout politics. The first principle of great change is that the effects are unforeseeable, and although one side or another may be right, the most likely outcome is a bit of this, a bit of that, and a lot of things that nobody had foreseen owing to other external events unknown at present. This book has sought to argue that the task of reimagining is far more complicated than after 1945, and that the result will be a process lasting not for a few years but for generations.

The differences between now and 1945 are both external and internal. Internally, society has become a great deal more complicated. The referendum was an unknown tool of political life in the 1940s, and populism was very restrained. There was negligible multiculturalism, and very little variation in major faith traditions, except within Christianity. Inequality was lower and poverty much greater. Austerity united almost all people. Most important of all was the absence of the effects of communications and electronic technologies. Although the war had seen vast improvements in some aspects of technology, there was no sense in which they had yet had a huge impact on popular culture. That was to come, foreseen by some, interestingly including the Church of England in a report called 'Towards the Conversion of England', published in 1944.

Today's society is faster, more complicated, more independent and more confused. Religious observance is far weaker, yet where it occurs, far more committed. Political life is very fluid, and nationalism is strong. The very existence of the UK is seen by some to be at risk at some point in the future.

Externally, the changes are also enormous, but very different. The biggest changes are those mentioned at the beginning of the Introduction to this book – technology and communications – to which is added globalization of trade, business, tourism and a million other things, and more than that, the outlook for globalization itself. The Empire has gone, but the countries that were liberated by its fall are now much closer in many ways. Most of all, there is the enormous uncertainty and/or opportunity of seeking a role outside the European Union, with very little idea of what it looks like, or even if it looks very different at all.

This book has been divided into three parts. One has been more or less theoretical – as is this Conclusion. The second part looked at the foundations of reimagining Britain, foundations on which all reimagining has taken place in the last 200 years: housing, health and education, as well as the economy and finance, and which added to the impact of the changes in families and households. The book argues that those areas are as foundational as ever, for in the absence of them functioning effectively for the common good it is very hard to see what else can possibly work, or indeed how the country can function well and with stability.

The third part dealt with the actors and with new influences in our national drama, some of whom are interpreting long-held roles in fresh ways, others of whom are appearing for the first time. It has been argued that their impact, and the need for their direction within a system of national virtues, practices and values, is so great that they can by themselves upstage the main historic elements. A fearful and defensive foreign policy, an incapacity to

deal with immigration and integration well, lack of effective progress in ensuring that climate-change impacts are
mitigated – all of these would undermine progress, or
our capacity to renew education, housing and health.

Even more foundationally, in a way that could not have
been conceived of in 1945, the rapid changes in patterns
of understanding of family and household and the deep
divides between different groups, challenge the institution that in one way or another has been at the heart of
much human stability. Of course families and households also sit at the heart of suffering in many cases, but
overwhelmingly they are places of healing and strength.
Yet they nowadays come in far more shapes and forms.
Living in a society where these shapes are present all at
once, and all competing, is an extraordinary novelty.

Foreign policy is an outlier among the issues addressed
in this book, and comes back to basic principles around
vision and ambition, as well as practices which develop
and strengthen a sense of solidarity more widely. It can
reasonably be argued that an effective and ambitious foreign policy is indispensable to trade, a protection against
terrorism, a generous and gratuity-filled approach to the
issues of people movements, and essential to enable any
impact on questions which are of a global nature but
which threaten our security, prosperity or sustainability.
An outward-looking, proactive foreign policy of global
reach in partnership with others – nations, and also mul-
tilateral institutions – is not a luxury for those who have
not yet realized that the Empire has ended, but is rather
a foundation for a country which has vulnerabilities.

For such an ambition to be validated in practice, if
Britain is to have a wise willingness to engage to a reasonable and sustainable level around the world, ambition
must also be deeply embedded in values, and contribute

to a sense of national identity. Values make a crucial statement about our understanding of what it is to be human. They ascribe worth to people whom we have never met and never will, simply because of the fact of their being human. They stand against the ideas of racism and cultural superiority, which are invariably a curse in our own country and around the world. They give us the moral standing to seek to better the world, not by Empire, or by force, but by persuasion. They deny the power of an inward-looking and fearful spirit.

The question still remains: what do we do now? The kind of changes necessary in this reimagining will take years to bring about and decades to show effect. The first step is thus to create a sense of reasonable but positive expectation, and to base it on values, not just self-interest. The world and our future in it may look threatening, but it also can be regarded as full of opportunities for those who engage it with confidence, and with a clear understanding of what is right and wrong. Values matter, and they must be carried through in practices. The policies with which we act must be critiqued for what they symbolize and not only for what they produce in GDP.

Second, there needs to be an exercise, which will be highly political and robustly debated, of defining the kind of education, housing and health system we want, in looking at the values underpinning households and families, the economy and finance, the environment, immigration and integration and so on. 'Make do and mend' has run out of life. Some of this work is starting, for example on the economy.[1]

---

[1] The Institute for Public Policy Research in 2016 started a two-year programme of seeking to look at the definition and necessities for a 'good' economy. To declare my interest, I am a member of the panel (which is not paid).

Third, practices must be related to values and virtues. So much of public and institutional life relies on what is implied rather than on what is said, but the implication may not fully be held or understood by anyone. The linking of practices and virtues has been applied in the past, most recently with the Beveridge Report and the resulting enactments of measures to combat the five giants; want, disease, squalor, ignorance and idleness. Legislation during and after the war consciously attacked these giants. It included the 1944 Education Act, the 1946 National Insurance Act, Industrial Injuries Act, New Towns Act and National Health Service Act, and the 1948 National Assistance Act. Politics remained fierce, but there was a clear link between values and actions that meant that the changes made lasted in some cases until today as fundamental principles of the way the UK understands human flourishing.

Fourth, there has to be constant feeding of intermediate institutions of all sorts and shapes and sizes.

In the commercial and corporate world, the role of companies as intermediate institutions requires a change in governance to include workers' participation, accountability of senior management, and responsibility for communities which they affect that is greater than a merely voluntary commitment to corporate social responsibility. To pollute a river with effluent should not result only in fines representing at most a few days' profit; concepts of corporate criminality need introducing that result in a lasting blot on a company's reputation and a permanent impediment to the careers of those responsible. Companies really can sin, and when they do it should be recognized and addressed.

By contrast, in the voluntary sector there should be incentives, such as tax deductions, for participation in the sort of institutions that build social capital and provide rich soil for the development of virtues, values and practices. Public recognition of the value of participation, of volunteering, needs signalling through every means at society's disposal. A robust and sustainable voluntary sector only minimally constrained by essential regulation will lead to the development of all sorts of currently unimagined small groups that increase the common good. There should be, and there already are, many intermediate institutions between the state and the individual, family or household. Schools and FE colleges often demonstrate values in their community activities, as faith groups and churches have done for centuries and continue to do. Regulation should encourage, not inhibit.

Fifth, there has to be some kind of narrative of the UK, and of the way in which values are understood, that captures the imagination and anchors what is said and done in a coherent pattern. This is the greatest challenge. As a country we no longer have a dominant moral narrative based in some great story or set of stories about who we are and for what we exist. It is a great challenge to achieve one in a country of competing and often incommensurable values and stories and narratives. Not only are those varied, but one of them – postmodern and radical individual autonomy – denies the legitimacy of all the others in a hegemonic and overpowering manner. This last has achieved supremacy in all kinds of areas, so that local government has become fearful of working with faith groups; the state hesitates to fund faith-based social interventions; free speech is encouraged, but street preachers may be arrested; historic stories of the great religious holy days have to be toned down . . . the list could be very long.

It would be both impossible and absurd to look for ways of compelling adherence to a national narrative. There is no way of identifying it, and even if this were possible there would happily be no way of forcing belief in it. It is possible, however, in the way we have done things in the UK, to recreate story through action. Parroting national values rapidly loses effect, especially if they are seen as inconsistently applied. Giving space and funding for different groups to work, encouraging a UK equivalent of the US Peace Corps for overseas service, advocacy of robust debate and critique of even the most widely accepted of ideas, all these build ways in which a national narrative emerges. Free speech, even the freedom to abuse precious beliefs, has diminished out of fear of offence. Universities should not be permitted to ban groups other than those manifestly advocating hatred or violence. Tenure for those who express controversial views should be introduced. We need an equivalent to the Bill of Rights that makes most views that do not advocate, promote or lead to violence, even abhorrent ones, permissible so that they can be equally robustly rebutted. It has worked well in the USA.

All this is written from the point of view of a Christian who looks with shame at the times the churches have sought the protection of the law against being offended, and yet have felt free to insult at will. The great modern heroes of the Christian faith were caught up in love for Jesus, gripped by the story of his life and the reality of his presence in their lives. William Wilberforce, Mary Sumner, Elizabeth Fry, Dr Martin Luther King Jr, Archbishop Desmond Tutu, Jean Vanier, Mother Teresa, Óscar Romero, Pastor Dietrich Bonhoeffer, Cardinal văn Thuận and millions of others have all practised values which transformed those who knew them, and in some cases changed much in the world. They were not perfect, but they provoked people to reimagine the future. Those of us who are Christians are taught by the story of our faith that God will raise up equally extraordinary people in the future. The UK grew from Christian roots: my hope is that in the future it rediscovers the power of the narrative that has shaped it for so long and set its values so deeply.

Acknowledgements

The number of people who have helped me write this book is enormous. Special mention must be made of Catherine Whittle, who did the lion's share of the research, and added numerous comments and challenges which have been invaluable. Jack Palmer-White has also read and thought and helped hugely. Emma Shelton in my office has collated comments and kept on top of things.

Caroline Chartres, my editor at Bloomsbury, has nagged tactfully, encouraged warmly, and as ever amused and prompted with witty and insightful comments. Her colleague Jamie Birkett has gone well beyond the extra mile to steer the book through production.

Robert Willis, Dean of Canterbury, and Charlie Arbuthnot very kindly read the text and commented. Mary Eaton read and encouraged; I am so very grateful.

I am deeply appreciative of my close working colleagues, David Porter, Bishop Nigel Stock, my former and current chaplains Jo Wells (now Bishop of Dorking) and Isabelle Hamley, Chris Russell, Sarah Snyder, Mark Poulson, Will Adam, Ailsa Anderson, Bishop Anthony Poggo, and Bishop Precious Omuku. They have very often contributed indirectly and accidentally in conversations which are always challenging and power-ful. To them must be added Archbishop Josiah Fearon.

Surprisingly to some (but not me), both the Church of England House of Bishops and the General Synod have been places of learning and education for me. I am especially grateful to a number of bishops who lead in areas mentioned in the book. They include Richard Chartres, James Langstaff, David Urquhart, Paul Butler, Tim Thornton, James Newcome, Stephen Conway, and many others. I would like to note especially Nick Holtam, who kindly assembled a wonderful group to help on the climate-change chapter, including – in addition to some of those already mentioned – Geoffrey Lean, George Marshall, Loretta Minghella, Professor Chris Rapley, Dr Meg Warner and David Shreeve.

Conversations with Sam Wells, Paula Vennells, Tim Cross, former colleagues in the oil industry such as Viv Gibney and Sir Graham Hearne, and many others have shaped my thinking over the years. Sam Wells also made invaluable comments on the text at a late stage.

The 'Association Internationale pour L'Enseignement Social Chrétien' (AIESC), currently led by Professor Paul Dembinski, has been a group of mainly but not exclusively Roman Catholic Christians with whom I have met annually for almost 20 years, and from whom I have learned of the riches of the Catholic Church's social teaching.

Finally, because although the list could last forever it has to stop somewhere, I would like to thank David Ford, and all those who have been part of the theological reflection group that has met in Canterbury over the last four years.

There could be literally thousands more, but only one person is responsible for messing up their good thinking, and that is me. This book does not cover everything it could, and events move so fast that it feels as though it is dating as quickly as ice cream melts in the sun. It is not a manifesto, nor an exhaustive list of areas to cover, but it does suggest some patterns and tools for thinking which I offer for what they are worth.

In all the ups and downs of writing, as well as my wonderful, generous and critical colleagues there is above all the humanizing and perspective-forming love of the family, most especially my wife Caroline, who finds a thousand answers to the moments of difficulty. To all mentioned here, and especially to her, thank you.

Index

abuse 47, 63, 64, 77, 82, 93,
    163, 236, 243, 282
  of children 43, 78
  elder abuse 109
  of environment 218–19
  of power 33, 46
  of vulnerable adults 43
academies 87, 102, 103
Acheson, Dean 28
Adonis, Lord (Andrew
    Adonis) 87
adult learning 102
Afghanistan 29, 183, 192
Alice in Wonderland
    (Carroll) 275
All Party Parliamentary
    Group (APPG) on
    Social Integration report
    205–6, 208
alt-right movements 31, 196
anarchy 48, 239
ancient Egypt 157
anti-cancer drugs 156
apocalyptic terrorism 29–31
APPG (All Party
    Parliamentary Group) on
    Social Integration report
    205–6, 208
apprenticeships 103,
    124–5, 167

Arche communities, L' 123
art therapy 119
aspirations 44–5, 47, 48, 54,
    85, 250
  of Christianity 2, 34
  economy and 149, 151, 154,
    161, 163, 169
  education and 89, 101, 103
  families and 72, 82–3
  health and 107, 117, 124–5
  housing and 137
assisted suicide 115, 260
asymmetries of power 155,
    159, 163–5
austerity 149, 276
authority 43, 243
autonomy 11, 65, 72, 153,
    260, 281

baby boomers 12, 72–3
banking industry 38, 52, 159,
    163–6, 167, 168, 238–9
Bazalgette, Joseph 109
Becket, Thomas 255, 263
Benedict, St 34
Benedict XVI, Pope 36, 37
Benedictine rule 34
Benson, Edward 158
Bentinck, William 18
Betjeman, John 119

Beveridge, William 8
Bible passages
　aspiration 44
　community in 32–4
　competition 46n17
　creation story 218–19
　creativity 45
　division of Israel
　　(Rehoboam) 239–41,
　　243–4, 247
　exodus from Israel 32, 33
　families 64, 69–72, 79–80, 82
　flourishing
　　communities 95–6
　immigration stories (Ruth)
　　200–3, 204–5
　Jeremiah 266–7
　Last Judgement 112–
　　13, 114–15, 116–17,
　　123, 152–4
　neighbourliness 177–80
　parable of Good Samaritan
　　178–80, 181, 183–4, 185,
　　186–7, 189
　parables about money
　　151, 152–3
　resilience 52
　wisdom 181–2
Blair, Tony 29, 86, 87
Boko Haram 30
Bonhoeffer, Dietrich 34, 282–3
Branagh, Kenneth 151
Brexit 9, 170, 175, 189, 274–6
　campaign focus 238
　impact of 10, 167
British East India
　Company 17–18
British Empire 271–2
British Humanist
　Association 259n
British Medical Council 260
Bromford HA,
　Wolverhampton 142

Buddhism 30
building societies 164
Burke, Edmund 8,
　227, 235

Cambridge, Duke and
　Duchess of 121
Cambridge University 89
Canary Wharf 163–4
Candide (Voltaire) 275
carers 73–4, 75
　Carers' Allowance 77
　children as 37, 74n
　crisis in care provision 29
　domiciliary care 109
Casey Review 91, 104
Catholic Social Teaching
　8, 35–47
　families 64–5
　principles 35–43
　values 44–7
census (2011) 256
change 16, 18
　cultural change 19–20
　history of 5–11
　see also climate change
chaplains 262
Chesterton, G. K. 98
child abuse 43, 78
Child Benefit 77
children 6, 55, 63, 119, 257
　abuse of 43, 78
　care of 37, 66, 76, 109
　as carers 37, 74n
　protection of 77–8, 251
　see also education
Christian Socialism 112
Christianity 30
　impact on national
　　identity 2–3
　privatization of 17
　and reconciliation 49–50
　and sustainability 53–4

Christianity and Social Order
  (Temple) 256
Church Commissioners
  165, 233
Church of England
  chaplains 262
  Foundation for Educational
    Leadership 104
  National Society 97, 261
  and subsidiarity 43
  'Towards the Conversion of
    England' report 276
Churches 253–70
  contribution of 257–8
  and education 261, 264
  incarnational ministry 264
  opposition to 258
  and public health 120
Churchill, Winston 28, 53
Citizenship Survey (2011) 257
City of London 163–4,
  166, 273
Civil Rights movement 33
Civil Wars 6
Clean Air Acts (1956) 110, 117
climate change 13, 32, 55, 197,
  215–34, 278
cohabitation 55, 65–6, 72
common good 38–9, 47, 48,
  118, 226, 231–2, 235–6,
  242, 244
  and climate change 229
  economy and 149, 150, 170
  finance and 161
  judgement and 112, 113
  and social care 124
Common Market 272
Commonwealth 6, 184
Commonwealth Summit
  (2018) 184
communication 18, 277
community 32–43, 45, 47, 48,
  54, 154

breakdown of 242
finance and 161
housing and 127–48
and human flourishing 95–6
and Last Judgement 112
minority communities 33
compassion 113
competition 46–7, 48, 155
Cook, Robin 184, 188
COP21 climate talks, Paris 228
Corbyn, Jeremy 12
Coriolanus (Shakespeare) 45
corporate criminality 280
corporate social responsibility
  budgets 38
courage 43–7, 54, 71–2,
  113, 154
  economy and 155
  finance and 161
  and Last Judgement 112
  and struggle to survive 117
Cranmer, Thomas 254
creativity 45–6, 48, 103, 154
  moral virtues of 227–8
  and struggle to survive 117
credit union movement 167
cultural change 19–20
culture 119
  changes in 17
  and identity 207–8
Cyrus, Persian Emperor 5

David Copperfield
  (Dickens) 150
debt 14, 51
  and Great Crash
    (2008) 158–9
  home ownership and 130
  international debt 273
*The Decline and Fall of
  the Roman Empire*
  (Gibbon) 255
democracy 48, 58, 59, 242, 260

Democratic Republic of the Congo (DRC) 40
depression (economic) 28, 239, 272
depression (mental illness) 75, 112, 116, 121–2
deprivation 37, 91, 92, 137, 192
development assistance 188
devolution 11, 246–7
'Devotions Upon Emergent Occasions: Meditation XVII' (Donne) 39–40
Dickens, Charles 14, 140, 150
disability groups 33, 260
disasters 38, 110, 127
  disaster relief 188
  natural disasters 110, 181, 186, 188
diversity 49, 82, 93–4, 101–2
divorce 65, 75, 261
domestic violence 63, 82
domiciliary care 109
Donne, John 39–40, 41
DRC (Democratic Republic of the Congo) 40
drug industry 156
Durham Cathedral 230–2

Ebola virus 183, 184
economic bubbles 157–8
economic migration 177
economics and finance 149–72
economy 32, 56
  and aspiration 149
  and common good 149, 150, 170
  and courage 155
  and international debt 273
  and public health 118
education 13, 32, 54, 85–104
  Christian worship in 97, 261–2
  Churches and 120, 261, 264

comprehensive system 86, 93
and development of values 101–4
and diversity 93–4, 101–2
GCSE grades and free school meals 91, 91–2
and human flourishing 98
and mental health 95
non-academic education 88–9
RE 97–8
and religious extremism 100
school meals 91, 91–2, 119
sex education 102
special schools 93
state schools 87
T-levels 103
'Trojan Horse' cases 100
UK schools fact sheet 88
Education Act (1944) 85, 97
Education Reform Act (1988) 86
EEC (European Economic Community) 19
elder abuse 109
elections 48
Elizabethan Settlement 6
employment 8, 16–17, 159, 164, 228, 233, 274
  banks and 239
  housing and 134, 139, 144–5
  and public health 118
  women in 76–7
energy supplies 220, 222
  renewable energy 233
  UK actual/projected energy consumption 226
English language 206–7
epidemiology 109
equal (same-sex) marriage 66–7, 80
equality 16, 155

Esso 156
European Coal and Steel
    Community 272
European Economic
    Community (EEC) 19
European Union (EU) 7, 28,
    227, 272, 273
    and refugees 176, 197
    see also Brexit
Eurozone 38–9
euthanasia 115
extremism 31–2, 100, 269, 275

fair trade 156, 190
fairness 211–12
faith groups 67, 253–70
    chaplains 262
    and Christian worship in
        education 261–2
    contribution of 268
    and introspection 265
    role of 259, 262, 264,
        267, 268–9
    views of 263
Falklands War 273
families 63–83, 278
    extended families 75, 76
    family breakdown 122
    historic understanding
        of 78–83
    Islamic understanding of 79
    nature of 55
    nuclear families 75, 76
    as place of safety 78
    structure of 63–6
    support for 73–7
famines 180, 190
FE (further education) 88, 101,
    102, 103, 249
fear 6, 26, 189, 205, 210,
    269, 282
female genital mutilation 190
fidelity 64, 65, 69

finance 157, 161, 246
    economics and
        finance 149–72
    international finance 163–4
    see also economy
financial engineering 28
financial policy 56
financial services 273
forced migration 177
foreign aid 188, 190
foreign policy 13, 32, 56–7,
    186, 188, 190–2, 277–8
    and immigration 197
    and national values 56–7
    requirements of 189–90
forgiveness 54
Francis, Pope: *Laudato Si'*
    encyclical 216
Francis Report 42
Francis, St 216
free markets 161–3, 166
free riders 236, 239, 242
free schools 102, 103
free trade 29
Freedom in the World report
    (2016) 191
Fry, Elizabeth 282–3
further education (FE) 88, 101,
    102, 103, 249
futures markets 157

Galbraith, J. K. 158
Gandhi, Mohandas
    Karamchand 58
GDP (gross domestic
    product): and stocks
    traded *160*
gender equality 260–1
gender minorities 33
gender pay gap 76–7
generosity 10, 15, 33–4, 36–7,
    50, 154, 161, 170, 187, 258
    ethical challenge to 177–8

generosity of spirit 64, 96
 and immigration 203, 204,
  205, 278
 and refugees 197
ghettoization 204
Gibbon, Edward 255
gig economy 162–3
globalization 29, 177,
  217–18, 277
Gooder, Paula 232
grammar schools 85, 86
gratuity 36–8, 76, 113, 161,
  170, 278
Great Crash (2008) 158–9
Great Recession (2008) 12, 28,
  169, 274
Great Smog, London
  (1952) 110
Greece 28, 38–9
Green Party, UK 225
Grenfell Tower fire (2017)
  29, 127–8
Gross Value Added
  (GVA) 159

Hadrian's Wall 198
hard power 182–3
Harry, Prince 121
hate crimes 13, 19
HE (higher education) 88,
  101, 103
health issues 32, 54, 85, 107–25
 anti-cancer drugs 156
 diabetes 119, 120
 GP service 108
 health inequality 116, 125
 infant mortality 218
 life expectancy 110, *111*,
  115, 117–19
 obesity 120
 public health 54, 109–10,
  114, 115, 116–17, 118, 120

social care 108–9, 114, 115,
  120, 124–5
 see also mental health
Henry II, King of England 255
Henry VI (Shakespeare) 45
higher education (HE) 88,
  101, 103
Hinduism 30
*Hitchhiker's Guide to
  the Galaxy, The*
  (Adams) 275–6
Hobbes, Thomas 50–1,
  117, 237
Hogarth, William 140–1
Homer 45
hope 25–8, 32
 apocalyptic terrorism
  and 30–1
 families and 63, 64–5
 foundations for 236, 245
 and resilience 52
House of Lords 255
households 48, 63–83, 278
 historic understanding
  of 78–83
 household wealth 14
 as safe places 55
 support for 73–7
housing 32, 54, 85
 and capital gains tax 146
 and community 127–48
 council houses, sale of 130
 deterioration in housing
  stock 134–5
 favelas and slums 33
 home ownership *129*, 130,
  135, 138
 houses built *131*
 housing provision changes
  128–30, *129*
 housing standards 127,
  128, 132

and identity 139–40
   as investment 13, 130–2,
      134, 138
   location 144–6
   new housing 147–8
   post-war housing provision
      128–9, 130
   and poverty 136
   private market 144, 146
   property values 144–6
   and public health 118
   redevelopment 135
   regional variations 132–4,
      133, 138–9
   rental market 132
   rising prices 130–2, 134, 135
   running costs and
      maintenance 134–5
   second homes 138–9
   social housing 136–7
housing associations (HAs)
   109, 136–7, 142–4, 146
Huguenots 198
human dignity 117, 123,
   125, 150
human flourishing 85, 95–6,
   139, 241, 245–6, 250
   climate change and 215, 217
   common good and 38
   competition and 46
   creativity and 45
   economy and 150, 170
   education and 98
   finance and 95–6
   reconciliation and 48, 49
   resilience and 225–6
human trafficking 186, 190
humanism 36
hypermodernity 11

I, Daniel Blake (film) 149, 171
identity 80–1, 82, 154

culture and 207–8
   housing and 139–40
   and language 206–7
   loss of 210
   UK national identity 205
   and values 227
ideological hegemony 262–3
IDPs (Internally Displaced
   Persons) 177
immigration 13, 57, 71–2
   control of 185–6
   impact of 68
   and integration 195–213,
      266–7, 277–8
   push/pull factors 197–8
   and religious influence 100
   and terrorism 189
income 26, 38, 99, 112,
   150, 159
income inequality 14–15
individualism 16
inequality 12, 14–15, 93, 169,
   176–7, 274
   and asymmetries of
      power 159
   health inequality 116, 125
   income inequality 14–15
   increase in 118–19
   public health and 116
   quality of life 110, 111–12
   wealth inequality 14
infant mortality 218
inflation 189
influence 242–3
infrastructure projects 13
injustice 74n, 92, 115, 155,
   162–3, 171, 210, 260–1
innovation 103, 117, 124,
   222, 249
insider trading 211
instability 41, 176, 191–2,
   203, 224

Institute for Public Policy
    Research 279n
integration 13, 57, 71–2
    and immigration 195–213,
        266–7, 277–8
interconnectedness 175
interest rates 13
intermediate institutions
    245–8, 250–1, 280, 281
Internally Displaced Persons
    (IDPs) 177
international finance 163–4
international terrorism 29–30
internet 175, 176–7, 268
intolerance 19, 262
introspection 19, 265
investment 13, 16, 155, 274
Iraq 29, 183, 192, 273
Islam 31, 264
Islamic State 30
isolation 71–2, 74–5, 112, 122,
    124, 175

Jerusalem 34, 244, 266
Jews 264
    diaspora 267
    exile story 5–6
    immigration 198
John Paul II, Pope St 250
justice 114, 148, 188n4,
    238, 242
    criminal justice 122
    economy and 149, 150,
        155, 169
    environmental justice 215
    social justice 112

Kennedy, Joseph 158
Kenny, Enda 195n
Keynes, John Maynard
    25n2, 158
Khmer Rouge 31
King, Martin Luther 58, 282–3

Kipling, Rudyard 51
Kuwait 273

Labour Election Manifesto
    (2017) 99
Langton, Stephen 255
language: and identity 206–7
Latin America 33
Laud, William 254
Lawson, Nigel (Baron Lawson
    of Blaby) 221, 222–3, 229
Leo XIII, Pope: *Rerum
    Novarum* (On Capital
    and Labour encyclical) 35
Leviathan (Hobbes) 237
Lewis, C.S. 15–16
liberalism 7, 69, 265
Libya 192
life expectancy 110, *111*,
    115, 117–19
lifelong learning 102
*Lion, The Witch and
    the Wardrobe, The*
    (Lewis) 15–16
living standards 161,
    217–18, 220
Lloyds Bank 164
Loach, Ken 149
local government 108,
    246–7, 281
    and housing 135, 141,
        146, 148
London Olympics (2012) 151
loneliness 71–2, 75, 143–4
love-in-action 4, 17, 69, 72, 95,
    114, 153, 178, 247
    gratuity and 38
    and values 44
loyalty 53, 59, 203, 237,
    241, 243–4

Magna Carta 255
Major, John 86, 87

Mandela, Nelson 58
markets 157, 161–3, 166
marriage 55, 66–7, 69, 80
Marriage (Same Sex Couples)
    Act (2013) 66
Marx, Karl 8, 238, 256
materialism 28–9
mental health 54, 75, 112, 114,
    115, 116, 120–4
  education and 95
  investment/divisions in 13
  personality disorders
    120–1, 122
  prisoners and 122
  see also depression
meritocracy 92
migration 13, 177, 185: see also
    immigration; refugees
Mill, John Stuart 265
minority groups 33
Mobil 156
modern slavery 190
monopolies 46, 155–6
moral responsibility: scope
    of 236–7
music therapy 119

National Church and Social
    Action (2014) 257
national identity 1–3, 208–9
National Offender
    Management Service
    (NOMS) 122–3
NATO 183
Near Neighbours projects 208
neighbourliness 139–40, 177–
    80, 186–7, 229
Newbigin, Lesslie 27
NHS (National Health
    Service) 73–4, 75, 107–8,
    120, 123, 187
Niebuhr, Reinhold 237–8
Nietzsche, Friedrich 36

Nigeria 30, 31
NOMS (National
    Offender Management
    Service) 122–3
Northern Ireland 20, 27, 33,
    167, 207
Northern Powerhouse 12
Norway 171

obesity 120
oil industry 156, 171, 273–4
opinion polls 225, 260
Oxford University 89

Palmerston, Lord (Henry
    Temple) 184–5, 188n4
panic 155
Papacy 263
parish councils 141
Parliamentary Commission on
    Banking Standards 165–6
participation 280–1
payday lending 167
Peasants' Revolt 255
peer-to-peer lending 13
people smuggling 186
personality disorders
    120–1, 122
Pew Research Center 100
Poland: Solidarność 39
Pole, Reginald 254
polygamy 79
Post Office 248–9
postmodernity 11
poverty 91, 92, 110, 136,
    161, 217–18
power
  abuse of 33, 46
  asymmetries of 155,
    159, 163–5
  hard power 182–3
  soft power threats 189
  practices

values and 3–4, 57–9, 280
virtues and 3–4
premature mortality 118–19
prison reforms 122
prisons 112
protectionism 29
public health 54, 109–10, 114,
    115, 116–17, 118, 120

QS World University
    Rankings 87

racism 26, 197, 204, 279
Reagan, Ronald 28
realpolitik 184
recession 12, 28, 39, 169, 274
reconciliation 47–50, 69–71,
    114, 191, 192
recycling 233
Reformation 157–8, 254
refugees 40, 176, 186, 198–9
    European Union and
        176, 197
religion 30, 264
    extremism 31, 100
    and national identity 208–9
    plurality of 3, 10
    see also Catholic Social
        Teaching; Christianity;
        Church of England;
        Churches; faith groups
Religious Education (RE):
    All Party Parliamentary
    Group report (2013) 97–8
rent-seeking 163
resilience 47, 51–3, 72, 101,
    103, 114, 227, 229–31
Richard III (Shakespeare) 45
robotics 209
Rockefeller, John D. 156
Romero, Óscar 282–3
Roosevelt, Theodore 156

Royal Bank of Scotland 164
Russell Group institutions 89

same-sex (equal) marriage
    66–7, 80
Sancroft, William 254
sati, ban on 17–18
Scotland 20, 29, 33, 89, 97, 207
Scott, Walter 230
Scottish Mental Health
    Strategy 121
secondary modern schools 102
secondary schools 103
secular stagnation 169
security 242
self-interest 155
self-pity 19
selfishness 238
sewage systems 109–10, 115
sex education 102
sexual issues
    double standards 67
    LGBTI sector 68
    LGBTIQ+ rights 261
    same-sex (equal) marriage
        67–8, 80
    sexual orientation 72, 260–1
    sexual violence 190
sexual minorities 33
sexual orientation 72, 260–1
sexual violence 190
Shakespeare, William 45, 254
Sharia law 79, 81–2
short-termism 155
Sierra Leone 183–4
Simon of Sudbury 255
sin 155, 162, 236, 280
single-parent households 66
slavery 33, 190
Smiles, Samuel 198–9
Smith, Adam 156
Snow, John 109

social care 108–9, 114, 115,
    120, 124–5
social contract 245
social housing 136–7
social justice 112
social media 67–8, 120, 175
Social Services 75
Social Value Act (2012)
    135n8
society
    generational division 12–13
    problems of 11–12
    secularization of 3, 10
Solar Impulse (solar-powered
    aircraft) 230–2
solidarity 39–41, 72, 118, 190,
    227, 230–1
    and climate change 229
    community health and 141
    economy and 149, 155
    public health and 116, 117
    and social care 124
Solidarność, Poland 39
Solzhenitsyn, Aleksandr
    46n17
South Sea Bubble 158
Southern Africa: ubuntu
    concept 139
Soviet Union 46, 161, 237–8
sport 119, 120
stability 47–54, 65, 154, 192
    and compassion 114
    economy and 149, 155, 162
    and Last Judgement 112
stakeholders 250
Stalin, Joseph 256
Standard Oil 156
start-ups 13
state pensions 77
Stern, Nicholas (Baron Stern
    of Brentford) 220–2,
    229, 233

stewardship 35, 152–3,
    154, 232
stocks traded: and GDP 160
subsidiarity 41–3, 121, 141,
    161, 190–1, 246
Sumner, Mary 282–3
sustainability 47, 53–4, 101,
    103, 114, 190, 227,
    229, 232–3
Sweden 119

Tallis, Thomas 266
Tawney, R.H. 8
taxation 146, 168
technical education 85,
    102, 103
technology 18, 277: see also
    internet; social media
television 175–6, 181
Temple, William 8, 256
Teresa of Calcutta,
    Mother 282–3
terrorism 29–31, 52, 189, 209
    9/11 attacks, USA 29
Thatcher government 86
Thatcher, Margaret 242
Times Higher Education:
    university rankings 86
torture 52
tradition 69, 78–83
Trafford Housing 142
Trump, Donald 228
trusteeship 35
tuition fees 99
Turner, Adair 14, 169
Tutu, Desmond 58, 282–3

ubuntu concept, Southern
    Africa 139
Uganda 198
UN Sustainable Development
    Goals 224–5

unemployment 12, 31, 272, 273
unfairness 239: *see also* fairness
universal destination of goods 35–6, 56, 92, 227
universities 86–7, 89–90, 90, 99, 249, 281
unsustainability 155: *see also* sustainability
USA (United States of America)
 2016 electoral campaign 209
 and climate change 219–20, 223, 228
 immigration into 195–6
USSR (Union of Soviet Socialist Republics) 46, 161, 237–8
utilitarianism 98–9
Utopia 25

values 15–17, 278–82
 British ix–x
 Catholic Social Teaching 44–7
 deep values 15–16
 economics and 150, 151
 education and 101–4
 fairness 211–12
 and identity 227
 implementation of 54
 imposed values 99–100
 and love 4–5
 and practices 3–4, 57–9, 280
 of stability 47–54
 and virtues 3–4, 280
văn Thuân, François-Xavier Nguyễn 27, 282–3
Vanier, Jean 282–3
venture capital 13

Victorian Britain 72, 76, 116, 140, 151
violence 77, 140, 169, 282
 domestic violence 63, 82
 sexual violence 190
virtues 15
 moral virtues of creativity 227–8
 and practices 3–4
 values and 3–4, 280
Voltaire (François-Marie Arouet) 275
voluntary sector 281
volunteering 281
vulnerable adults 43, 76, 77–8, 109

Wales 20, 33, 207
Walesa, Lech 39
water supplies 109, 115, 117, 224
wealth inequality 14
Wells, Sam 235–6
Western Christianity 2–3
Whitehead, Henry 109
Wilberforce, William 183, 282–3
Williams & Glyn bank 165
Wilson government 85–6
wisdom 181–2, 241
Wolf, Martin 165
World Trade Organization: Doha round 228

xenophobia 19

YouGov poll (2011) 259

zero-hour contracts 109, 162–3

A Note on the Type

The text of this book is set in Linotype Stempel Garamond, a version of Garamond adapted and first used by the Stempel foundry in 1924. It is one of several versions of Garamond based on the designs of Claude Garamond. It is thought that Garamond based his font on Bembo, cut in 1495 by Francesco Griffo in collaboration with the Italian printer Aldus Manutius. Garamond types were first used in books printed in Paris around 1532. Many of the present-day versions of this type are based on the Typi Academiae of Jean Jannon cut in Sedan in 1615.

Claude Garamond was born in Paris in 1480. He learned how to cut type from his father and by the age of fifteen he was able to fashion steel punches the size of a pica with great precision. At the age of sixty he was commissioned by King Francis I to design a Greek alphabet, and for this he was given the honourable title of royal type founder. He died in 1561.